THE LIBRARY OF PHILOSOPHY AND THEOLOGY

Edited by

JOHN MCINTYRE AND ALASDAIR MACINTYRE

THE CHRISTIAN MESSAGE AND MYTH

Nihil Obstat Carolus Davis, S.T.L.
Censor deputatus.
Imprimatur E. Morrogh Bernard. Vic. Gen.
Westmonasterii, die 26 *Septembris,* 1957.

THE
CHRISTIAN MESSAGE
AND MYTH

The Theology of
Rudolf Bultmann

L. MALEVEZ, S.J.

*Professor at the Jesuit Philosophical and Theological College
of Saint Albert, Louvain*

SCM PRESS LTD
56 BLOOMSBURY STREET
LONDON

Translated by Olive Wyon, D.D., from the French LE MESSAGE
CHRÉTIEN ET LE MYTHE, published 1954 by Desclée de Brouwer,
Brussels, Bruges and Paris.

Appendix II translated by Bernard Noble from the French
EXEGÈSE BIBLIQUE ET PHILOSOPHIE, published in NOUVELLE
REVUE THÉOLOGIQUE, Vol. 78, November and December 1956,
pp. 897-914, 1,027-1,042.

First published in English 1958

© SCM PRESS LTD 1958

Printed in Great Britain by
The Camelot Press Ltd., London and Southampton

GENERAL INTRODUCTION

In the last hundred years the relationship between philosophy and theology has been radically transformed twice over. The theologians of the nineteenth century were accustomed to treat idealist metaphysics as an ally against unbelief, and the philosophers were equally accustomed to treat the knowledge of God as a central philosophical theme. But in both disciplines the rejection of idealism was followed not so much by a hostility to as by a lack of interest in the preoccupations of the other. Moore, Russell, and Wittgenstein initiated the conception of philosophy as logical analysis; Barth proclaimed the task of theology as elucidation of the biblical revelation. Philosophers were often preoccupied with questions of method, theologians with problems of biblical exegesis. And in each discipline an uneasy and ill-informed suspicion of the other was too often entertained.

This interim period is now happily over. In the last ten years philosophy and theology have once again begun to converse. The methods of philosophical analysis have been applied to religious concepts, and some theologians have begun to look to philosophy for aid with their own problems. At the same time Continental theology has been reacting to the powerful influence of existentialist philosophy and existentialist concepts have entered even biblical studies in the controversies over demythologizing. *The Library of Philosophy and Theology* has played an important part in the furtherance of these discussions and its first Editor, Professor R. Gregor Smith, deserves much of the credit for the renewed prestige of philosophical theology.

The present editors hope to continue the admirable tradition of the series in publishing works which are designed either to break new ground in this topic or to present in a form available to a wider public work which has already been done. The books published in the series represent a wide variety of standpoints. The series itself is to be identified with none of them, but only with the desire to promote a fruitful conversation in contemporary terms between philosophers and theologians.

ALASDAIR MacINTYRE
JOHN MCINTYRE

CONTENTS

7

TRANSLATOR'S PREFACE

THE author has read this translation in manuscript; at some points, in the interests of clarity, he has emended the text. These changes have been incorporated in the present version. My cordial thanks are due to Father Malevez for the care and courtesy with which he has dealt with various questions which have inevitably arisen in the course of this work. My gratitude is also due to Mme Marsh, Ph.D. (Sorbonne) for her invaluable help in the preparation of this translation for the press.

OLIVE WYON

FOREWORD TO THE ENGLISH EDITION

THE French original of this work appeared in 1954. Since then work concerning Bultmann's theology has been published in various countries, and there is of course no reference in our introduction to these recent publications. However, we ourselves contributed a new study of Bultmann to the *Nouvelle Revue Théologique* of December, 1956 (Vol. 78, pp. 897-914 and 1027-1042). It is in this study that we have paid due regard to several important publications of the years since 1954. For this reason we believed our English-speaking readers would find it helpful if we were to add a translation of our article to that of the larger work. It will be found in Appendix II of this volume under the title 'Biblical Exegesis and Philosophy: two opposed conceptions of their relationship—R. Bultmann and K. Barth'. It would doubtless have been preferable if, instead of publishing this article as a separate appendix, we had inserted its content into the body of the work: it would have found its natural place in Chapters II and III, which are devoted respectively to 'The Principle of Existential Interpretation' and to 'The Existential Interpretation of the *Kerygma*', for the article seeks to contribute to the understanding not so much of Bultmann's actual doctrine as of his principles of interpretation and hermeneutics. In making such an insertion we would have eliminated a certain amount of duplication: on the other hand we would have been obliged to recast the whole of our work—as to form, that is, not as to matter. For a revision of this magnitude we have not had time.

We wish to express our sincere gratitude to Dr Olive Wyon and Mr Bernard Noble, translators respectively of the book and of the article, for all the care and insight with which they have rendered our text into English.

L. MALEVEZ

INTRODUCTION

THE idea of the Christian message has not been dominant in Catholic Christian thought, and before the emergence of the most recent *kerygmatische Theologie*, it does not seem to have aroused much interest in the minds of its theological scholars. Protestantism has often reproached the Catholic Church for the extreme importance it attaches to the doctrinal character of the Christian faith. It is, however, a remarkable fact that Catholic theologians have never composed a treatise dealing specifically with the concept of the 'Gospel', the Good News, nor with that of the 'Word of God': is this not due to the conviction that the message should never be considered apart from the messenger? If it is important for the Catholic Christian to be always on the alert for 'news' hitherto unheard, which one day resounded in history, it is still more important for him to be attached by a mysterious link to the person of the ever-living Christ, his Saviour.

Our title suggests that we are breaking this tradition of silence, a rupture which might cause some astonishment. Further: we here associate the Christian message with the idea of myth. But to speak of a 'myth' surely suggests that we are speaking of a fiction? Do we actually mean to suggest that there is some common ground between the Christian message and the tales of mythology?

The subject which we treat in this book, however, leaves us no choice. Our aim is to interpret the thought of the Protestant theologian Rudolf Bultmann; and Bultmann is mainly concerned with the effort to confront the Christian message and the mythical element in Christianity: that is, with *Kerygma und Mythos*. Thus the title was dictated to us. Let us say, however, from the very outset, that in the thought of Bultmann himself, his concern is not with a 'union' of ideas, but with a separation: he claims that where the message is understood in its purity there is not, or there can no longer be, any question of 'myth'; and where the

11

element of 'myth' persists, there is grave danger that the message itself will be stifled.

The principal work of Rudolf Bultmann, which we examine critically in this book, consists of a small book of barely forty pages; it is a simple sketch presented to the judgment of the Christian theologian. None the less, it has struck a tremendous blow at certain Protestant theological positions; the vigour of this reaction has been surprising, even for the author himself; it has also caused a good deal of perplexity in the minds of younger men, drawing them away, in an unfortunate manner, from traditional Christianity, and leading them (against the author's intentions) into the path of a purely philosophical existentialism, which risks retaining nothing of Christianity but the name.

The simple text of the lecture published first of all in 1941 in the *Beiträge zur evangelischen Theologie* under the title: 'Offenbarung und Heilsgeschehen', is now known by a fresh title: 'Neues Testament und Mythologie' ('New Testament and Mythology'); it also has a sub-title indicating the purpose of the work: 'Das Problem der Entmythologisierung der neutestamentlichen Verkündigung' (The Mythological Element in the Message of the New Testament and the Problem of its Reinterpretation).

Traditional Christianity presents the substance of the Christian message in a mythological form: the Son of God, eternally pre-existent, assuming in Christ a human nature, and expiating by his death the sin of mankind; when he rose from the dead, he appeared to his disciples; having ascended into heaven he sent his Spirit, an energy acting inwardly, and the guarantee of our own future resurrection. All this 'mythology', says Bultmann, obviously cannot be accepted by contemporary thought. Hence, if Christianity is not to perish, it must set to work to 'demythologize' itself. Positively, in the Christian message it will conserve only those elements which are relevant for the intelligence of man and his existence before God. This does not mean that the message will be reduced to a pure philosophy; it will retain the idea of revelation, and also that of an 'intervention'

—but not a mythological one—of God in history: through Christ, and by means of him, God speaks to man and calls him; he shows him his condition as a creature: which is both that of a sinner, and of one who is justified; he also saves him, and that means that he gives a certain 'authenticity' to his earthly existence; to enter into this new 'existence' it is enough for man to renounce all pharisaical trust in himself, and to surrender himself to God's free forgiving grace.

In his other works Bultmann does not explicitly express this interpretation of Christianity, but he frequently hints at it. It is suggested here and there in several articles collected by the author in the two volumes of *Glauben und Verstehen*; naturally, the most recent articles are from this point of view the most explicit, especially 'Das Problem der Hermeneutik' (1950) (*Glauben und Verstehen*, Tübingen, Vol. II, 1952, pp. 211-235) (ET, 'The Problem of Hermeneutics', *Essays Philosophical and Theological*, London, 1955); but we can find traces of this point of view in earlier works of his, such as in 'Kirche und Lehre im NT' (1929) (*Glauben und Verstehen*, Tübingen, Vol. I, second edition, 1953, p. 167; observations on the conception of the Sacrament in St Paul). This same theology inspires the exegetical work of Bultmann: we shall have occasion, as we go on, to call attention to the *Theology of the New Testament*, in order to illustrate this affirmation of the essay of 1941. In any case, all this is implicit or simply allusive. Only two studies have appeared since 1941 to complete the first essay, or to clarify obscure points in his thought: the first one, an answer to objections raised by the theologian Schniewind, bears the title: 'Zu J. Schniewinds Thesen, das Problem der Entmythologisierung betreffend' (1943) (ET, 'A Reply to the Theses of J. Schniewind', in *Kerygma and Myth*, London, 1953); the second one, 'Zum Problem der Entmythologisierung' (1951) (partly translated as 'Bultmann Replies to His Critics', *Kerygma and Myth*), is just as important as the essay of 1941; we shall take full account of it in our exposition.

We have just suggested that the work entitled 'Neues Testament und Mythologie' (1941) aroused certain criticisms of

13

Bultmann's ideas; in actual fact these criticisms were numerous; to put it more plainly, his theology raised a storm of controversy, in which some scholars took his part. The major documents in this debate have been collected by H. W. Bartsch in the three volumes *Kerygma und Mythos*; Vol. I, 1951; Vol. II, 1952; Vol. III, 1954 (Herbert Reich, Evangelischer Verlag, Hamburg), which we shall quote respectively as B. I, II, and III: in the first two, in addition to the three works of Bultmann which have already been mentioned, we find contributions from several Protestant theologians: here I will only mention the names of Lohmeyer, Sauter, Schniewind (Vol. I) and of Karl Barth (Extract from his *Dogmatik*, III, 2, pp. 531-537), Buri, Hartlich, Sachs and Kümmel (Vol. II).

The third volume, recently published (1954), bears the sub-title: *Das Gespräch mit der Philosophie*. This title is explained by the reproduction of an important passage from the writings of Karl Jaspers, a lecture given at Basle by the philosopher on 27 April 1953: 'Wahrheit und Unheil der Bultmannschen Entmythologisierung', which was published first of all in the *Schweizerische Theologische Umschau*, Vol. 23, 1953, pp. 74-106. In this passage Jaspers exposes Bultmann's essay to a severe criticism, to which the latter was not slow to respond: 'Zur Frage der Entmythologisierung Antwort an Karl Jaspers': a response published for the first time in the *Theologische Zeitschrift* (published by the Theological Faculty of Basle), Vol. X, 1954, pp. 81-95, and reproduced in the third volume of *Kerygma und Mythos* (B., III, pp. 47-59), immediately after the article by K. Jaspers.

These three volumes do not include another important study to which we shall be referring from time to time: K. Barth, 'Rudolf Bultmann, Ein Versuch ihn zu verstehen',[1] Zürich, 1952 (in the collection *Theologische Studien*, Cahier 34).

In English-speaking countries, the most important work on this subject is the partial translation (by R. H. Fuller) of the two works of Bartsch (already mentioned), under the title *Kerygma und Myth*, 1953, in one volume, which closes

[1] An attempt to understand him.

14

with an Anglican criticism by Austin Farrer, also fairly severe, of Bultmann's attempt. We shall refer to this volume as *KM*. Ian Henderson's *Myth in the New Testament, Studies in Biblical Theology*, No. 7, London, 1952, can also be read with profit.

In French we may mention the study by K. Prenter: 'Mythe et Évangile', in the *Revue de théologie et de philosophie* of Lausanne; Vol. XXV, 1947, pp. 49-67; and that of G. Casalis, 'Le Problème du mythe', in the *Revue d'Histoire et de Philosophie religieuses de l'Université de Strasbourg*, Vol. XXXI, 1951, pp. 330ff.

All the works which have been mentioned hitherto come from the Protestant side. Of Catholic theologians we mention some pages from O. Simmel, S.J., 'Mythos und Neues Testament', in *Stimmen der Zeit*, Vol. CL, 1952, pp. 33ff.; in the *Theologische Revue*, Vol. 49, 1953, pp. 122ff., a critical study by A. Kolping, 'Sola Fide, Aus der Diskussion um Bultmann's Forderung nach Entmythologisierung des Evangeliums'. In the *Revue Nouvelle*, Vol. XVII, 1953, p. 639, the Rev. Fr. J. Hamer has given a good introduction to Bultmann's theology under the title: 'Une orientation de la pensée protestante: Rudolf Bultmann'. The *Recherches de science religieuse*, Vol. 41, 1953, pp. 612ff. contains the *bulletin critique* of R. Marlé, 'Théologie Protestante: R. Bultmann et la "Demythologisation" du message néotestamentaire'. In Dutch, the articles by P. Fransen, *Entmythologisierung*, in the *Bijdragen*, Vol. XI, 1950, and of J. de Fraine: *Evangelische boodschap en modern denken*, in *Streven*, Vol. 6, 1953, pp. 203ff.

In my own exposition of Bultmann's thought I have not sought for an impossible literal fidelity. The English translation mentioned above is doubtless a remarkable achievement; but when we compare it with the original text, it becomes evident that in several passages the translator has had to interpret as much as to translate. Further, Bultmann's thought presents certain obscurities at several points; this is the opinion of all the critics, and the very title that Barth gives to his book: *Ein Versuch ihn zu verstehen* (An attempt to understand him), which shows that his work is an effort at interpretation, also suggests the difficulty of the subject.

THE CHRISTIAN MESSAGE AND MYTH

First and foremost, one of the most difficult points in his thought is this: What is the part played in Bultmann's thought by the Christ of History in the economy of salvation? It seems to me that at this point his thought lays itself open to two interpretations, which we might describe respectively as 'objective' and 'subjective'; I shall deal with them both in succession. The critics, on the whole, only take the second interpretation into account. But to me this seems to do less than justice to the real intention of Bultmann. I had almost come to this conclusion when I came across a recent book by F. Gogarten: *Entmythologisierung und Kirche* (Stuttgart, 1953) (ET, *Demythologizing and History*, London, 1955), in which the author lays great stress on the objective realistic interpretation; a fact which swept away my final misgivings.

In the present work the exposition of Bultmann's thought is followed by a final chapter which contains a criticism of his thought as a whole. After having gathered up the positive elements in Bultmann's theology, which are of value for Christian theology as a whole, we shall then indicate its faults and weaknesses. In any case, here we have to make a selection, in dealing with the questions raised by Bultmann. The very fact that Bultmann's work is an attempt to interpret Christianity as a whole opened up for Christian theologians the totality of problems which the Christian religion provides for thought. Here it is impossible to deal with all these controversies. Since other authors have dealt with these questions, I shall omit the question of the dependence of faith on the conclusions of historical research, as well as the value of the Resurrection stories in the Gospels, and in the Pauline Epistles. For the rest, we shall be dealing with the major problems: problems of the incompatibility of the message in its traditional form with modern scientific, philosophical and religious thought, and, finally, a comparison between tradition and the theology of Bultmann, from the point of view of their religious value respectively. In the end, it will appear, as we think, that Bultmann has not shaken the foundations of the traditional theology of the Incarnation and of the Holy Spirit.

I

THE DEMYTHOLOGIZING REQUIRED

BULTMANN'S essay opens with the following challenging statement: there can be no agreement between contemporary scientific thought and what he calls the 'mythical', traditional expression of the Christian message. In the world of our experience (or in the world of the present day as we know it) modern science cannot admit the idea of any intervention by so-called 'supernatural' forces, which do not conform to the law of empirical causality: there are no demons, and no angels, there is no divine power permeating this world, and influencing it in a 'supernatural' way. Now the Christian message, as the Churches present it, gives a quite different view of the relation of the world to God: the traditional preaching of the Gospel remains, even today, completely impregnated with mythological conceptions which cannot be reconciled with the world of science. It is this contradiction which Bultmann is trying to make us understand first of all.[1]

Now what do we mean by 'myth' and 'mythical thought'? Such a way of thought does not only mean that faith affirms the reality of a higher, transcendent world, but that it believes that this transcendent world actually intervenes and indeed bursts into the affairs of human life, upon this earth, to which we naturally belong; it claims that certain familiar

[1] The two works which we are here trying to expound: 'Neues Testament und Mythologie' and 'Zum Problem der Entmythologisierung', are found respectively in B. I, pp. 10-48, and B. II, pp. 179-208. An English translation of the former work, 'New Testament and Mythology', appears on pp. 1-44 of *KM*, and of most of the latter, 'Bultmann Replies to His Critics', on pp. 191-211 of *KM* (see Introduction, pp. 13-14, above).

phenomena are due to the action of supernatural forces, or to divine powers, which it sometimes personifies in the shape of 'gods' or 'heroes'.[1] It believes in strange forces, often disquieting and uncanny, which not only dominate nature, but man himself: his sensations, his thoughts, his desires, his highest spiritual life, which they nourish sometimes by means of material food, or which they relate to the magical powers of a mysterious 'spirit' (*pneuma*).

Naturally, mythical thought does not introduce these transcendent forces into our human world without endowing them with certain terrestrial attributes, without representing them in a form which is derived from realities with which we are familiar. For instance, the transcendence of God (*die Jenseitigkeit*) will be expressed in spatial terms (as a *räumliche Ferne*); or it will speak of a World Egg (*Weltei*) or of a World Tree, in order to make the foundation and origin of our universe intelligible; thus mythical thought described strife among the gods—conflicts which it posits as the origin of our historical situation and institutions—in the language usually applied to wars which devastate the life of nations. In short, mythical thought represents the transcendent world in which it believes, in this-worldly, human terms. And when these somewhat speculative views are carried further, it will also conceive the actual cult, with its religious actions, as operations in which these non-material forces are imparted to us through material and perceptible gestures such as magical rites and sacraments.[2]

Now let us turn to the New Testament: it is evident that much of its message is expressed in mythical terms. The picture of the world which it presents is mythological: the universe consists of three spheres: heaven, earth, and hell. The earth is not its own master, for both the supernatural forces—God and his angels—and the demonic forces from below, are struggling for its mastery; its view of nature is utterly different from that of the view of modern science, with its strict adherence to the orderly scheme presented by natural law; above all, in some way man is alienated

[1] B. II, p. 180. [2] B. I, p. 22, n. 2, ET, *KM*, p. 10, n. 2.

from himself, torn asunder in the depths of his being by the conflict between the Spirit of God and the demonic world-powers; his history takes place within an era, a present aeon, given over to the domination of Satan and the 'forces' of sin and death, and it is rushing downhill towards its end, which is imminent, to be swallowed up in a cosmic catastrophe.

Still more serious is the fact that the New Testament proclamation of the saving event is equally mythical: the action of God in Christ, the principal theme of the message and ministry of the Christian Church, is presented in the mythological terms of Jewish Apocalypse, or of the Gnostic myth of redemption. 'When the days are accomplished', behold, the divine power irrupts into our human world, by his mission upon earth and in his appearance in the form of man, as of a Son of God who is supposed to be pre-existent. His death on the Cross secures the pardon of our sins. His Resurrection inaugurates the great upheaval of the Last Days, when death, the result of the sin of Adam, will be vanquished. He himself, already exalted to heaven, at the right hand of the Father, is nevertheless the King and Lord of this world, and already—at least to some extent—controls and dominates the demonic forces which had previously enslaved us. Further, in the near future he will come again on the clouds of heaven, for the universal judgment of men who have been raised from the dead. In the meantime, through Baptism and Holy Communion, the believer is now united with him, and unless he forfeits this union by unworthy conduct, he is assured of his resurrection; he receives the guarantee of this in the Spirit, an active interior force which makes him, inwardly, a 'child of God'.[1]

Here it is interesting to note that this New Testament mythology is neither particularly original, nor even distinctively Christian; it is confined to reproducing, in essentials, the mythology of Jewish Apocalyptic, and that of the Gnostic myth of Redemption.[2] These two schools of thought

[1] B. I, pp. 15-16, ET, *KM*, pp. 1-2.
[2] B. I, p. 26, ET, *KM*, p. 15.

hold the same dualistic conviction: that the world and men, enslaved by satanic forces, long for a divine liberation: only an intervention from above could set men free from these evil forces of the under-world. These two views differ only in certain forms of expression; for instance, Jewish Apocalyptic proclaims that God will save us by sending his Messiah; with him here upon earth the present age will come to an end and a new age will dawn; the Gnostic view, on the other hand, believes in the descent of the Son of God himself from the world of light; he will clothe himself in the body of man, he will liberate his own by his action and his teaching, and he will lead them towards their heavenly fatherland.

Now, according to Bultmann, modern scientific thought has finally destroyed all these mythological views, and has made it impossible for the modern world to accept them. Take the natural sciences first of all: in the light of their discoveries what can the three-decker universe mean—implied in the phrases *descendit ad inferos, ascendit ad coelos*—or the idea of the Coming of the Son of Man on the clouds of heaven, or the prospect of believers being 'caught up in the clouds, to meet the Lord in the air' (I Thess. 4.17)? The discovery of the laws of nature has destroyed our belief in spirits; sickness and disease are due to purely natural causes, all of them belonging to this world—they are not due to spells cast by demons—the modern scientist says frankly: 'Make full use of all the methods of modern medicine, and at once you will cease to believe in the demonic forces of the New Testament!' Miracles, too, as miracles—that is, the operation of a supernatural power in conflict with the powers of the lower regions—are equally incredible. So far as the eschatological views of the New Testament are concerned, they may be written off as 'finished', since Christ did not return. Some people may say that recent developments in the sphere of natural science have changed the scale on which the law of causality works, owing to the discoveries of the atomic age. That may be so, but this does not allow us to think of the world as passively open to the operation of transcendent forces; even if scientific results must be subject to a process of continual revision, none the less, the modern scientist believes that the universe is controlled by 'this-worldly' forces which are accessible to their methods of experimentation.[1]

Still more than the natural sciences, however, the sciences which concern man himself—or to put it better, the know-ledge which modern man has acquired about himself—prevent him from accepting the mythical conception of the New Testament. Modern man regards himself as a unified being (*einheitliches Wesen*) composed of thought, sensation and will; he does not feel that he is inwardly torn in two by the strange forces which are struggling to gain posses-sion of his soul; the term he applies to people who believe that they are possessed by divine or demonic forces is simply this: 'schizophrenic';[2] normally he does not believe either in divine intervention or in the presence of Satan or of demons in the phenomena of his inner life.[3] Biology and psychoanalysis, it is true, reveal to him the profound de-pendence of his natural being; although he is spirit, he is also a natural reality; by his bodily condition he is part of a system of physical forces which exert their influence upon him; but this dependence does not mean that he is at the mercy of supernatural forces outside himself; thus he seeks to master these physical forces, and to organize his life along reasonable lines. For him, in a closed world of natural phenomena, no 'supernatural' power can enter; his mind is autonomous; he is responsible to himself alone, and no out-side 'spiritual' force can affect him in the way he is affected by natural forces.

Thus the New Testament doctrines of the Spirit and the Sacraments are beyond his comprehension. How can the water of Baptism impart to him a mysterious life? or the Holy Communion a spiritual force? and can an unworthy participation in the Lord's Supper bring in its train sick-ness and death?[4] Further, it is impossible for him to regard

[1] B. II, p. 181.   [2] B. I, p. 19, ET, *KM*, p. 6.   [3] B. II, p. 182.
[4] B. I, p. 19, ET, *KM*, p. 6, here quoting I Cor. 11.30.

death as the result of sin, since it hangs over him as a menace before he has committed any sins at all. If he hears of 'Original Sin', and the sin of the first man, he replies: but how can guilt attach to any action that is not strictly personal? In the same way he cannot accept the doctrine of vicarious atonement through the death of Christ: how can my sins be expiated by an innocent being? and what a primitive and barbarous idea of God is implied by this doctrine! For if we think of the death of Christ as a sacrifice, do we not at once recall the savage character of the idea of expiation of sin through blood? Similarly such a man finds it impossible to regard the Resurrection of Jesus as an event which liberates a vital force which man can assimilate through the Sacraments, as if the return of a dead man to life (in a physical sense) and the re-animation of a corpse, could have anything to do with the realities of the life of the spirit! Finally, when in Rom. 5.12 and I Cor. 15.21-44, the death of Christ and his Resurrection are expanded into a great cosmic event (into which we are integrated), modern man feels that he can do no more than reject such views out of hand; for he feels that such ideas reduce man as a human being to the level of a natural creature, and the saving event to a merely natural process: now, we can no longer believe in an assimilation into a material universe even if it be 'from heaven', nor can we believe that the so-called 'spiritual body' will lead to the creation of a true 'spiritual life' and the achievement of our 'authenticity'.[1]

This being so, it is obvious that Christian preaching will be simply beating the air if it tries to link its message with the conceptions of a pre-scientific age, which otherwise (as we have already noted incidentally) are not specifically 'evangelical' in their origins. The fact that so many people have given up Christianity is surely due to the fact that for far too long the message of Christianity has been presented in mythical guise, which is definitely out of date. If the Church wants to preserve the *kerygma*, and to secure its

[1] B. I, p. 21, ET, *KM*, p. 8.

acceptance by succeeding generations, it is urgent that, as soon as possible, she should set about 'demythologizing' her message, believing that this task is possible. At the same time, she must guard against the danger of trying to keep this process of 'demythologization' within certain prescribed limits. For instance, the Church may wish to retain the mythical idea that material food, the body of Christ, will effect spiritual changes, but she will abandon the idea of baptism for the dead, or that the Holy Communion cele-brated unworthily has a bad effect upon the health.[1] 'No such thing!' says Bultmann; he insists that such a com-promise is impossible; demythologizing must be without reserve, and it must deal with fundamental ideas.[2] And although Bultmann does not express himself very clearly on this point, we can see the reason for this absolute de-mand: modern scientific thought cannot endure the idea of any kind of divine intervention in our human world: hence, wherever this idea emerges, as, for instance, in the traditional idea of the Incarnation of the Son of God, the Christian theologian must submit to criticism and must be willing to 'purify' the message.

But, it will be said, there is no need to urge this duty of 'demythologizing' the Christian message on the younger generation of theologians: for it has already been done—by the old school of Liberal Christianity!

At this point, Bultmann makes two main criticisms of the previous efforts at demythologizing;[3] in so doing he makes a critical examination which enables him to define posi-tively his own idea of the work that needs to be done.

Here is his first criticism: the 'Liberal' process of demytho-logizing was made at the expense of the *kerygma* itself, which it destroyed at its very heart. The Liberal school regarded

[1] B. I, p. 21, ET, *KM*, p. 9.   [2] B. II, p. 185.
[3] Bultmann distinguishes two recent processes of demythologization, that of the Liberal Christians, and that of the school of comparative religion (*religionsgeschichtliche Schule*) (B. I, p. 25, ET, *KM*, p. 13). We can omit, without harm, the verdict which he passes upon the latter.

mythical conceptions as non-essential; they were like the shell which encloses the kernel. But how did it define this kernel? In its view, the essence of the Gospel consisted merely in a collection of religious and ethical truths immanent in the human mind. Christ did not confront us with a divine event, coming from outside at the same moment to judge and to pardon (in one act) our unhappy existence; the saving truths and values are within us, but like a mystical soul asleep; like a good angel, Christ came to awaken this soul; on the whole he confined himself to revealing man to himself, to the process of reawakening and making explicit what man already knew implicitly, the supra-temporal truths by which man was already living, although he did not realize it. Doubtless these truths reached the reflective consciousness of man within history, and they were clarified by the historical conditions of the fact of Christianity, but the significance of this fact was hardly anything more than pedagogic; once these values had been discovered (Harnack: the Fatherhood of God and the infinite value of the human soul) their recognition was no longer connected with belief in a divine act of salvation. That too is the reason why—according to the Liberal view —the New Testament does not hurt us, nor do we find it a 'stumbling-block': we accept the truths which it reveals without effort since before they were made explicit we already possessed them and they were the basis of our inner life.

Now, in all this, the Liberal Christians have falsified the Christian message. For—anticipating his own interpretation of the *kerygma*, from this point Bultmann insists that the Gospel message is essentially the proclamation of an act of God, of an event which is not human at all, by which God saves man; the revelation of the radical incompatibility between God and the world, a revelation which, far from throwing man back upon himself and asking him to believe in himself (as if he were the measure of all things), forces him to renounce the false security of human values, and to go out of himself in order to abandon himself to God; that

THE DEMYTHOLOGIZING REQUIRED

is, the revelation of the Cross. Also this revelation does not meet in us a spirit already prepared to accept it; but, rather, it demands from us a decision in which we have to conquer ourselves. By its very nature it gives us a shock, it confronts us with a 'stumbling-block'.[1]

Doubtless, all genuine efforts at demythologization will have to eliminate some 'causes of offence' due to the preaching of the *kerygma* today: and indeed, precisely those 'causes of offence' which have been already mentioned, which bring out the incompatibility of these mythological conceptions with the modern view of existence. But, over and above these unnecessary hindrances, caused by an archaic way of preaching, the message ought always to present the 'stumbling-block' of the Cross. There will always be the man or woman who does not want to have anything to do with it, and who rejects it with a sense of sheer revulsion. This fact was not understood by the Liberal school of thought, and that is the first reason why its effort at demythologizing was a failure.

Now for the second reason: the Liberal school regarded the process of demythologizing as the elimination of the mythological element. We, however, should regard it as an existential interpretation of myth.[2] This can be explained quite easily. Mythical thought, as we have already suggested, consists of two elements. It is animated by the following *intention*:[3] it desires to express its belief in the dependence of man: dependence not only in familiar things like the food we eat and the air we breathe, but upon

---

[1] This idea of 'shock' and 'scandal' or 'stumbling-block' is not much stressed in *Neues Testament und Mythologie,* but it is emphasized in Bultmann's *Theologie des Neuen Testaments,* second edition, Tübingen, 1951, pp. 386-396, ET, *Theology of the New Testament,* Vol. 2, pp. 40-48, London, 1955. Here he points out that the 'world' (in the Johannine sense of the word) is bound to feel that the Christian revelation is an attack (*Angriff*) made by God upon it; it gives man a shock, and is a stumbling-block (*Anstoss*). This indeed is the theme of the Fourth Gospel (see mainly pp. 393-394, ET, Vol. 2, pp. 46-47). In his recent reply to Jaspers (*Zur Frage der Entmythologisierung*) Bultmann frequently recurs to this idea of the character of revelation as *Anstoss* (B. III, pp. 51, 58).

[2] B. I, p. 24, ET, *KM,* p. 12.   [3] B. II, pp. 183-184.

mysterious transcendent forces: in this second kind of dependence man hopes that the fact that he is aware of it will enable him to influence the forces with which he is familiar, and use them for his own needs; so he asks God to give him his daily bread. We should note that this belief in the divine forces which control our life is equivalent to a conception of the existence of man; it suggests that human life is based upon, and grounded in powers which are beyond its reach: in so doing it acknowledges that in some way or another man's existence is controlled by the action of God.

In order to interpret Bultmann's thought at this point we might describe this *intention*, this first element, as the soul of the myth. The second element, its body (which is the mythological element proper) consists in its 'this-worldly' presentation (which can only be described as unfortunate) —which the myth ascribes to the operation of these higher powers. The myth suggests that these forces operate in our world in the same way as the 'this-worldly' forces themselves. Think, for instance, of the mythological conception of miracle: it presents the action of God as a process which both interrupts and prolongs (*unterbricht und doch gleichzeitig verkettet*)[1] the natural or psychological course of history; it introduces transcendent causality into the chain of events in this world. Similarly, the myth regards the gods as 'heroes', men of superior endowments, and makes them act as such. Or, again, mythical thought tends to speak of the divine omnipotence and omniscience as 'attributes', which can be understood by speculative thought, or by the human reason in general; and on this basis it draws up a whole list of doctrinal propositions; now the only valid function of speculative thought is to give a scientific interpretation of the universe. Thus inevitably the theology which it produces brings God down to the human level; the divine 'omnipotence' and 'omniscience' which it affirms does not differ from the rest of human power and knowledge; the difference is merely quantitative.[2] In short, myth transforms

_____
[1] B. II, p. 183.   [2] B. II, p. 184.

that which is 'other-worldly' and divine into something 'this-worldly' and human—that is, an object—which can be manipulated by man;[1] it constructs a whole system of 'this-worldly' representations of God in his essence and in his action.

Now, ought the demythologizing of the New Testament to renounce equally both these component elements of mythical thought and then eliminate mythical thought entirely? This was the view taken by the Liberal Christian school of thought. It rejected not only the body of the myth but the conception of dependent existence which it was trying to express. At least, this school did not believe that religious thought ought to be controlled by the New Testament view of existence, as an intangible norm; with great audacity, for the biblical knowledge of human existence it substituted the views of a religious *a priori*, a 'spiritual life' on a humanistic level.

This extreme, however, cannot be justified. What is it, in fact, in mythical thought, which arouses the reasonable objection—already mentioned—of modern man? Is it his belief in the operation of a mysterious force which affects our life, its conviction that our existence is based upon, and conditioned by the power of a Being who far transcends humanity? By no means. What modern man refuses to accept is this: the idea that transcendent forces operate in our world in exactly the same way as the natural forces around us; and, further, the idea (which really amounts to the same thing) that this transcendence can be attained by our ordinary faculties of observation and experience, and consequently can be expressed in the terms of 'objectivizing' thought; to put it briefly, modern man does not object to the idea that transcendence exists, that it confronts and challenges us, but it does reject the idea that in becoming immanent it ceases to exist, that is, to be itself.

Thus it is evident that, negatively, an authentic 'demythologization' will confine its efforts to eliminating the anthropomorphic presentation of transcendence which characterizes

[1] *Der Mythos objektiviert das Jenseits zum Diesseits* und damit auch zum Verfügbaren (B. II, p. 184).

27

the myth of the New Testament. It will reject all speculative doctrines of God both in his action and in his Being, as he is 'in himself'; it takes this line because it holds that a doctrine which has been 'objectivized' and universalized reduces the God of whom it speaks to the level of this world. Positively, however, it will try to meet the contention of the myth, that is, to bring out the *intention* which animates it. As we have already said, the secret purpose of myth is not to give us a pseudo-scientific view of the world, of its origin and its nature, but to express its belief in the dependence of our human existence upon the God who calls us as persons; unfortunately the 'mythologizing' process frustrates this purpose: the objective mythological representations absorb our attention, and distract us from the real point; and, since modern man cannot believe in this corpus of Christian myth, the whole Christian message is imperilled. A genuine demythologizing process will eliminate this danger: in the New Testament, it will bring out the significance of human existence in the sight of God; from those incidents in the Scriptures which speak of transcendent powers controlling the world and man, it will single out the concept of existence, the 'possibility' which it offers to man of understanding himself; in short, it will give an existential interpretation of the Christian myth—an interpretation to which, in principle, modern man will offer no objection.

II

THE PRINCIPLE OF EXISTENTIAL INTERPRETATION

'EXISTENTIAL INTERPRETATION': in this context, what does it mean? Here, it means that Bultmann is influenced —quite consciously, by the philosophy of Heidegger. His interpretation of this philosophy may not be always in harmony with the intention of the author of *Sein und Zeit*; in fact, he seems to tend towards what has been called the 'nihilism' of Heidegger. The observations which appear in the book entitled *What is Metaphysics?* in 1943, should have shown that this is a mistaken interpretation.[1] About 1940, however, many of Heidegger's readers held this view, and Bultmann agreed with them.

The philosophy of *Sein und Zeit* is essentially a transcendental analysis of *Dasein*. We must distinguish this term from that of *Vorhandensein*: the latter term signifies 'something-which-is-present' (or a given object), 'something-at-hand, present', 'existing', in the ordinary sense of the word, as 'something which can be affirmed of all that surrounds us',[2] the being of inanimate objects, or more generally of phenomena which can be grasped by the process of 'objectivizing' thought.[3] *Dasein*, on the other hand, stands for the 'being of humans' or the human being in that which is characteristic of him, which is the possibility of asking himself the question of Being in general, interest in the totality

---

[1] Cf. Max Müller: *Crise de la métaphysique*, Paris, 1953, the chapter entitled (in question form) 'The "Nihilism" of Heidegger?', pp. 54-59.

[2] Here we are quoting K. Rahner, *Introduction au concept de philosophie existentiale chez Heidegger*, in *Recherches de science religieuse*, Vol. 30, 1940, p. 161.

[3] B. II, p. 193, ET, *KM*, p. 194.

of Being, to which is added the power of understanding oneself, and of ordering one's life as one chooses. Bultmann observes that—so far as he is concerned—*Dasein* does not exist without possessing a knowledge of itself which is not derived from thought or philosophy, but from life itself:[1] it is not a theoretical knowledge, under the sign of the Logos, but an experience, or state of soul, which Heidegger regards as elemental, fundamental (*Grunderfahrung, Grundbestimmung*).[2]

Precisely, existential analysis seeks to lift this knowledge which has been thus exercised on to the plane of reflection: but we should be careful to note that it abstracts from the concrete conditions in which that existence is realized and placed (for instance, the existence of the believer or of the atheist);[3] it is an analysis of existence in general,[4] which makes a great effort to discern the 'general and formal structure which belongs to *Dasein*, which is the specific mode of being human':[5] this is a general statement which, it is generally agreed, is covered by the word '*existenzial*' (existential) (the word '*existenziell*' (*existentiel*) being reserved for the concrete practical possibilities of the individual *Dasein*, with which we shall be dealing later on):[6] a general statement, furthermore, which, in the mind of the author of *Sein und Zeit*, is meant to prepare the way for a doctrine of Being in general.

Nevertheless, in spite of this universality, existential analysis has nothing in common with a science of the abstract essence of man, with an anthropology whose method consists in deducting by the way of logical necessity more particular notions of a more comprehensive notion; think, for instance, of certain classic deductions about the immortality

---

[1] B. II, pp. 191, 192, ET, *KM*, pp. 192-193.
[2] K. Rahner, *loc. cit.*, p. 166.
[3] B. II, p. 194, ET, *KM*, p. 195.
[4] *überhaupt*; B. II, p. 192, ET, *KM*, p. 193; *allgemein*; B. II, p. 194, ET, *KM*, p. 195.
[5] K. Rahner, *loc. cit.*, p. 161.
[6] Cf. *An Existentialist Theology*, J. Macquarrie, London, 1955, p. 34 (Tr.).

of the soul derived from the notion of its spiritual nature. An anthropology of this kind is regarded as having lost contact with reality; and that it simply consists of a set of rather formal concepts. Here we must remind ourselves of the phenomenological method: it alone permits 'that which shows itself, as it is revealed to itself, to be seen in his own self-disclosure as existing'.[1] Existential analysis will thus be the application of the phenomenological method to the understanding of human *Dasein*: it will keep existence in view continually: it will wait, so to speak, for it to reveal itself, its fundamental structures; or to put it better, emphasizing a feature which has already been indicated: it will confine itself to clarifying the knowledge of existence exercised in the position of existence itself, to make explicit, to develop this knowledge by giving to it, at the stage of reflection an appropriate conceptual expression.[2]

Proceeding in this manner in *Dasein, Sein und Zeit* disengages from anguish (experience of the fundamental situation) the existential elements which are called: dereliction, power-to-be, and fallenness, which are organically connected with 'care' (*Sorge*), that is to say in 'Being anticipating that which-is-already-thrown-into-the-world-in-which-it-is-lost',[3] and which throws itself constantly ahead of itself, towards an absolute term, death. In a general way, in his picture of man, Heidegger accentuates the features which emphasize his distress and his radical sense of finitude. It is of course true that he will tell us that the privileged gesture of *Dasein* —that which distinguishes it from *Vorhandensein*—is to constitute the being of the world, to give it its meaning, its intelligibility, but this giver of Being who is man, remains,

---

[1] 'Phenomenology says then ἀποφαίνεσθαι τὰ φαινόμενα "*Das was sich zeigt, so wie es sich von ihm selbst her zeigt, von ihm selbst her sehen lassen*".' M. Heidegger, *Sein und Zeit*, Tübingen, sixth edition, 1949, p. 34.

[2] Thus, at least, this is what Bultmann says: 'The "correct" philosophy is, quite simply, that philosophical labour which makes an effort to develop the understanding of existence which is "given" with human existence, in suitable terms' (*Begrifflichkeit*), (B. II, p. 192, ET, *KM*, p. 193).

[3] A. De Waelhens, *La philosophie de Martin Heidegger*, Louvain, 1940, p. 130.

in this very gesture, a bare existent, thrown among the existents, issued from nothing and destined for Nothing: he does not transcend his Being-in-the-world; the power which he has of projecting his possibilities is not the power of surmounting or suspending his condition of 'being-thrown-there' in order to die.[1]

But, while existential analysis reveals man's distress, it also illuminates his *Dasein* by showing him the conditions of his authenticity: it teaches him that he is menaced by the danger of being sucked down into *Vorhandensein*, of becoming a *thing*, instead of developing personality, of becoming confused with the impersonal and the neuter (or *man*); instead of reaching the condition of the true 'self', of losing himself in anonymity, instead of releasing his authenticity, of seeking his security in the realities of this world, instead of facing his destiny (and especially death, which forms part of life), of regulating his behaviour according to ready-made norms, all due to social pressure, instead of deciding for himself the conduct he chooses;[2] if he wants to avoid this shipwreck in 'the banality of daily life' 'in the dispersion and dissipation of himself in contact with things',[3] in order to do this he ought to accept himself as a whole and ratify his destiny (in spite of any obscurity he may still have about this); that is what existential analysis teaches man, by the mere fact that it makes him appreciate the difference between *Dasein* and *Vorhandensein*; thanks to that, *Dasein* becomes aware of itself (on reflection) as a being who is responsible for himself,[4] and who cannot become fully himself save in becoming personally involved in this or that concrete existential possibility, in a personal *existentiel* decision: the acceptance, in solitude, of a task of which the existent alone sees that it is his own, at the moment when he accepts it.[5]

---

[1] After M. Dufrenne and P. Ricoeur: *Karl Jaspers et la philosophie de l'existence*, Paris, 1947, in the chapter 'La vérité et l'être, III Une philosophie à deux foyers: Jaspers en face de Heidegger', pp. 365, 366.

[2] M. Heidegger, *Sein und Zeit*, pp. 127, 128, 130, 179.

[3] K. Rahner, *loc. cit.*, p. 169.

[4] *der sich selbst überantwortet ist*, B. II, p. 193, ET, *KM*, p. 193.

[5] Cf. M. Müller, *op. cit.*, p. 25 (see also pp. 80-84).

This brings us to the point at which Bultmann's thought on what he calls the 'existential interpretation' of the Christian message is clarified. In his thought this expression has a complex meaning, in which we can distinguish three affirmations which become more and more precise as time goes on.

1. First of all, it covers only these elements in the exegesis of the New Testament which refer to the understanding of ourselves. Bultmann believes that these are the only points worthy of the attention of modern man. We must note very particularly that here Bultmann gives the principle of existential interpretation the value of a unique and strictly exclusive norm. This means that when we are reading the Bible, we can safely ignore its 'objectivizing presentations', the doctrines which are of interest to speculative and impersonal thought—as we have already seen, these presentations can only be mythological; all we have to ask of the Scriptures is this: what do they tell us about our existence, and the conditions of its authenticity?

The biblical message is rigorously existentialist and personalist in character: it is never theoretical: it never moves on the plane of speculation,[1] or, when it does so, it no longer commands our assent. It does not teach us any general doctrine about God, about his operation in the world, or even about predestination or reprobation: we can look for no philosophy of life (*Weltanschauung*) from it; it summons *you*, the concrete human being, in your equally concrete existence, in your *hic et nunc*, and summons you to welcome it; it places you in the I-Thou relation; it knows one dimension only: the call of God—and the response of man: 'the

---

[1] We are quoting here from E. Brunner, 'Prédestination et liberté' in the *Revue d'histoire et de philosophie religieuse* published by the Protestant Faculty of Theology of Strasbourg, Vol. 32, 1952, p. 95. Brunner's remarks here do not occur in any context dealing with Bultmann's theology, but they seem to me to express very aptly the thought of the latter on the precise point with which we are here concerned. But while sharing Bultmann's views on the necessity for an existentialist, nonspeculative interpretation of the New Testament, Brunner by no means accepts Bultmann's theology as a whole. See his critical remarks in Vol. 2 of his *Dogmatics*, Zürich, 1950, pp. 311-316; ET, London 1952, pp. 186ff.

dimension of responsibility'.[1] Doubtless, it is possible, as we shall see later on, that among these conditions of our authenticity there figures the existential (*existentiel*) acceptance of a divine saving act, but if this divine act is not conceived on the lines of 'this-worldly' action, modern man will not reasonably be able to refuse it; it will confront him with the 'offence' of the Cross, but already we know that this 'offence' has nothing to do with the unnecessary 'offence' of the mythological interpretation.

If the demand for the existential interpretation in Bultmann's thought did not go beyond the first meaning, it would provide the Catholic theologian with the basis for a partial possible understanding—partial only, because in its exclusiveness the principle of existential interpretation is unacceptable: it is not true that the Christian message applies to man alone. But if the principle were confined to stressing the importance of human interest in all religious truth, related to God himself, the Catholic theologian would not refuse to admit this: for him too in itself faith also involves charity, and the revelation of the most sublime mysteries ought to help us to understand ourselves in our relation with God, and to achieve our destiny.

2. But in Bultmann's thought the existential interpretation implies a good deal more than this: he says explicitly that only the existential elements in the New Testament can be accepted. Yet they are claimed to be the fulfilment of our natural self-knowledge; it must be clear that they correspond to a latent possibility in the human *Dasein*. But *why*? Because, if one of these existential elements, revealed by the analysis of existential philosophy, fails to meet a human situation, then these existential elements in the New Testament must rightly be called 'mythical', an irruption of the divine into the human realm, which is inadmissible, it is a violent rupture—like that of miracle—of the conditions of our existence; then, fundamentally they themselves would no longer be existential.

[1] E. Brunner, *ibid.*

34

Let us explain by an example.[1] The Christian message charges us with our sinful condition and regards this condition as an *aversio a Deo*: in a more general way, it invites us to confess our sins and to receive the grace of God; the preacher on Sunday morning summons his hearers, and urges them to decision, in order that they may all, together, accept the fact of their misery and of the divine pardon. But so long as the man in the pew does not receive this message as a 'word' which responds to a secret desire in the depths of his being, the idea of an *aversio a Deo* will be quite beyond him; it will not even interest him; it will not reveal to him his existential condition; it will simply remain a '*mythologoumenon*' without force and without any truth for humanity. First of all he needs to be helped, by a natural process of existential analysis, to realize that he is a 'lost' sinner, in dire need of God's mercy, and then to perceive within himself the point at which he may eventually experience God's forgiveness and a new life in Christ. This is a philosophical task whose results will be limited: doubtless the Fall, the *Verfallenheit*, of which you speak at this level of thought, will not coincide with that of the Fall in the light of the Christian message; you will not realize fully the deceitfulness of sin; further, you will not know the Fall as sin, as *aversio a Deo*, because as a philosopher you will ignore the effective encounter with a personal God, the existence of relations, whether friendly or hostile, between you and him, all that you can do is to explain what 'a personal encounter usually means, in what it can consist' ('. . . *sondern nur zeigen kann, was personales Geschehen* überhaupt *bedeutet*', B. I, p. 124, ET, *KM*, p. 104). None the less, these philosophical reflections on human misery will be very effective in helping you to show the existential and human character of the reflections which are definitely Christian; and they will therefore justify people in accepting them; they will disturb the man who listens to the

[1] Bultmann himself gives us this explanation in his reply to the theologian J. Schniewind, *Zu J. Schniewinds Thesen*. B. I, p. 124, ET, *KM*, p. 104.

message: for, showing him that the confession of sin and the acceptance of grace correspond to the possibilities of his existence, he will see that to reject the *kerygma* is culpable unbelief. They will not eliminate the element of 'offence' from the *kerygma*: the natural man will still be summoned to make a painful renunciation of his own works, to give himself for his salvation into the power of Another, but they will eliminate the mythological, unintelligible and foreign elements from the message.

We must also note that this existential philosophy, indispensable for the demythologized interpretation of the New Testament, is, for Bultmann, an existential form of analysis universally valid for human existence. Doubtless, it is confined to releasing the natural knowledge which man has of himself, and acts simply by existing: from this point of view, it has nothing in common with an artificial or abstract anthropology; nevertheless, it does claim to provide the existential universals of *Dasein*; it contains no element of simple personal trust, nor of confession; based on the phenomenological method, it believes that it is able to make explicit the constants of human existence, to establish a general anthropology (preparatory moreover to a knowledge of the nature of Being in general), and to the extent in which it succeeds, this generalization, and in some way, this ontology, is supposed to provide the appropriate instrument for the existential interpretation of the message, and for its acceptance.

Again, if Bultmann's claims were confined to this second, more precise meaning of the existential interpretation, the Catholic theologian might very well suggest that, in substance, Bultmann's contention coincides with other attempts at re-interpretation with which he is already quite familiar; that is, for instance, all the research that has been devoted to the question of the relation between Nature and Supernature; here we are not only thinking of the contribution to apologetics made by Maurice Blondel, but of many other theologians, both past and present, who have moreover gone far more deeply into this question than Bultmann has done;

his views are mediocre, in comparison with theirs, yet he ignores their work entirely.

3. But Bultmann pushes his claims further: the existential analysis which he believes to be necessary for the existential interpretation of the Christian message is precisely that of the philosophy of Martin Heidegger. Why appeal to one particular brand of philosophy? Bultmann believes that this philosophy alone can render him *two services* which he regards as indispensable.

On the one hand, as we have seen, the philosophy of *Sein und Zeit* (at least in the way in which Bultmann and many others understand it) accentuates, in the concept of *Dasein*, the features which emphasize man's fall and misery. On the other hand, in his thought Bultmann has already a preconceived idea of the Christian message, fairly typical of Protestant thought, which lays great emphasis upon the idea of the Fall: the *aversio a Deo*, which is man's sin, constitutes a radical fall, a fundamental corruption of nature, a total loss of the image of God. So Heidegger's philosophy was chosen because, in order to understand the scriptural conception of sin, and of the *aversio a Deo*, existentially, and the Christian message in general, Heidegger's existential analysis, and his understanding of the desperate condition of *Dasein* (human existence or human life) seemed to Bultmann the most appropriate instrument to use. In short: we ought, says Bultmann, to interpret the Christian message with the methods of Heidegger's philosophy because it reveals the distress of *Dasein*, and thus prepares us for the knowledge of a Gospel of the Fall and of forgiveness.

But there is more in it than this: Bultmann claims that Heidegger's analysis, and still more precisely the ontology which it implies, can render a second service to Christian thought, and one which is very different from the first; moreover, it is independent of the 'nihilist' features of his interpretation of Heidegger, and more closely attached to a less controversial element in the thought of the author of *Sein und Zeit*. This 'second service' is stated as follows:

anticipating his interpretation of the *kerygma*, Bultmann has already given us to understand that the message includes, in his view, the announcement of a divine saving event, wrought historically through Christ; now, he believes that the ontology of Heidegger alone is able to provide us with the categories appropriate for a correct expression of this divine history which are acceptable to the philosopher.

First of all, *negatively*, let us see why the classical ontology is not adequate to this task. Bultmann writes: 'In my opinion Christology ought finally to shake off the domination of an ontology of objectivizing thought and present itself in the terms of a new ontology (*in einer neuen ontologischen Begrifflichkeit*).[1]

'Objectivizing ontology'; these words obviously refer to the 'ancient ontology' (*die antike Ontologie*) which Heidegger criticizes in *Sein und Zeit*.[2] According to Heidegger, the dominant feature of this ontology is essentialism: it presents itself exclusively as a philosophy of essences, to the detriment of the philosophy of Being: indeed, it does not really face the question of Being. 'Certainly, the "essence" with which this philosophy is preoccupied represents the essential *place* of Being, the regions which are ordered are *modes of Being*. . . . Being sustains the essences, sanctions order. The philosophy of essences has therefore Being for its horizon and it is on this account that it is truly a philosophy. . . . It moves within Being, as in its right setting. But this setting, the space and context of all questions, and of all raising of questions, is never itself the explicit theme of reflection. It is like a light which illuminates everything and makes all investigations possible, but which is never examined in itself.'[3]

Another feature of the classical ontology, at least from the time of Descartes, is this: the objectivization of Being (*das Seiende*). This term also designates the essence, not however the abstract and universal essence, the 'species', but

---

[1] B. II, p. 206, n. 1, ET, *KM*, p. 209.
[2] M. Heidegger, *Sein und Zeit*, pp. 19-27 (p. 22: *die antike Ontologie*).
[3] M. Müller, *op. cit.*, p. 17.

THE PRINCIPLE OF EXISTENTIAL INTERPRETATION

essence in its *concretion* and its individuality. Now the Cartesian ontology has seen in existence an object, something which is confronted by the representation, an 'entity' entirely foreign to the subject, confining itself to offering itself to it as a means of taking or of possible seizure (*Angriff*)[1]; in other words, Cartesianism has separated the subject from the object; instead of seeing, as it should have done, that the mind is a being-in-the-world, where it appears to be, and to which the connexion with the world was intrinsic (there is no 'self' save by and in an actual relation with something other than myself),[2] the Cartesian philosophy has conceived the subject as a pure 'self', a simple capacity of apprehending the real in the representation. The consequence of this view was that the classical ontology was diverted from its proper object, Being: already too unmindful of Being on account of its exclusive attention to essences (abstract), in addition it increased the distance still further by its attention to objectivized 'existents' or objects.

This is not difficult to understand. If the 'existent' instead of being objectivized, had been considered in its immanence in *Dasein*, its knowledge would have furnished the basis for a knowledge of Being itself. We must not forget that it is *Dasein*, and that alone, which opens up the way into Being for us; if ever a science of Being becomes possible for us, it is on condition that it is articulated in terms of existential analysis, the man 'who wants to know what Being is' must 'brood over himself'; the reason for this is that Being 'is not something in addition which can be isolated from the whole, and thus—if we can put it so—attain its pure state. Its notion as the *a priori* and necessary universal propositions show, pre-exists, underlying all particular knowledge.'

---

[1] Here we would refer the reader to F. Gogarten's *Entmythologisierung und Kirche*, Stuttgart, 1953, pp. 53, 54, ET *Demythologizing and History*, London, 1955, pp. 50ff., where he criticizes the 'subject-object' pattern inextricably linked with the Cartesian view of the world of reality: more strongly even than Bultmann himself, Gogarten tries to show the importance of this criticism for the understanding of Bultmann's theology.

[2] A. De Waelhens, *op. cit.*, p. 36.

We cannot then seek to define it save in going back to 'that initial notion which the human mind possesses of it, in other words, to man himself: the subject who is seeking becomes the object of the quest'.[1] But here is an ontology which objectivizes the 'existents', tears them away from their natural immanence, holds them to be essences, physical realities interesting in themselves, beyond their attachment to *Dasein*, and thus also to Being itself; it is obvious that such an ontology is forced to ignore Being; the 'existents' cease to be for it the means of the 'unveiling' of Being, the place from which the mystery of Being could be elucidated; all the constructions which it could erect from these objects, all the hierarchies of essences, all the general categories of physical realities (substance, accidents, etc.) are doomed in advance to defeat: they will never permit ontology to attain the possession of the reality which it seeks, the ontological reality.

Now do we begin to see some of the disastrous consequences of this distortion of ontology for Christian theology? Let us suppose that the theologians borrow their concepts from this essentialist ontology for the Being of God and his action in history, for the salvation which he brings to us in Christ (and it is a fact that this has taken place, that theologians have actually done this): the result cannot help being a failure. For if God exists and acts, that is to say, if he reveals himself and communicates himself in history, it is obvious that his existence and his revelation are situated on the side of the interior mystery of Being and cannot be grasped save through this mystery which has been previously elucidated; the essentialist ontology, blind to Being, could only blind theology itself about God and the divine mysteries of salvation; it could only conceive God as the supreme objective existent, as the principle and the foundation of objects: the supreme Being of nature, a sort of *natura naturans*; and so far as the historical action of God is concerned and the history of salvation, it could not conceive it otherwise than as the supernaturalization of physical

[1] K. Rahner, art. cit., p. 157.

realities and in terms of the consecration of a secular world. (This really amounts to saying that it was doomed to 'mythologize'.) For there is myth—so Bultmann says—making his definition of mythology more explicit—not only in all the instances where the action of God is conceived as revealing itself to the senses in nature, but already in those cases where the divine action is simply expressed in physical categories, or compared with a natural force, even if it is not supposed to manifest its divine character in such an event.

Now we understand Bultmann's desire which he expresses thus: 'Christology ought finally to free itself entirely from the domination of an ontology of objectivizing thought.' In a very general way, in his thought, this desire is applied to the interpretation of the message as a whole; it is the totality of the saving event which ought to be severed from the influence of the categories of essentialist ontology, for instance, that we ought to cease conceiving the reality of the Spirit in the (mythical) terms of a physical force, secretly influencing our minds. But particularly in Christology we begin to see that later on, in the doctrine of the Incarnation, we shall be urged to renounce the essentialist conceptions of the two natures, human and divine, and of their union in the unique Person of the Word.

Positively: Bultmann believes that the service which the essentialist ontology cannot render to Christian theology, can be expected from the ontology of Heidegger. We may well ask: on what does Bultmann base this hope: Heidegger may indeed have described that which has been called 'the roots of the comprehension of Being'[1] in an original way: it is, as we know, the existential analysis of *Dasein*; but up to this point he has scarcely given an explicit answer to the question: What is Being? In short, we do not know what his ontology is.[2]

Here, however, Bultmann himself is going to try to fill

---

[1] B. Welte, 'Remarques sur l'ontologie de Heidegger', in the *Revue des science philosophiques et théologiques*, Vol. 31, 1947, p. 380.
[2] I.e. because Heidegger has not yet published his ontology.

this gap. Here we must remember that the analysis of Heidegger's philosophy—interpreted by Bultmann—has revealed to *Dasein* the condition of its authentic existence: man can only fulfil himself in a personal existential decision. Now—Bultmann suggests—nothing can prevent us from thinking that this decision ought to bear upon a divine event coming suddenly into our existence: God would then intervene in our history and it would be our free acceptance, in faith, of this divine event which would assure our authenticity; on condition, however, that the act of God must not be invested with the characters of an 'objective' (or physical) intervention; we must not conceive 'divine history' in terms of the objects of representative thought: we know already that God and his action cannot be placed on the side of the 'objective existents'; to think the opposite would be to return to the mythological errors of an essentialist theology. It remains to be seen whether another type of divine action can be conceived: a Word of God, and a message from God, challenging us, so to speak, from the mystery of Being, hidden in the depths of *Dasein*. On this very difficult and important point, what is Bultmann's conception? And how can certain expansions of Heidegger's ontological analysis succeed in helping us at this point? He will tell us this later in explicit terms when he expounds his theology of the saving event.[1] For the moment it is sufficient for us to be enlightened, to some extent, about the nature of the second service which he expects from Heidegger's ontology. Contrary to the essentialist ontology, it is capable, he believes, of procuring us concepts appropriate for the expression of God and his eventual historical encounter with man.

Here, we believe, are the elements which enter, dimly, into Bultmann's programme for the existential interpretation of the *kerygma*. In short, this interpretation will obey three laws: it will consider only those elements in the message which are related to the knowledge of ourselves; it will make clear the agreement between the Christian message

[1] See below, pp. 92, 93, and especially pp. 95-101, 142.

and the existential element in *Dasein*; it will proclaim the *kerygma* in the specific terms of Heidegger's philosophy (and here it will even ask from Heidegger's analysis two very distinct services).

It was necessary to distinguish these three elements, in order to spare Bultmann from a criticism which would be too devastating. Jaspers has reproached Bultmann for giving to his existential analysis the character of a personal belief: whatever we may say of Heidegger as interpreted by Bultmann, the reduction of *Dasein* to 'the spirit of despair', says Jaspers, 'is not in any way the truth about man as a whole; it is simply the way in which certain men, and even several, though not all, understand themselves'.[1] In my opinion this protest is justified; but it does not affect the desire for an existential interpretation not based specifically on Heidegger's philosophy: even if it be found that Bultmann is mistaken in basing his interpretation on an existential analysis exclusively derived from Heidegger's philosophy, we have still to ask whether in principle, he is not authorised to call in the aid of an existential analysis, of universal validity, whose conclusions would omit Heidegger's 'nihilism'.

From several quarters, indeed, many serious criticisms have been made of the very effort to make use of existential philosophy at all, and more generally, of the actual principle of the existential interpretation of the New Testament. To claim that the only valid element in the Christian message is that view of existence which it gives us, really amounts to saying that the human mind, *a priori*, dictates to the Word of God the conditions on which he will believe; by that very fact the Bible is placed under the control of a preparatory philosophy; this means putting the Word of God under the domination of human learning,[2] thus robbing God of his sovereignty. If we decide in advance

[1] Cf. K. Jaspers, 'Wahrheit und Unheil der Bultmannschen Entmythologisierung' (B. III, p. 42).
[2] B. II, p. 191, ET, *KM*, p. 191.

that God can only will to reveal to us the conditions of our authentic existence, it seems that we are infringing his absolute sovereignty, both in his Being and in his action upon us.

Another way of expressing the same criticism is this: that Bultmann borrows from Heidegger's philosophy the categories of 'authentic' and 'inauthentic existence', of 'anguish' and 'care', and even of the Fall (*Verfallenheit*), and that Christianity must express and define itself in these categories, or we shall not be able to accept Christianity at all. Or again, it has been said: according to Bultmann, the Christian myth, if it wishes to be accepted, must be interpreted existentially, that is to say, in terms of the biblical conception of existence; this affirmation is based upon the following postulate: it is impossible for God to act upon us in the manner of 'this-worldly' forces; certainly, we do not deny the very idea of divine action; but this can only consist in a transformation of the natural knowledge we have of ourselves; our 'being as humans' is *Dasein*, in the sense given to this word in Heidegger's philosophy, as we have already seen; that is to say, it is essentially *Erschlossenheit*, being open to oneself, and self-knowledge; henceforward the only action that God could exert upon me would consist in a change in the knowledge of myself; the only possible divine event would be scarcely more than a phenomenon of consciousness.

These are all different expressions of one fundamental criticism: namely, *that Bultmann makes the Christian message depend upon a philosophy*. In the eyes of Protestant theology this is a very serious charge, above all if it is tinged in the slightest degree by Barthian conceptions: we know that for a very long time Barth refused to accept the idea of a point of contact, in revelation, with our nature: the Word of God will not submit itself to any kind of *a priori* dictated by the human mind, but it brings with it, and kindles within us, the actual conditions of its acceptance: by the gift of the Holy Spirit, God confers on man possibilities which he does not naturally possess.

Bultmann has met this criticism; the way in which he

answers it helps us to deepen our understanding of his positive conception of the existential interpretation.

First and foremost, if the *kerygma* is subjected to an existential analysis, we do not believe that this means placing it under the control of an 'objectivizing' theory, impersonal and speculative in character, the aim of which is to 'objectivize' the reality with which it is dealing into a 'this-worldly' reality. We must recall the fact that the existential analysis is nothing more than the clear and reasonable explication of the knowledge of existence exercised in existence itself.[1] Expressed in the categories of *Dasein*, and to this extent subordinated to them, for all that, the message will not be 'rationalized'.

Ought I, at least, to say that it is thanks to them that the message is 'intelligible'?[2] Even here we must make distinctions. I do not really comprehend friendship, fidelity, and love, I do not find them intelligible save in the experience of existential (*existentiel*) encounter, that is to say, in my personal 'engagement' (involvement) in these values, in their exercise (an *'existentiel'* knowledge which still does not prevent me from grasping them as a pure mystery, and further, which reveals to me their mysterious character). Before this 'engagement' or apart from it, I had no satisfying knowledge: neither a philosophy of love, nor a psychological analysis, not even the existential analysis will reveal to me the essence of love; doubtless, the existential analysis has this advantage over these other methods in that, at least, it reveals to me my openness (*Erschlossenheit*) to these values, the need which I feel of them when I am deprived of them, because it reveals to me my existence, my *Dasein*; now that is precisely their living appeal; thus, through existential analysis, I acquire, it is true, some knowledge of fidelity and of love, in a rather vague way, if I may put it so, and in the question that I put existentially on this subject.[3]

---

[1] '*die klare und methodische Ausbildung des mit der Existenz selbst gegebenen Existenzverständnisses*' (B. II, p. 189).

[2] '*Verstehen ist etwas anderes als rational erklären*' (B. II, p. 190).

[3] '*ich verstehe sie dann in der Frage nach ihnen*', (B. II, p. 190).

It is the same in that which concerns the *kerygma*, which is—as we already know—the message of the grace of God. Before I have even heard the Word—let us freely admit this—I could know, in the analysis of my existence, a certain aspiration after grace; but it is evident that this sense of 'absence' did not mean more to me than a very vague and uncertain knowledge; *I do not reach authentic knowledge until the moment when the Word having met me in my concrete existence, I shall have freely welcomed it myself*; and even then, grace will not cease to be a mystery to me, because I shall be infinitely astonished that God has deigned to meet me.[1] In short, says Bultmann, I leave to a philosophy, to a natural existential analysis, a certain knowledge of the message, which is however not positive knowledge in its fulness.

Let us observe, further, that it is impossible to make contact with the Scriptures, and try to make any kind of interpretation, without being disturbed by questions which already imply a philosophy of some kind. In other words, even those, Bultmann says, who reproach him with having a preparatory philosophy are not without one themselves. If there were no questions put by the mind on the nature of reality, the text would remain silent. Doubtless this way of putting the questions (*Fragestellung*) cannot prejudge the content which is being examined, nor anticipate the conclusions of exegesis; rather, it should open our eyes to the meaning of the text; but precisely, without that, our eyes will not be opened. Now, it is reasonable to think that the appropriate way of 'questioning', when we want to read the Bible aright, is that which concerns the meaning of our existence. That is usually the main reason for interest in historical documents of any kind. *A fortiori* this applies to the Bible; does not the Church tell us to go to the Bible because it is 'the place where I am going to hear something decisive about my existence'?[2] And the Bible is not limited to showing me a possible way of understanding my existence —all historical documents do that—it confronts me as a Word which summons me, personally, and offers me

[1] B. II, p. 190.   [2] B. II, p. 191, ET, *KM*, p. 191.

authentic existence. So that if the critic drives his point home still further by saying: the right spirit in which to examine a passage requires from us beforehand a certain vital attitude, a certain behaviour (*Lebensverhältnis*) towards the reality with which the text is dealing; now apart from faith I cannot have any 'attitude' with regard to the divine revelation which the Bible contains—we must here repeat a remark which has already been made: actually, even before we have faith, every one has an attitude towards God; this is finely expressed in Augustine's phrase: *Fecisti nos ad te Deus et inquietum est cor nostrum, donec requescat in te*; whether man is aware of it or not, God's desire towards man has begun to 'draw' him towards God.[1]

Now, this preliminary philosophy, used in the form of a question, raising the whole problem of the meaning of our existence, is of great moment for the reader of the Bible, for the exegete, enabling him to translate this philosophy from the implicit into the explicit state, even before the interpretation of the text begins; once again this is what existential analysis does: by means of thought it releases the existential categories (*Begrifflichkeit*) which in every way already inspired the reader at least secretly, as we have shown. This means, it is true, that the exegetical work is made to depend upon a philosophy henceforward aware of itself. But we should be careful to observe that this is not dependence upon an organized philosophical system, like, for instance, Hegelian Idealism,[2] nor even with regard to responses already acquired concerning the meaning of my existence: existential analysis does not define for us a material ideal of existence, it does not claim to teach us how we ought to exist; it does not even say 'you ought to exist' (it does not found a system of ethics); quite simply it shows us in what *Dasein* differs from *Vorhandensein*, and that it is not itself save on conditions of freely being oneself in an existential decision of any kind; there is no content, nothing but a form, nothing but the categories which the *Dasein* exercises where it is set.

[1] B. II, p. 192, ET, *KM*, p. 192.   [2] B. II, p. 192, ET. *KM*, p. 193.

Here a more subtle objection has been raised: but the practice of existential analysis already conceals, in its author, a decision for that determinate conception of existence;[1] it is not true that his analysis is purely formal; it does not eliminate every '*existentiel*' attitude, all effective conduct with regard to existence. In fact Bultmann replies, decision is there already, but it is simply the decision to exist, but not to exist in any particular manner; an initial decision which does not close the mind, which on the contrary, opens it to the eventual concrete possibilities of the conception of existence. Without that, without the previous will to be a man, to accept one's being in responsibility no one could understand a single word of the Scriptures: at least those words by which the Scriptures call us and challenge us to decision. Further, let us concede something more to the critic: existential analysis conveys a sort of general knowledge of the phenomena of existence which it examines: hence we can say that it constitutes a norm by which existence must be regulated; nevertheless, it remains true that it is purely formal. We can illustrate this from the example chosen by the critic himself: the 'phenomenon of love': existential analysis shows me that I can only understand 'my love' 'existentielly' (i.e. only in accepting or in rejecting it freely); this means that it constitutes a norm; but it does not reveal to me in any way 'how I have to understand it' (whether I ought to accept it or reject in a particular instance?); it tells me nothing about the content involved in my power of loving; if something has become clear to me it is precisely that existential knowledge cannot be replaced by any existential analysis.

In Bultmann's view this is how the principle of existential interpretation is justified. At the same time his meaning becomes clearer. We see that the demand for an existential interpretation is equivalent to the demand for a certain proof, addressed to the message: if the latter wishes to be

---

[1] That is the criticism of *F. K. Schumann*, in his article 'Die Entmythologisierbarkeit des Christusgeschehens' B. I, pp. 197, 198, ET, 'Can the Event of Jesus Christ be Demythologized?' *KM*, pp. 185, 186.

received, it must show that it corresponds to the natural knowledge which man possesses of himself: far from being in opposition to this knowledge, the message ought to assume and fulfil it.[1] The Word of God challenges us to faith, but in such a way that it opens up for us the possibility of understanding ourselves. That is why faith and unbelief are not a blind and arbitrary decision, but an intelligent 'Yes' or 'No'.[2] By this we can see that though Bultmann claims that faith must not be based upon exterior 'miraculous' signs (which would be only mythology), on the other hand he urges the necessity for a sort of interior motivation; he restores the idea of a certain apologetic of immanence, he renounces the absolute fideism so characteristic of so many schools of Protestant theology. This is a fact, of which he himself is aware: for instance, he criticizes Barthian theology severely, saying that it inculcates an attitude of blind surrender, at the price of intellectual sacrifice; the reason for this statement is the fact that Barth lays so much stress on faith as based upon itself alone, and on the sovereign rights of the Word apart from any 'point of contact' with man.[3]

Finally, Bultmann warns us against an excessive emphasis on this demonstrative rôle of the existential interpretation of the message: when it is presented to us, we shall take care to regard it as an anthropology whose universal and scientific validity claims our consent; enabling us to gain the knowledge of ourselves, it will nevertheless offer it to us as one possible interpretation, among others, of existence; precisely because it is 'existential' it will show us that nothing can release us from the need for decision. Thus, even demythologized, even discovered in its correspondence with existence, Christianity will not be like scientific truth which forces us to accept it: it will still summon us to 'take sides', to make a free choice in the present, as in the past, to have a faith.

[1] B. II, pp. 191ff., ET, *KM*, pp. 191ff.   [2] B. I, p. 46, ET, *KM*, p. 141.
[3] Cf. *R. Bultmann*, 'Das Problem der Hermeneutik', in *Glauben und Verstehen*, Tübingen, 1952, Vol. II, p. 235 . . . "Akzeptieren mittels *eines* Sacrificum Intellectus", cf. ET, 'The Problem of Hermeneutics', *Essays*, London, 1955, p. 261.

III

THE EXISTENTIAL INTERPRETATION
OF THE *KERYGMA*

CHRISTIANITY as preached by the Churches to-day remains profoundly mythological. Its demythologizing, its existential interpretation, can only be the joint work of the theologians of tomorrow. Bultmann does not claim to offer us more than a first attempt, in broad outline.[1]

In the conception of existence presented by the Christian message, the New Testament itself distinguishes two pictures: the existence of man outside of faith and the existence of the Christian in faith.

Existence without Faith. According to the Christian message, man has become the slave of the world and its 'powers': he belongs henceforth to 'this world' (ὁ κόσμος οὗτος), to 'this age' (οὗτος ὁ αἰών). Nevertheless, here, there is a difference between the New Testament and Gnosticism: the New Testament does not place matter among the evil 'powers', nor does it regard the human body as evil; we never find in its pages any protest against the exile of the soul within matter, or against the influence of the senses upon the spirit. In short, there is no trace of dualism; the world, matter, and the body are creatures of God, and because of this they are works of goodness; if the world has become 'this world', that is, the realm of evil and of death, this degradation must be derived from man himself: it is due to his own fault, not in the least to that of Fate (*Verhängnis*) that man has forged his own chains, Rom. 6.23; I Cor.

[1] B. I, pp. 27-40, ET, *KM*, pp. 17-33.

50

15.56.[1] Paul, it is true, assigns to the father of the human race, to Adam, the empire of death over our existence; but, without trying to reconcile the two statements, he does not minimize our individual responsibility when he writes: that since Adam, death has struck all men because all have sinned (Rom. 5.12): as if perhaps, in his thought, Adam only introduced into the world the possibility of death and not its necessity.

'This world', thus constituted by man, is called the world of the flesh. What does this mean? The 'flesh' does not describe our bodily life, the life of the senses (*die Körperlichkeit und Sinnlichkeit*) but the sphere of the visible, of 'being-there' (*die Sphäre des Vorhandenen*), of that which can be 'manipulated' (*des Verfügbaren*), of that which can be measured, and also that which is perishable (*des Vergänglichen*). It becomes a power which dominates man when man puts his trust in it, bases his whole existence on the methods which it offers him, lives 'according to it', instead of living 'according to the invisible'.

Further, this 'carnal' organization of life can take two forms: either man abandons himself lightheartedly to his own desires and to all 'the tempting possibilities' which life offers, or he dominates his own existence, he wishes to control it, but by leaning on his own strength and on the 'works of the Law': in this second case, his conduct, although it is less 'material', is no less 'carnal'; for according to the Bible, the 'flesh' includes all those activities which aim at procuring for us all the advantages 'within the visible world', merits, tangible results like that of legal justice (Gal. 3.3; Phil. 3.4ff.). Every man, according to Paul, is a prey to anxiety (μεριμνᾶν, I Cor. 7.32ff.), he is always 'making plans': the man without faith is always anxious about his own security; in order to achieve it, he depends upon his own efforts, upon the tangible resources which the world offers, and trusts entirely in his own cleverness; and when

---

[1] Here we use the Scripture references which Bultmann quotes. But it is obvious that we do not necessarily regard them as valid proofs of his statements.

he believes that he has 'secured' his future, he is proud of it, and boasts about it (καυχᾶσθαι). But his assurance is nothing but a superficial illusion; actually he has lost his life and his authentic existence (*seine eigentliche Existenz*); because he has put his trust in purely human methods, he has become enslaved to the world around him, and he has unleashed forces against himself by which he believes himself to be surrounded by sinister powers which he represents to himself as gigantic myths. The result is that in man's social life jealousy and conflict predominate; or at least, if man does succeed in establishing a certain order of justice, he does so by means of contracts and conventions, instead of by the triumph of love; what else can we expect if every one is competing with others in order to secure for himself, selfishly, all that gives pleasure to the senses, and can be acquired by his own effort. All this is impregnated with the universal sentiment of anxiety: everyone clings to the wretched 'security' which he has gained for himself, yet secretly convinced that everything is crumbling away, and that he is losing his real life.

Existence within Faith. Authentic existence lives by that which is invisible and eternal: by the very fact of living in this dimension it renounces all security which could be procured by oneself by means of 'this-worldly' methods. The New Testament calls this 'life according to the spirit': it is essentially faith in the 'grace' of God, the confidence that the unknown, the incompatible, the wholly other, comes to meet man as love, in order to offer him his own future, his life, his security. Grace itself proclaims that it is a grace which pardons: and by this the believer understands that it liberates him from being enslaved to the perishable; until then he had rejected the invisible and had trusted only in himself, and that was his sin; now he opens himself up to the omnipotence of the other; he gives himself into his hands for all things, he expects from him all good: in all this he attains authentic freedom. It is not that the believer renounces the world, practises asceticism, refuses to take part in cultural activities, or in social and political life; on the contrary, the Christian takes part in the life of the world in order to further the victory of God's purpose; but at the same time, he keeps his distance from the world, and he shares in the life of the world as though 'it were not' (ὡς μή: I Cor. 7.29-31). This gives him a kind of mastery over all things (I Cor. 3.21-23); he can deal with everything: 'All things are lawful for me . . . but all things are not expedient' (I Cor. 6.12; 10.23ff.). He can be gay with the joyful and weep with the sorrowful. 'Free from all men, I brought myself under bondage to all' (I Cor. 9.19-23). 'I know how to be abased, and I know also how to abound . . . to be filled and to be hungry . . .' (Phil. 4.12). He is crucified to the world and the world to him (Gal. 6.14). The strength of his new life is seen in his weakness, in suffering and death (II Cor. 4.7-11; 12.9ff.); for it is precisely when he is conscious of his nothingness, and accepts it, that he can receive anything from God (II Cor. 12.9ff.; 6.8-10).

To exist thus is described as existing 'eschatologically', and to be a new creation (II Cor. 5.17): the former things have passed away, and the day of salvation, the νῦν δέ of the time of the End is already here, the life to come is anticipated. When it speaks like this, the New Testament itself 'demythologizes', it detaches itself from the Jewish eschatology, it eliminates from the message the representations of a transcendent world of which until then it was said that it would come down to earth from heaven; the work of existential interpretation has already begun, in the first Christian generation. More than any other, John gets rid of apocalyptic eschatology: for him, there is no longer a universal judgment conceived as a cosmic event which is still to come: the world has already been judged by the act that Jesus has called men to believe (John 3.19; 9.39; 12.31): man believes, and this means that he has eternal life (John 5.24); all has been accomplished for him; he is no longer the slave of the world, he has already won the victory (I John 5.4).

The same remark applies to the Gnostic eschatology. If

the New Testament had posited for the believer a new 'nature', if it had thought that his redemption consisted in the deliverance of a spiritual element which had gone astray in matter, of a pre-existent nature, it would have used the language of the Gnostics, like them, it would have used mythological language; but no; nothing of the kind, redemption is not conceived in terms of a cosmic process. Man is saved by faith, by his response to the God who calls him. And in this faith, there is no superior spiritual state, infallibly guaranteed (which would have opened the way to libertinism), nor is it incessantly menaced (which would have opened the way to asceticism) : there is nothing but an existential encounter, expressed by an imperative just as much as by an indicative; the decision of faith is not achieved once for all; it has to be renewed and confirmed in each concrete situation the believer has to meet; it is not a seizure in the sense of distraint, it is not an act of surrender, once for all; rather it is the state of 'being seized' (or apprehended); and thus the life of faith consists in a continual tension between 'not yet', and 'however, already', the incessant pursuit of an aim (Phil. 3.12-14); and the liberty which it brings does not get rid of the claims of duty: it is a liberty for obedience (Rom. 6.1ff.).

There is another difference between Christianity and Gnosticism: in the latter, the participation of the redeemed in the cosmic process of redemption is supposed to be effected and manifested under the form of a 'this-worldly' reality: it should evoke pneumatic phenomena and especially ecstasies. All this is mythology. There is nothing like this in the New Testament: here, in principle, there is no room for phenomena whose function would be to manifest in this world that which comes from the world beyond, to make it an immanent fact. St Paul had experiences of ecstasy, it is true (II Cor. 5.13; 12.1ff.), but he rises above the temptation to regard this as a proof of the action of the Spirit; nowhere is there any question of forming or disciplining the spiritual experience, nor of designating such a privileged experience as the summit of Christian existence to be desired: that experience is not characterized by psychical phenomena but by the pure decision of faith.

Paul shares the popular conviction, it is true, that the Spirit makes his presence felt by miraculous results. But in view of the emphasis on 'spiritual gifts' at Corinth, he becomes aware of the equivocal character of these phenomena. And if he sometimes conceives the Spirit as a mysterious power whose possession guarantees the resurrection (Rom. 8.11), if he speaks of this as a supernatural reality (I Cor. 15.44ff.), he also interprets it more deeply and simply as the possibility of a new existence understood in the decision for faith: the Spirit does not act like a force of nature; it is not a transcendent good that the believer appropriates for himself; it is only the accomplishment of the command not to live after the flesh: 'Walk by the Spirit, and you shall not fulfil the lusts of the flesh' (Gal. 5.16).

Further, there is the fruit of the Spirit: 'love, joy, peace, longsuffering, kindness, goodness, faithfulness, meekness, self-control . . .' (Gal. 5.22): this shows us that the liberation from the world, acquired by faith, does not dispense the believer from being involved in the life of the world, and from brotherly intercourse with other men. Freed from anxiety and enslavement to the seen and temporal, the Christian becomes free for other people. It is in believing in God and in loving his brothers that he realizes and confirms his condition as a 'new creation'; and all this defines his Christian existence.

That is true, but is that all? We have sought to demythologize the New Testament conception of human existence, and to give it a purely existential interpretation. Is our task then over? Have we exhausted the Christian knowledge of the human being, by saying that man realizes himself in faith, in his abandonment to God, and in his interior liberation from the world? If the answer is 'yes', then we ought to admit that the New Testament conception of human existence is no more than the natural conception of man (*das natürliche Seinsverständnis des Menschen*, B. I, p. 32, ET,

KM, p. 23): the anthropology of the *kerygma*, once it has been divested of its mythological garment, would coincide —to put it in a word—fairly closely with the anthropology of certain schools of philosophy of the present day.

Let us take for instance, the existential philosophy of Heidegger. We have already compared it with the existential interpretation of the New Testament: a first comparison, simply from the formal point of view. Let us compare it now from the point of view of content: we observe a substantial agreement between the analysis of Heidegger and the New Testament conception of existence as we have conceived it up to the present. Heidegger tells us: *Dasein* is exposed to the danger of being lost in the *Vorhanden*, in the impersonal and the neutral. Does it desire to escape this menace and to save its authenticity? Then it must renounce all the false security offered by the *Vorhanden*, and must abandon itself without reserve to the future, 'give itself up to life in all that this means of uncertainty and risk'.[1] We may well believe that we are listening to a Christian message which has been secularized: the 'man after the flesh' of St Paul finds his counterpart in the 'inauthentic existence' of Heidegger; the man 'after the Spirit' corresponds to 'authentic existence', the passage from the one condition to the other being effected, in both instances, by an existential decision which we may regard as an act of faith, for it is an abandonment to the future; and at the end, the same *Entweltlichung*, the same distance taken with regard to the world of objects of the *Vorhanden*. Similarly, in the work of Kamlah:[2] let us renounce, he says, all

---

[1] Quoted from R. Prenter, *Mythe et Évangile* (article mentioned in the Introduction, p. 15), p. 58.

[2] W. Kamlah is an old pupil of Bultmann from the University of Marburg: the work of Kamlah to which Bultmann here alludes, *Christentum und Selbstbehauptung*, Frankfurt, 1940, came out in a second edition, revised and completed, under the title, *Christentum und Geschichtlichkeit. Untersuchungen zur Entstehung des Christentums und zu Augustins 'Bürgerschaft Gottes'*, Stuttgart, 1951. According to Kamlah, no divine event is necessary for 'surrender' or for 'authentic existence'. We need not look to Christian sources for anything more than an indispensable inspiration for the natural knowledge of the human being.

confidence in ourselves, let us abandon all the ties which hold us back, in order to surrender ourselves to Being as a whole, more exactly to its foundation, to God; in this abandonment, we shall know the meaning of the real. And Kamlah himself observes that the structure of this 'abandonment' is related to the Christian Faith, thus suggesting that in its essence the latter is a purely natural attitude, and that the comprehension of existence is not the fruit of a divine revelation.

But it is evident that the New Testament interpretation of existence includes elements of which philosophy knows nothing.

First of all, it does not confine itself to placing Christian existence in an existential decision for a future of any sort, nor even in a simple faith in God: the faith on which the authentic existence depends is faith in Christ; to speak more exactly: the New Testament requires of man that he should believe in the intervention of God in history, in a divine event of salvation in Christ. Now our existential interpretation has not, till now, left any room for this relation to Christ, which is, however, apparently essential.

Further, the New Testament positively refuses to regard faith as a natural attitude, which man can create within himself by means of simple philosophical reflection, and without the aid of revelation. Doubtless, in its eyes faith is not a mysterious quality, a supernatural and mythological reality, by which we are divinely enriched (nor is love, in the Christian sense, a mysterious practice): it is its very nature; when the New Testament speaks of the believer as a 'new creature', it simply means that it verifies human existence, authentically, in accordance with the creative idea. But this condition, this perfection of his nature, according to the New Testament, does not lie in man's own hands, and it is not sufficient for him, in order to realize it, to depend upon his own powers of reflection and the recollection of his own thought.

Here we see very clearly where the New Testament and philosophy part company. Certainly, philosophy is well aware that man has lost himself, or at least that he is always in danger of losing himself, and of misunderstanding his authentic nature, and that, in consequence, he does not possess 'authenticity' directly, but that he has to make some effort to attain it. Sooner or later all philosophy becomes more or less imperative: thus the aim of idealism is to open the eyes of man to his true being; it tells him that he is spirit, and that he must not let his real life be side-tracked into the life of the senses; 'become what you are' (what you are called to be); Heidegger's philosophy shows man his lost condition in the *'man'*, and seeks to call him back to himself; and even Kamlah is well aware that man's authentic existence is as it were 'buried' (out of sight); 'abandonment' (*die Hingabe*), he says, is not, for man, an attitude which can be taken for granted; it is an order, a command (*Gebot*) and the liberation which it procures is always the fruit of an act of obedience. But in spite of all this, philosophy retains the conviction that once man becomes aware of his 'authentic' nature, he will be able to realize it; in short, philosophy is convinced that it alone can disentangle the true being of man and thus set it free to make the act of surrender. It is at this point that it differs from the New Testament: for here, man is fundamentally incapable of breaking away from his state of alienation in the world. From the New Testament point of view an act of divine love alone can save us; indeed, it is not too much to say that the Christian message is not primarily a doctrine of the nature of our 'authentic existence', but the proclamation of the saving act, the saving event, which is accomplished in Christ: and while philosophy cannot admit that man's situation is really desperate (because it regards itself as the hope and salvation of man), the New Testament tells us that there is no hope for us anywhere outside the salvation of God.

Bultmann regards this comparison between the New Testament and philosophy with its emphasis upon the conditions of achieving our authenticity as so important, that he feels bound to concentrate upon it, and to try to carry it further.[1]

[1] B. I, pp. 35-40, ET, *KM*, pp. 27-34.

Let us note first of all a point of contact: according to philosophy, man can only become what he already is. Idealism declares: if man can live a spiritual life it is because he is spirit: 'become what thou art'. Heidegger says: man is invited to accept himself in face of death, because existential analysis has revealed to him his situation of 'being-thrown there' (*Geworfenheit*) in the Nothing. The New Testament uses similar language. Paul urges believers to be 'saints' because they are already sanctified (I Cor. 5.7; 6.11); to walk according to the Spirit because they are already in the Spirit (Gal. 5.25); to destroy sin because they are already dead unto sin (Rom. 6.11). John says: it is precisely because believers are not of the world that they can triumph over the world (John 17.16); because they are born of God they do not sin (I John 3.9). Thus man cannot live his 'authentic' life save in virtue of the fact that he is already living in it, that he already possesses it: philosophy and the New Testament agree on this point. Bultmann does not lay any special emphasis on the point of this remark. But it is evident that in his eyes this is the point: just as philosophy completely ignores the mysterious and supernatural condition of man (for when man attains his authentic existence he is merely achieving self-realization) the New Testament also says 'become what thou art'; faith will not elevate you to a mysterious sacred existence, it will not confer upon you a 'supernature'—as Gnosticism thought, as Catholic dogma still thinks—it will not introduce you into a system of divine gifts and graces and infused virtues (that would be 'mythology'), it will confine itself to revealing to you your true being, and permitting you to realize it.

Now let us turn to the point where the two views diverge: the New Testament only speaks in this way to those who are already believers, that is to say, to those who have allowed the saving work of God to be accomplished within them; it does not use this language to men as such (*zu den Menschen als solchen*, B. I, p. 36, ET, *KM*, p. 28). From the New Testament point of view those who exist apart from Christ are not alive; they are dead, for they have fallen below the level of their own nature; they cannot 'become what they are', because in fact they 'are not', and to exhort them to lead their 'authentic existence' would fall on deaf ears, for such men would be wholly incapable of hearing or answering such a challenge.

In other terms: the difference between the New Testament and philosophy comes out in their views on the Fall (*Verfallenheit*). Philosophy does not ignore it, but it does not appreciate its depth; for it, the Self has not really succumbed; it is not 'lost' in the depths of its being, it always retains a zone of 'authenticity'; the proof of this is the language it uses about man; it says to him: face the fact of your distress; for when you see your misery you can liberate yourself from this condition; you have not lost all possibility of liberation. Surely, this is only another way of saying that man is not utterly fallen? The New Testament says the exact opposite (and here Bultmann speaks as a disciple of Luther): for him the Fall is complete, nature itself is lost; that is why the Christian believer alone, whose nature has been renewed in Christ can be invited to live an 'authentic' life.

Philosophy will say: but man is not totally 'fallen'; if he were, how can we explain the fact that his eyes are open to the reality of his fall? Does not this ultimate clarity about his condition show that an element of 'authenticity' has been preserved? Not so long ago Barth would have answered this question in the negative: left to himself, he would have said, man is unconscious of his guilt; but the Word of God alone, in the act of granting him forgiveness, shows him that he is a sinner. Bultmann, if we read him aright, gives a different answer. He says: it is true that man recognizes, at least to some extent, his situation as fallen man; let us also admit that of himself, and to the same extent, he also knows the nature of his authentic existence: the awareness of a privation always implies a certain knowledge of the wealth of which one is being deprived. Further: this sense of apprehension—even if dim and confused—of authentic existence, enfolds and impregnates the whole of human life, even if only in the form of anxiety and regret; it is on account of this quality that a man deserves to be called a man. Let us go further: man can even know, of himself, that he cannot re-conquer his true being save in an existential decision (we have seen above that the existential analysis sufficed to reveal to him this condition of his authentic existence[1]). But, Bultmann goes on, from the point of view of the New Testament, philosophy goes wrong at this very point: it believes (wrongly) from a purely Socratic point of view that this natural knowledge of his authenticity enables fallen man to regain it.[2] *Du kannst, denn du sollst*: when man sees that he *ought* to do something, he understands that he can do it. To which the New Testament objects: he cannot; he has lost all power to do so. Now it is this total impotence which shows the totality of the Fall: he may indeed have a certain awareness of his condition, but the fact remains that he is incapable of putting himself right, this is enough to give us the right to say that there is a radical corruption in man's nature. Further, the very consciousness that man possesses of his fall, and through it of his authenticity, is seriously vitiated because it is accompanied by the mistaken idea that man can attain his true being by his own efforts.

If then we ask why, according to the New Testament, man has lost the power of regaining his authentic life, we must answer (this is a typically Protestant reply): 'every step taken by fallen man is a step of fallen man'.[3] The older Protestant theology used to say: all the actions of sinners are sins; how could a sin 'justify' us or restore to us our true image? Still more, it is precisely our confidence in ourselves which constitutes our main guilt: every act based upon it takes us further away from our true being. Paul declares that the Jews did not know righteousness precisely because they sought to start from themselves, and, in order to achieve this they relied on their own 'works'. Above all the

[1] See above, p. 32.
[2] 'Aber sie (die Philosophie) ist der Meinung, *dass den Menschen das Wissen um seine Eigentlichkeit ihrer schon mächtig mache*', B. I, p. 37, ET, *KM*, p. 29.
[3] B. I, p. 37, ET, *KM*, p. 29.

New Testament blames fallen man for his pride, his claim to be able to live in his own strength (*Eigenmächtigkeit*). If our true life is the life of surrender, then the man who lives wholly in the realm of the seen and temporal is not alone in ignoring the true life: this fault is committed equally by the man who believes that it is possible to live this life of surrender in his human strength alone—as if this attitude of surrender began with us—as if the authentic life could be something which we can achieve by our own efforts, when it is simply due to grace, and is a gift of God! Now, fundamentally, this Jewish presumption is shared by philosophy. As we have already seen, philosophy is aware of the necessity for surrender: apart from it we cannot be true to our own nature; but, by a singular contradiction, it claims that man can live his life by his own efforts.

While the New Testament shows man the depth into which he has fallen, and his fundamental incapacity to surrender himself, it also tells him that what he cannot do for himself, God has done for him: he has delivered man from himself, and from all his impotence, in Christ. God has reconciled the world unto himself in Christ, 'not reckoning unto them their trespasses' (II Cor. 5.19); 'him who knew no sin, he made to be sin on our behalf, that we might become the righteousness of God in him' (II Cor. 5.21), not on account of the false righteousness of our own works, but because of the righteousness of God himself. For those who accept this message in faith the past has been wiped out; it is 'finished', the 'old man' has disappeared. They now enter into the 'new age'—towards the end, for, by their decision for God, the present has eschatological value: 'Wherefore if any man is in Christ, he is a new creature: the old things are passed away; behold, they are become new' (II Cor. 5.17). The 'new life' consists in the recovery of freedom. For the 'forgiveness of sins' of which the New Testament speaks is not to be understood in the simple sense of a release from punishment, as if man's situation were otherwise unchanged; rather, in this forgiveness, man is delivered from sin itself, from this sin to which he was enslaved up to the very moment of liberation. A liberation and a liberty on the other hand which, we must repeat, is not conceived as a mysterious and sacred quality, as in Gnostic thought, but as liberty for obedience: man has been made capable of welcoming God, of surrendering himself actively to him; it is this which proves the juxtaposition, already indicated, of the imperative and the indicative: to walk in freedom. All our new duties are summed up in the commandment of love: the man who has been set free from himself by the forgiveness of God is set free to devote himself to others (Rom. 13.8-10; Gal. 5.14): according to St Paul. St John, on his part, insists that the knowledge of the 'truth' of God manifested in Jesus liberates man (John 8.32) from being enslaved in sin (John 8.34); by Jesus man is called from death to life (John 5.25), from darkness to light (John 9.39); the believer is 'born anew' (John 3.3); he no longer belongs to the world, he has triumphed over it by his faith (I John 5.4).

Finally, Bultmann expresses the thought of the New Testament in the following terms: 'Faith, in so far as it sets man free from himself, in so far as it enables him to face the future with confidence, is only possible in the form of belief in the love of God. But faith in the love of God remains confidence in oneself, so long as this love is scarcely more than an idea, a symbol shaped by our 'wishful thinking' (*Wunschbild*), so long, that is, as God has not revealed his love. The Christian Faith is faith in Christ, in this sense that it is faith in this love of God which is revealed in Christ. Only one who has been gripped by the prevenient love of God, is able to love; only one who is freed by God can trust him in return; only one who has known the gift of God can give himself in return. If then we are set free in order to surrender ourselves to God, it is because God has first of all given himself for us. 'Herein is love, not that we loved God, but that he loved us, and sent his Son to be the propitiation for our sins' (I John 4.10). We must love him, because he first loved us (I John 4.19).[1]

[1] B. I, pp. 39-40, ET, *KM*, pp. 32-33.

In short, according to the New Testament, it is the gift of God (and not our own nature) which makes it possible for us to give ourselves. It is at this point that the Christian message is clearly and profoundly distinguished from that of philosophy: a distinction which we may express in these terms: in contradiction to the natural and philosophical conception of existence, the Christian message affirms the existence of God's action; it is this action alone which makes it possible for man to surrender himself, to live a life of faith and love, which is authentic human existence.[1]

But, by that very fact, the New Testament faith confronts us, Bultmann continues, with a very serious problem. We must remember that, where modern man is concerned no mythological element in the expression of the Christian faith is permissible; that only a strictly existential interpretation of the Christian message can claim our acceptance. We may have succeeded in demythologizing the thought of the New Testament as it deals with the existence of man without faith, and within faith. But now, in that which concerns the passage from the one form of existence to the other, and the conversion of 'flesh' to 'spirit', the Christian message proclaims a divine event in Christ: it is this Christ event he declares, against philosophy, which is the unique and indispensable principle of our liberation; it alone which enables us to enter our authentic existence! But if we admit this, do we not at once re-open the door to myth? Is not the notion of the *Christusgeschehen* 'mythological' through and through? Let us consider the way in which the New Testament expresses it: the Christ, of whom it is said, he saves us—or that God saves us in him—is a divine pre-existent Being who has mingled with the world and has taken upon himself our flesh; his sacred reality worked miracles in the world of things and in the minds and hearts of men; after having expiated our sins upon the Cross he was raised from

[1] 'Das Neue Testament redet und der christliche Glaube weiss von einer Tat Gottes, *welche die Hingabe, welche den Glauben, welche die Liebe, welche das eigentliche Leben des Menschen erst möglich macht*', B. I, p. 40, ET, *KM*, p. 33.

the dead, and by the communication of his Spirit he gives to those who are baptized into him a pneumatic (spiritual) existence, which is something like a heavenly nature. Are not all these features of the event distinctively mythical? It is impossible to resist the conclusion that, by a salvation understood in this sense, the Christian message has very largely re-assumed the character of a mythology. Henceforth, one question confronts us: is it possible to demythologize the Christ event absolutely (as must be done to make it acceptable) without losing it altogether, to separate in this theology of the act of salvation the mythological garment from a substance wholly purified, to give to the saving action of God an interpretation which is exclusively existential?

We can see the gravity of the question. Let us suppose that this new 'demythologizing' proves to be impossible: in this case, modern man could no longer conserve anything of the Christ event; in his faith there would no longer be any room for the fact of Christianity; there would no longer be anything for him to gather from the New Testament save the idea, expounded above, of the two forms of existence. Now, as we have seen, this conception can be held not only without reference to Christ, but without any reference to the idea of a divine event. It coincided, we said, with the natural conception of existence, with the anthropology of various schools of modern philosophy; an anthropology which speaks of a surrender, certainly, but which assigns the power to do so to man himself. Henceforth, the profession of the Christian Faith would no longer be distinguishable from an existentialist philosophy. To sum up, we would have to say that the New Testament confines itself to offering us, under the cloak of a mythology, the natural knowledge of human existence; the Western philosophies would have rendered us the great service of peeling off this garment and of giving to the conception of existence which it obscured a more correct and considered expression. Christian theology would then have prepared the way for philosophy,[1] and by this, provisionally, would have been the

[1] *die Vorgängerin der Philosophie*, B. I, p. 32, ET, *KM*, p. 23.

great educator of the Western mind, but to-day it would be absolutely out of date, and its contemporary champions would fight in vain to put it in competition with the work of the philosophers.

It is evident that certain contemporary philosophical works offer themselves to us in the manner of a secularized Christianity. But it is no less sure that Bultmann does not mean to join their ranks. He himself means to remain a theologian, and he does not ask those who have the cure of souls to cease to regard themselves as the preachers of a message. In other words, he persists in giving a meaning to the divine event in Christ, he believes in the possibility of its demythologizing. That is what we now have to expound.

IV

THE SAVING EVENT

HERE we must begin by pointing out an ambiguity in Bultmann's thought. In order to sum up Bultmann's thought in a few words, it has been aptly said, that *'while orthodoxy as a whole* speaks of an event which can be objectively established *(von einem objektiv festellbaren Geschehen redet)*, something which happens, and remains outside of us, to which faith is ultimately related, Bultmann—and this is something which he has very much at heart—relates this event so exclusively to faith that faith absorbs it entirely . . .'[1] thus, according to Bultmann, the saving event, which takes place in Christ, when demythologized, would have no recognizable objective reality. But we must note the ambiguity of this expression. It can have two meanings: *either that the divine event has an objective reality*, that God has *done* something in Christ, apart from us; but, says Bultmann, we cannot see this 'something', this 'object', nor can we prove it (it is not *feststellbar*); on the contrary, it eludes all our methods of historical investigation; reason cannot fathom it; it is apprehended by faith alone. Or, on the other hand, it can mean that *the divine event has done nothing outside the believer*; but that during the preaching of the Word, or the reading of the Bible, God speaks to us; *the reality of the divine act consists wholly in this intimate approach to the soul,* and in the response, which is equally intimate, which we give to him in faith, in this decision by which I choose to say (in imitation of Christ?) that I owe my salvation, my authentic existence, to God and his free grace.

[1] C. Wehrung, 'Theologie, Kirche, Kirchenleitung', in the *Zeitschrift für systematische Theologie*, Vol. XXII, 1953, p. 179.

We assume that the first meaning alone represents Bultmann's real thought. Generally, however, his critics (and Wehrung himself) present the second interpretation, which is extremely subjective; and we shall have occasion to show that his critics can give solid support to this view. To sum up, we must admit that on this point it is difficult for the reader to be quite sure of Bultmann's real meaning.

This uncertainty, this ambiguity in the conception of the event, i.e. whether it is subjective or objective in character, is due to a fundamental lack of clarity in Bultmann's thought; this affects his idea of myth, and in consequence also his conception of a radical demythologizing.

Sometimes, 'myth' seems to indicate, vaguely, every kind of divine intervention in the human sphere (in this sense we may speak of 'myth' in the broad sense). But on the whole, Bultmann uses the word in a more limited sense ('myth' in the strict sense of the word): he has already told us that in his view the notion of the mythological does not cover, properly speaking, the simple belief in the action of a transcendent power upon our life: he would describe as 'mythical' only that transcendent action which is assimilated with 'this-worldly' action, or the sphere of immanence, and doubtless, as we have already seen, this second meaning could be subdivided: sometimes the intervention of the divine reality is conceived simply in the essentialist categories (substance, accident) of physical realities, without necessarily claiming that this intervention is manifested in its divine character: for instance, the working of the Holy Spirit may be ascribed to a force hidden within nature; or at other times the divine intervention will be proclaimed as recognizable as such; here the transcendent is supposed to act in nature and in history in such a way that it produces marvellous effects, miracles, which reveal its own excellence; for instance, the θεῖος ἀνήρ, the divine man who is Christ, is presented as a 'transparency' of the transcendent; this transcendent is not only compared with a causality of this world; in addition it is accessible, to some extent, to our faculties of observation and experience.[1] But in both cases, in the first as well as the second, because the divine action is compared to physical causality, we have 'myth' in the strict sense of the word.

'Myth' in the broad sense, on the one hand, 'myth' in the strict sense of the word on the other: it is plain that Bultmann's view of the extent to which the demythologizing of the event is required, will depend upon the way in which he is using the word 'myth': if he is thinking of it in the broad sense, it is evident that his conception of the event will be more 'subjective' than if he is using it in the narrow sense. If 'myth' is defined in a vague and general way, as all divine intervention in human life, then in the name of a radical demythologizing we must do away with every notion of an objective reality, wrought by God, in the Christ of History: this would necessitate a conception of salvation as something wholly inward, in which indeed

[1] In his *Theologie des Neuen Testaments.* first edition, Tübingen, 1948, pp. 128-129, ET, *Theology of the New Testament*, Vol. I, London, 1952, p. 130, Bultmann reminds us that 'the Hellenistic Age knew a series of θεῖοι ἄνδρες who were supposed to be sons of God (υἱοὶ θεοῦ), or who passed as such, and as such were venerated in the worship ritual'. In the same book, second edition, Tübingen, 1951, pp. 388ff., ET, Vol. 2, pp. 42ff., he puts the question whether the evangelists and especially the writer of the Fourth Gospel, have not applied this Hellenistic idea to Jesus: 'Is the human figure of Jesus in some way a "transparency" (*das Transparent*) through which his divine nature shines? At first sight we might think so; for some passages in the Gospels describe Jesus as the θεῖος ἀνήρ in the Hellenistic sense of the words; a "divine man" with marvellous wisdom and knowledge, who works miracles, and is able to evade all the traps set for him by his enemies.' But this is only in appearance. Certainly, 'the meaning of the historic figure of Jesus, of his human story, is the revelation of his glory, and, through that, of the Glory of God; it is the eschatological event. But it is not visible to the world, to which the glorified Lord does not and cannot manifest himself' (John 14.22), for the world cannot receive the 'Spirit of Truth' who gives the knowledge of the truth to believers, and to them only (John 14.17; 16.13ff.) (p. 396, ET, Vol. 2, p. 49). Thus, according to Bultmann, for the Gospel of John, Jesus was not a θεῖος ἀνήρ anxious to show or to reveal a transcendent mystery to the impersonal gaze of reason (whether through miracles or some other 'signs'). The Gospel of John has always 'demythologized' the story of Jesus.

it would be difficult to define our relation to Christ; further, Bultmann would have to face a new difficulty: if all God's action, all his intervention in history comes under the category of 'myth', can we speak of a divine saving event at all? even an inward one? Can faith itself still be related to God as to its principle? Can our achievement of authentic existence still claim to be due to divine grace? And are we not once again menaced by the danger of reducing Christianity to a pure philosophy? Or again, if we regard 'myth' from the narrower point of view as divine intervention manifestly affecting human life, or conceived in terms of physical reality: in this case, in order to be true to the demand for a radical demythologizing, it would not be necessary to eliminate all objective reality from the event; we could say, without mythologizing: God has accomplished something in our favour, and not only in us ourselves, but also outside of us in Christ; then all we need to eliminate from the Christ event is not the divine act itself, but simply those elements which evidently manifest its transcendence, or declare its connexion with God in the terms of essentialist ontology (the pre-existence of the divine being, his intervention in this world, his manifestation by his miraculous power, by a certain divine grandeur of his life, of his doctrine, etc.) elements which are, properly speaking, 'mythological', since they assimilate the act of God with an action within this world. Bearing this ambiguity in mind, we shall present successively two theories of demythologizing, two absolutely possible interpretations, subjective and objective, and we shall conclude by deciding firmly in favour of the objective one. And in expounding this objective interpretation we shall examine Bultmann's thought successively in the two following works: 'Neues Testament und Mythologie'[1] and 'Zum Problem der Entmythologisierung'.[2]

[1] B. I, pp. 40-48, 'New Testament and Mythology', ET, *KM*, pp. 1-44.
[2] B. II, pp. 179-208, ET, partly *KM*, pp. 191-211.

I. THE OBJECTIVE INTERPRETATION OF DEMYTHOLOGIZING

(i) According to 'Neues Testament und Mythologie' (1941)

The question which Bultmann has to answer may be formulated as follows: we have seen that the existential and demythologized interpretation of the New Testament ought to leave a place for the divine event in Christ, otherwise we would reduce the content of Scripture to the simple anthropology of contemporary philosophies. But, on the other hand, the divine event, as the Bible presents it to us, is expressed in mythological terms. Is it possible to demythologize it wholly, as should be done? And after this process has been completed, what remains of the act of God, what remains of the event which the Christian message offers to our faith?

The Life of Jesus

According to the New Testament, the saving event, the act of God, begins before the death of Jesus, during his life itself. In other words, according to the Scriptures, the earthly life of Jesus forms part of the history of salvation. Here it assumes a mythological form. We then ask: is this mythology separable from the very essence of the event? it may seem—and Bultmann even thinks so—that the New Testament itself begins this process of demythologizing (or at least, that here and there it suggests a demythologizing interpretation). As a proof of this Bultmann points out that in contrast to the gods of the mystery religions, in the New Testament, the Christ has a definite historic existence: a pre-existent Being, he is none the less quite clearly a human being—a man—Jesus of Nazareth; and his destiny is also that of a man, which ends on the Cross. The historical and the mythical elements are here blended in a very singular way; to such an extent that the New Testament itself has not been afraid of making some contradictory statements, e.g. the affirmation of Christ's pre-existence, but also of his birth at a precise date; kenosis, taking on the 'form of a servant'—identification with man (Phil. 2.7); but, on the other hand, he is a divine Being, distinguished by 'mighty works, and wonders and signs' (Acts 2.22). Now, it is possible to suggest that the New Testament has acted quite deliberately in clothing the historical element with the garment of myth. The mythological element is not chosen for its own sake: it is not used in order that we ought to accept its own content, its objective representations; quite simply it is used in order to emphasize the historical importance of Christ and of his story, and the significance and the bearing of his human figure in the history of salvation. If we have grasped his meaning, this is what Bultmann means: in the story of Christ, God wills to reveal to us that he himself has wrought our salvation; the Christian mythology has been chosen by him as the appropriate instrument for this revelation. So far as the affirmation of Christ's pre-existence, and of the Virgin Birth, are concerned we can see the point: these views are intended to help us to understand that the meaning of Christ and of his history is not exhausted by his appearance in human life, by what our human faculties of observation and of induction can establish, as is the case with other men. Confronted by Christ, do not try first of all, in order to understand him, to get clear in your mind about his human origin, do not explain it by its 'this-worldly' (*innerweltlich*) setting; rather, renounce this point of view, and try to discover *what God has to say to you* through this form, through this story of Christ,[1] for indeed, through it and by it God wills to speak to you. Precisely, in order to help us to enter into this spirit, to adopt this attitude of a listener, the New Testament has clothed the figure of Christ in mythological representations: his pre-existence and his heavenly origin, his birth of a virgin. But these representations are only a garment: they are not the saving act itself, they do not enter into the object proposed to our faith.[2]

---

[1] '*was Gott mir durch sie sagen will*', B. I, p. 41, ET, *KM*, p. 35.

[2] All this is beside the mark. The New Testament does not give any impression of wishing to demythologize the 'Christ event', so far as

But it is obvious that the New Testament goes far beyond the life of Jesus upon earth, and sums up the whole saving event in his death on the Cross, and in his Resurrection.

The Cross of Jesus

It is evident that the New Testament surrounds it with 'objectivizing representations' which are mythological in character: the crucifixion of the pre-existent Incarnate Son of God, the victim whose blood expiates our sins, making vicarious (*stellvertretend*) 'satisfaction' for the sins of the world, taking upon himself our punishment, and by this delivering us from death. From every point of view, this conception is wholly unacceptable. Further, it does not agree with the profound purpose of the New Testament itself; according to this conception our sins would be remitted, only in the sense that we shall be spared the punishment we deserve. Now, what faith should express is something quite different: the Cross means, not only remission of punishment, but liberation from sin itself, victory over the power of sin, which until then had kept us in bondage.

But, in point of fact, it is possible to divest the Cross of this mythological form, with the added advantage that in so doing its true purpose comes out more clearly.

In order to grasp Bultmann's thought at this point, we must take into account a distinction (which he makes here and there in his writings) between *historisch* and *geschichtlich*; if I am not mistaken, he has not taken the trouble to explain this distinction in any of his books, but this is what it means: *historisch* means an event, a fact, which took place on a certain date, which can be verified in our ordinary experience with the aid of the historical method; *geschichtlich* also describes an *event*, it is not a non-temporal reality, like the Platonic doctrine of Ideas; here, however, the event is not necessarily connected with a date, nor can it be proved by 'historical evidence': the Creation is an 'event'

the questions of pre-existence and the Virgin Birth are concerned. Bultmann interprets this blending of the mythical and the historical as a 'sign' of its supposedly 'demythologizing' intention—but he has no proof whatever for this argument.

73

of this kind, and so is the divine work of salvation; and the world and man, which are involved in these 'divine events' themselves constitute *Geschichte* (or history); such 'events' are described as *geschichtlich*, as far as they are related to the purpose of the divine accomplishment 'in events'.

Let us apply this distinction to the Cross. It is an historical event (in the sense of *historisch*); when he says this, Bultmann wants us to understand that, as an historian, he admits the fact of the crucifixion of Jesus. Now, in the Christian message this 'historicity' has assumed cosmic dimensions, as expressed in the mythological representations which we have already mentioned. Why was this done? It was done in order to help us to understand the significance, the historical (*geschichtlich*) implication of the Cross; according to the New Testament, in the divine purpose, the Cross has the value of a *geschichtlich* event, that is to say, an event which affects the whole of humanity in its relation to God; the significance and the value of this event is as follows: the Cross (in its *geschichtlich* significance) achieves the liberating judgment[1] on men; upon those who have fallen a prey to the powers of the 'world'.[2]

What is the judgment to which this statement refers? It is God who judges us, and that means that he shows us our condition as sinners; or, to put it still more precisely, our powerlessness to conquer sin by our own efforts, to achieve our authentic existence in our own strength; but this judgment is liberating, in this sense: while it shows us our impotence to save ourselves, at the same time it reveals to us our salvation by grace: God says to us: you are fallen men, in yourselves there is no hope of resurrection; but if you confess your helplessness you are also regenerated creatures, 're-born' as the result of a quite unmerited mercy.

But in what sense are we told that this judgment has been accomplished upon the Cross? Here, we believe, is what

---

[1] *das befreiende Gericht*, B. I, p. 43, ET, *KM*, p. 37.
[2] . . . *dass in ihm* . . . —*dem Kreuze—das Gericht über uns selbst*, die den Mächten der "Welt" verfallenen Menschen, *vollzogen* ist', B. I, p. 42, cf. *KM*, p. 36.

Bultmann means by this (to the extent in which his thought is patient of an objective interpretation): this certainly does not mean that Christ has earned our salvation, our liberating judgment, by his death: such an interpretation would reintroduce the doctrine of vicarious satisfaction into Christian theology, and we already know that Bultmann considers this to be mythological. But this is what he says: the judgment of God upon us is an act of God, which, considered from the point of view of its divine principle, is in some way outside time;[1] *the Cross accomplishes judgment in this sense, that it gives it its temporal expression*: on the historic Cross of Christ, God manifests the condemnation which he has passed upon all men; it is there that he makes known to us our personal condition as sinners, condemned, crucified. To sum up: the Cross of Christ is rather a statement of fact than something 'done'.

To which we must now add that this statement of fact is prolonged, by God himself, all through our history: in order to do this, the act of God, after having erected the Cross of Christ in history, through the apostles creates the *kerygma*, the message of the Cross, and in the Church the preaching of Christ Crucified; and thus, by means of the apostolic *kerygma* from that moment the judgment is always present, and always contemporary. This is so true that we may even speak of the *kerygma*—as Bultmann says himself —as a sacramental event: 'It re-presents (in the sense in which Dom Casel uses the word) a past event in such a way that it renews it, and in so doing realizes the conditions of a personal encounter.'[2] An eternal act of God, in the act of preaching the judgment becomes an act which is always temporal, and a truly historical (*geschichtlich*) event, since it accompanies us throughout the course of history, and continually summons us to obedience in the duties and claims of the present moment.

[1] *jenseits der Zeit*, B. I, p. 42, ET, *KM*, p. 36.
[2] 'Es (das Kerygma) vergegenwärtigt das Geschehen der Vergangenheit so, dass es dasselbe erneuert und mir so selbst zum Begegnis wird'. This sentence comes from another of Bultmann's works: 'Zu J. Schniewinds Thesen, das Problem der Entmythologisierung betreffend', B. I, p. 132, ET, 'A Reply to the Theses of J. Schniewind', *KM*, p. 115.

Finally, this judgment, which is proclaimed in the message, is appropriated by us, by faith (or, we reject it in unbelief). By faith alone: we cannot insist on this too strongly: the event happens outside us; but being 'outside of us' it does not reveal any sign of its transcendence (otherwise, it would be mythological); and that is why it escapes observation, and more particularly the speculative, impersonal consideration of the historian; the latter only sees, and can only see in the Cross a simple fact of the past, absolutely similar to so many other dramatic events which are purely human; he does not grasp the lasting value, the *geschichtlich* significance of the crucifixion; for him, there is no announcement of the divine judgment, no Word of God. There is no apprehension of the act of God as such save in the act of faith itself. That is so true, the appropriation of the event belongs so exclusively to faith, that we may even say that it is here that the saving event is accomplished; at least it is here that it receives its full actuality. Faith, says the Bible, is itself the operation of the Spirit, that is to say, it is the gift of God, the act of God, *the* saving act *par excellence*. But to conclude, we cannot repeat too often that defined by its object, faith does not make us confess in mythical terms: 'Christ has expiated for me and in my place; by his death the Son of God has won my authentic existence', but quite simply: 'God judges me, God crucifies me, by revealing to me my powerlessness to liberate myself from myself, and by inviting me to accept this'.

It is precisely by this confession, understood in this sense, that I reach authentic liberation. Faith verifies, for me, the condition of ultimate realities: in it, the meaning and the purpose of time and history is already reached. The end of history has not to be pushed back into a state of the world to come; it realizes itself, from to-day, in the encounter with, and the acceptance of the *kerygma*. The time of the end is already present, the age of the *eschaton* has begun. This is what John means when he writes: 'Now is the judgment of this world' (John 12.31).[1]

[1] B. I, p. 133, ET, *KM*, p. 116.

These explanations, we believe, will help to clarify certain difficult passages in Bultmann's writings, such as the following: 'In permitting the crucifixion of Jesus, God has set up the Cross in our favour: to believe in the Cross of Jesus, is not to consider a mythical fact which has been accomplished outside of us and of our world, an event which can be known objectively in the manner of an object—an event which God is supposed to have imputed to us for our advantage (in other words, to 'believe' does not consist in confessing that Christ has won our salvation by an objective redemption, as Christian theology of the traditional kind believes), but to believe in the Cross consists in taking up the Cross of Christ as our own, and allowing ourselves to be crucified with him. In so far as it is a saving event (in its saving impact), the Cross is not an isolated fact, which took place in Christ as in a mythical character; it is only in its significance that it has a cosmic dimension. (Now) its significance in the transformation of history (*geschichtsumgestaltende Bedeutung*) is expressed in the fact that the New Testament presents it *as the eschatological event*; that is to say, it is not a past event, to which we look back; but it is the eschatological event in time and beyond time, in so far as it is understood in its significance and that it does not cease to be present (*Gegenwart*) for faith'.[1] 'Thus the Cross of Christ, in so far as it is a saving event, is not a mythical fact, but it is a *geschichtlich* event, based on the *historic fact* (*in dem historischen Ereignis*) of the crucifixion of Jesus of Nazareth. This historical fact is, in its significance, *geschichtlich*, the judgment passed upon the world, the judgment which liberates mankind. And it is to the extent that this is so that Christ is crucified "for us"—and not in the sense in which these words are used in support of a theory of "satisfaction" or sacrifice. Thus the historic fact does not reveal its character as a saving event to mythological knowledge, but to "historical" knowledge (in the sense of *geschichtlich*); and it does so to the extent in which a genuine "historical" knowledge (in the sense of *geschichtlich*) succeeds in

[1] B. I, p. 42, ET, *KM*, p. 36.

understanding its significance. At bottom, the mythological terminology in which the New Testament expression of the saving mystery is embedded, simply aims at enabling us to understand the significance (and the implication for *Geschichte* and for eschatology) of the historic fact (*historisch*). The historic fact of the Cross has, by the significance which is peculiar to it, opened up a new *"geschichtlich"* situation; the proclamation of the Cross as the saving event summons the listener to decide whether he will apply to himself this significance and allow himself to be crucified with Christ'.[1]

The divine saving event of the Cross, understood and presented thus, is completely 'demythologized': that at least is Bultmann's opinion.

But we can also see at what a price. According to Bultmann's theology, the Christian is no longer authorized to hail Christ as his Saviour: no redemption has been objectively accomplished in him and by him. Certainly, Bultmann does not wish to break the link between our salvation and Christ entirely. The New Testament connects salvation— the passage from inauthentic existence to authentic existence —too closely with the historical phenomenon, with the name of Jesus, with his life, and above all with his death, for any form of Christian theology to dare to suppress this relation absolutely. But here, in Bultmann's thought, this connexion is interpreted in such a way that the historical figure of Christ has no other meaning than that of being the origin, the point of departure for Christianity. He is simply the starting-point of the 'statement' of the liberating judgment upon mankind. As has been said already, in the traditional interpretation, Christology, without being separated from soteriology, and remaining in close and vital connexion with it, did in some way or another precede it, and was indeed its founder: the Person of Christ is indeed the basis of salvation, or, to put it better, it is by him, in his life and his death, that the 'Red Sea' is crossed and the 'Passover' of all mankind is celebrated; hence, Christ is truly the

[1] B. I, p. 43, ET, *KM*, p. 37.

substance, the backbone of the Christian message.[1] For Bultmann, on the contrary, Christ is little more than the name
and the title of soteriology; if Christ is retained, it is simply
in order to ensure to the latter a historical (*geschichtlich*)
character: it is with Christ that the act of the divine Saviour,
the eternal Self, enters into time and into history. But his
Person is not the subject whose condemnation to death has
already wrought our redemption: it has inaugurated salvation, it has not achieved it.

On the other hand, we must beware of regarding Bultmann's soteriology as a purely subjective theory of salvation.
Arguing from the fact that Bultmann does not allow for
any interpretation of the Christian message save in strictly
existential terms, it has been said that, in order to be true
to his own logic, he ought to 'subjectivize' the saving event
absolutely: God's action is to be conceived solely as a change
in my knowledge of myself; the only possible divine event
is a phenomenon of the human consciousness.[2]

We must admit that here and there, the text of Bultmann
(which is extremely confused) does imply this subjective
interpretation of his thought (an interpretation to which
we shall return later on). But it would be wrong to regard
it as the only possible one, or even as the most likely, shut-
ting our eyes to the objective aspect of his thought, which
in our opinion is more strongly emphasized. We have
already called attention several times to Bultmann's views
on the significance of the Cross; now it is this significance
which is the substance of the saving event; and it is obvious
that the Cross does not acquire this meaning save in the
heart of one who hears the *kerygma* and accepts it, just as
a passage in a book does not 'come alive' save in the mind
of the reader; thus the saving event is only realized at the
moment when the hearer receives the Cross of Christ as
his own; allows himself to be 'crucified' with him, and
'commits himself to the way of condemnation to death as

[1] K. Barth, *Rudolf Bultmann, Ein Versuch ihn zu verstehen* (quoted in
the Introduction to this book), p. 17.

[2] We have already encountered this objection: see p. 44 above.

THE CHRISTIAN MESSAGE AND MYTH

much as to the way of grace and of life'.[1] Starting from this
point, only one more step is needed to reach the following
affirmation: there is no act of God outside of us; the whole
work of salvation takes place within us. But it would be
wiser to refuse to take this step. The real thought of Bultmann seems to be something like this: it is true, we have
admitted this already, the appropriation of the 'judgment'
by faith alone gives it full actuality; but nevertheless this subjective faith is the appropriation of an objective act, written
in history, that is to say, the Cross of Christ proclaimed by
the apostolic *kerygma* and the preaching of the Church. It would
not be simply and entirely correct to think that, according
to Bultmann, God has not achieved anything in the death of
Christ save in the hearts of those who have heard the message.

But while some critics would admit that there is an 'objective' element in Bultmann's view of the saving event, and
that this event is not exclusively 'subjective' in character,
other critics have given us to understand, that, according
to Bultmann, this 'objectivity' is not in the Cross itself, but
in the *kerygma*, in the witness of the apostles and of the
Church, who speak to us of the Cross: the death of Christ,
it is said, does not become a saving event until it enters
into the *kerygma*.[2] This would mean that the 'objective'
element is not entirely eliminated, that it is limited to the
kerygma. From this point of view, one would have to raise
a far less serious objection to Bultmann's view, namely:
because Bultmann would admit in this case a certain 'objectivity' of the saving event (at least in the *kerygma*), his
theology would not come so dangerously near to the 'subjectivism' of Liberal theology.[3]

[1] K. Barth, *op. cit.*, p. 19.   [2] K. Barth, *op. cit.*, p. 20.
[3] If Bultmann's thought were exclusively 'subjective', it would come
nearer to Liberal theology, but it still would not be equated with it.
After all, even when Bultmann is most 'subjective' in expression, he
maintains, at least in intention, the existence of a divine saving act,
at least inwardly, of a decisive divine intervention in man's history,
of a direct revelation within time, to which, furthermore, man owes
allegiance which is not derived from purely rational motives, nor from
religious sentiment: all of which distinguishes his thought from that
of Liberal Christianity.

This objection is still a serious one, however, for if it were justified it would follow that Christ, considered in himself, and independent of the apostolic *kerygma*, would have no claim to enter into the structure of the objective saving event. This objection could invoke in its favour the following support: Bultmann declares explicitly that, outside of the *kerygma*, apart from the witness of the apostles which interprets it to us, which shows us its meaning, the Cross of Christ is only 'an historical fact of the past' without interest for faith. Without interest: for thus considered in itself, apart from the soteriological interpretation which the Church gives to it, it depends on our methods of historical research, on those methods which we apply impartially to the study of all the facts: now, in the light of historical research, the Cross of Christ appears to us certainly as a grim human drama, but in no way as the beginning, willed by God, of the saving event. In other words, the Christ of the historian is, according to Bultmann, absolutely foreign to Christ, the Saviour known to faith.

Again, we must admit that here and there the text does lay itself open to such an interpretation. But the whole suggests a conception which traces the objectivism back to Christ himself. Doubtless Bultmann affirms the absolute impotence of the historical method, applied to the phenomenon of Christ, to discover what he calls the 'eschatological' significance of this phenomenon. A Catholic theologian would deny this at this point: he would dispute the statement that without the light of faith, the sincere mind applied to the study of Christ could have no inkling of his transcendence. But this controversy is here without any immediate interest. For Bultmann, it is true, the eschatological significance of the Cross of Christ and its saving power is only recognized in faith, as it is only conveyed to us by the message (the external design of the message, offered to our faculties of observation and of induction, does not allow anything to come through to us); but from this we must not conclude that in the eyes of Bultmann the apostolic message introduces into the historical fact of the Cross a significance of which this fact would be, of itself, deprived; sometimes at least, Bultmann makes us think that the message does not introduce this significance, rather that it proclaims it, or better still perhaps that it discovers it; it is doubtless the only one to do it, but it only succeeds because this soteriological meaning was previously written in the fact itself. Thus the Cross of Christ, taken in itself, realizes the objective event of salvation. Not of course in this sense that it effects, mythologically, our redemption, but simply in this sense, that it constitutes the beginning of the objective statement of our liberation.

Whatever we may think of this last point, and even supposing that the Cross of Christ does not form part of the saving event save through entering into the apostolic *kerygma*, the fact remains that in Bultmann's theology, in any case, the saving event receives an objective character, at least in this *kerygma* itself.

In my opinion, we cannot doubt that Bultmann means to maintain this 'objectivity' of the event. But it is a question whether he *can* do this without contradicting himself. In purifying the theology of the Cross from all theories of satisfaction and of sacrifice, he flatters himself that he has succeeded in demythologizing it absolutely. But has he really succeeded in doing so? Since he maintains the idea of the act of God, since above all he gives to this act an expression in external history (in the Cross or in the *kerygma*), does this not suggest that he is reintroducing into his theology an element which he ought to regard as authentically mythological?[1]

The Resurrection

It is beyond doubt that in the view of the New Testament the Resurrection is just as much part of the saving event as the Cross. Bultmann, however, believes that the need for demythologizing requires us to pronounce a verdict on the Resurrection which is very different in principle from that which we have pronounced on the Cross. We could admit,

[1] We shall return to this question later on, pp. 149, 150.

without being unfaithful to the demand for an absolute demythologizing, the reality of the historic fact of the Cross, and as historians we have done so: Jesus of Nazareth was really crucified under Pontius Pilate. But the Resurrection is a very different matter: we would be denying the need for a radical demythologizing if we would accept the phenomenon of the Resurrection and its character as an 'empirical fact': for, in this phenomenon, everything is mythical, not only the New Testament setting, but the tangible fact itself: the re-animation of a corpse, 'the return of a dead man into the life of this present world',[1] the miraculous irruption of the divine into the human sphere. Thus Bultmann writes that the Resurrection is an absolutely mythical event: *ein schlechthin mythisches Ereignis.*[2] In short, as it was said (by Barth), Bultmann thinks that there is nothing to be said about the Risen Christ, about his life after death, about the assurance of his victory over death which he brought to his disciples, about his intercourse with them before they were called (by God) to be the bearers of the message; the disciples did not really behold the glory of God in his Incarnate Word, risen and living before their eyes.[3]

Can we say at least that although it could not be discerned empirically, the Resurrection took place *effectively*, but in a dimension where it could not be proved by the disciples? Can we say that the Christ did really conquer death, but that his victory was not revealed to his disciples on the plane of sense experience? No, we cannot even say that. Actually we cannot be sure that Bultmann denies the fact (not manifested) of the resurrection of Christ, nor that he is obliged to deny it in order to remain logically faithful to the claims of demythologizing. But at least it is clear that, in his eyes neither as an empirical fact nor as a transcendent fact (not manifested), does the Resurrection form part of the saving event.[4]

[1] 'Die Rückkehr eines Gestorbenen in das Leben der diesseitigen Welt' (B. I, p. 45, ET, *KM*, p. 39).
[2] B. I, p. 44, ET, *KM*, p. 38.   [3] K. Barth, *op. cit.*, p. 22.
[4] Other Protestant theologians, E. Brunner for instance, also regard as mythical a resurrection consisting in the re-animation of a corpse.

Now, positively—Bultmann continues—this is how we interpret the soteriological rôle which the New Testament assigns to the Resurrection: we have seen that in the Cross of Jesus, in some way, within time, God achieved the *liberating* judgment which he passes *ab aeterno* upon our existence. It was indeed true that the Cross not only achieved our condemnation, but our salvation: according to the New Testament it is the Cross which saves us, which lifts us to the plane of authentic existence. Only, although by itself, by its dramatic design, the Cross revealed our condemnation to death (the aspect according to which the judgment is condemnation), it did not manifest to any extent our salvation, nor the victory which God has given us over death. Thus the story of the Resurrection was introduced into the

But they do not deny, on the contrary, they affirm, the triumph of Christ over death: they hold that Christ has reassumed a complete human nature, he possesses a living body but his body is not related to the body which was laid in the sepulchre; he is living a transcendent life entirely superior to the conditions of physical, earthly life; finally, this Risen Christ manifested himself to his disciples: these appearances were of a quite different order from purely subjective visions or hallucinations. This is what we gather from the work of E. Brunner: *Das Ewige als Zukunft und Gegenwart*, Zürich, 1953, p. 158, ET, *Eternal Hope*, London, 1954, p. 144. In comparison with these views, Bultmann's negative conclusions seem to be: (*a*) that there was no 're-animation' of the corpse; (*b*) there was no objective appearance of the Living Christ. But does Bultmann go further, and deny that Christ is alive? Some writers seem to think so; Brunner, for instance, who thinks that Bultmann's eschatology would do away with all hope of a future life, and thus also denies the Resurrection of Christ (cf. E. Brunner, *op. cit.*, p. 147, ET, p. 134, and 232, ET, p. 217): there could be no transfiguration of physical life, nor the hope of survival of humanity as such, because such a transfiguration would imply an irruption of the supernatural into this present world and the sphere of human life: the demand for an existential interpretation would force us to abandon all cosmological eschatology. In support of this interpretation, Brunner only quotes one passage from Bultmann: '*Die eschatologische Existenz ist . . . nur im Glauben, nicht . . . im Schauen realisiert, das heisst, sie ist kein weltliches Phänomen*' (B. II, p. 205, ET, *KM*, p. 208). This passage is not decisive: it certainly rejects the apocalyptic idea of those biblical passages which proclaim the future life in terms of the resurrection of the flesh, but it could leave the question open of a survival which would not be the result of a divine action upon our present world. But even if Bultmann admitted the reality of Christ Risen and Living, it is plain that he does not believe that he would play any part in the plan of salvation.

content of the *kerygma* in order to assure us of this victory.

In other words: God created the belief in the Resurrection in the minds of the disciples: we must not forget that the disciples shared the mythical views of the world of their own day; God's action was adapted to their state of mind, and this produced the idea of a physical resurrection in their minds; but in the guise of a mythical story, the true divine content which God poured into their hearts, was, quite simply, *the knowledge of the triumphant value of the Cross*, the discovery of its saving significance, the grasp of its liberating aspect. It is this experience of being 'grasped' by God, known wholly inwardly in our hearts, which is the sole paschal event, as it is that alone which constitutes the content of the joyous message (and not of a physical resurrection, which is supposed to be objective). So when the message invites us too, to confess our faith in the Resurrection of Christ, it does not ask us to affirm a marvellous fact, accomplished and manifested in our empirical world; nor even an event which could be distinguished adequately from the Cross, and would be added to it. The message simply says: with the disciples, with the eyes of faith, gaze at the triumphant significance of the Cross. For 'his death is already the victory won over the power of death'.[1] There is only one drama, one event: that of the death on the Cross. The Resurrection is no more than the *expression* of its liberating value. Indeed, this was the view of the New Testament itself; in the Fourth Gospel does not John say that the Passion of Jesus is the hour of his exaltation? Does he not find a twofold meaning in the *exaltari*? exaltation to the Cross and exaltation to glory?[2] The death of Jesus should

[1] *sein Tod selbst ist schon die Überwindung der Todesmacht*, B. I, p. 44, ET, *KM*, p. 39.

[2] *M. A. Vergote*: 'L'exaltation du Christ en Croix selon le quatrième Evangile', in *Ephemerides theologicae Lovanienses*, Vol. XXVIII, 1952, pp. 5-23, shows that in the Gospel of St John the 'exaltation and glorification' is already 'implied' in the 'lifting up' of the Son of Man on the Cross, but without prejudice to its full manifestation in the *reality* of the Resurrection and Ascension, the 'exaltation' on the Cross is the symbol of the approaching Ascension: Bultmann has no right to regard the two events as one (cf. A. Vergote, art. cit., p. 12, n. 29).

not only be regarded as a simply human death, nor even as a judgment which would confine itself simply to condemning us: it is the divine statement of grace and pardon: we do not say more than this when we confess that Jesus is risen from the dead.

Presented in this way, the message of the Resurrection is certainly demythologized; and nevertheless, it still has some content, since it proclaims the triumphant significance of the Cross. On the other hand, the demythologizing proper to the Resurrection is of a different character from that applied to Calvary. The Cross as an historical fact, says Bultmann, of itself, forms an integral part of the saving event, quite apart from its incorporation in the apostolic *kerygma*. We cannot say the same of the Resurrection: not only is it not an historical fact, but the actual triumph which it is supposed to express, is not manifested in the drama of Golgotha; the triumphant significance of the death of Christ only exists in the mind of the disciples, in what it says to them, and in the message they have to give to us. Here, Barth is quite right to say: according to Bultmann, 'It is only in the message of the Risen Christ and in faith in the Resurrection that the Resurrection has its effect. It seems then that the knowledge of the (triumphant) significance of the crucifixion is not derived from Jesus Christ himself'.[1]

Besides, we cannot repeat it too often, the Cross of Jesus and his triumph over death are only an expression of the 'event of grace' which is being accomplished at every moment for each one of us. We come back continually to this conception, which is the essence of the message: the liberating judgment of God, which, considered from the divine point of view, takes place beyond time, also takes place within time, in the faith of those who accept it as a statement of fact: it is this realization in our existence as believers which constitutes the saving event in the full sense of the word; just as it also transforms history (*die Historie*) into *Geschichte*, the divine history of redemption. The Cross

[1] K. Barth, *op. cit.*, pp. 22, 23.

of Christ, and the triumph which it contains (stated in the message under the form of the Resurrection) are merely a manifestation—the first in a series—of this saving cosmic event: but this cosmic event will continually have a profoundly effective influence to the very end of time.[1] Evidently, we could express the fact of our individual faith in terms of participation in the death and Resurrection of Christ, precisely because this death and Resurrection constitute the first manifestation of the saving event: this is how the New Testament speaks of it; but in a more profound sense, we may express it in terms of participation in the eschatological and historical (*geschichtlich*) event which is always present, always contemporary.

By 'participation' Bultmann says, and in actual life this means not only faith, but obedience and love: participation in the death of Christ, in the judgment of God which condemns sin consists, as we have said, in being 'crucified with Christ': we not only renounce our passions and our greed, but we accept ourselves, as we are, as fallen human beings, incapable of setting ourselves free, in contrast to the philosophers—we renounce all pharisaical self-confidence (I Cor. 5.6), all trust in our own efforts; similarly, participation in the Resurrection of Christ, which is an experience of liberation, will consist in 'rising again' with Jesus: that is, we shall believe not only that God sets us free, but also that we *are* truly liberated; this liberty is not only expressed in the indicative of love, but also in the imperative: raised to the level of authentic existence, we shall love others with the love with which God loves us, that is to say, with a free and generous love, which springs from no other source than from God himself. The whole of salvation, of our eschatological existence, of our last end, consists in this; but we must be on our guard against conceiving all this in *future* terms, at least in the apocalyptic manner of a resurrection of the flesh: otherwise, we shall again succumb to the temptation of mythology.

[1] '*nur dass sich dieses kosmische Geschehen auf den Zeitlauf verteilt*', B. I, p. 45, ET, *KM*, p. 40.

The Gospel Message (die Verkündigung)

The Cross and the Resurrection of Christ are proclaimed to us as saving events in the witness of the disciples and in the message which was entrusted to them, in their preaching. In other words, apart from this message, the Cross would only seem to us—men and historians of the present day—as an historical fact of ambiguous significance; it is only through the message that we receive its eschatological significance, its value as a saving event. Therefore, it must be said that faith in the Cross and in the Resurrection is, in reality, faith in the Word of preaching as the Word of God.

In the face of that Word we cannot ask whether it has authority.[1] Indeed, what kind of authority could this be? Are we to demand that the transcendent should prove its reality by tangible signs? that it should manifest itself in 'this-worldly' phenomena; in short, that it should be 'mythologized', and thus cease to be what it is, namely the reality which cannot be translated into the world of our experience. All we are asked is simply this: when the Gospel is preached, will you accept it or refuse it? We may however add, that in inviting us to believe in the death and Resurrection as an eschatological event (in the *presence* within time, of the liberating judgment) the Christian message offers us the true knowledge of ourselves; until then, we might indeed, in the light of our existential knowledge, have some light on our true being, about its distress, about our 'being-thrown-into-the-world'; but the reality of our fall would remain mysterious, and our efforts at liberation and authentic existence would be useless; now, however, when we hear the Word, we realize that we are sinners who have been graciously pardoned and set free; we perceive the connexion between the message and the system of existential analysis, and the fact that it answers our secret longings; further, we are involved in the divine process of genuine liberation. In all this, in this affinity and in this fulfilment of desire, we can see a kind of verification of the Word, a testimony to its

[1] B. I, p. 46, ET, *KM*, p. 41.

truth. And that is why our faith, although deprived of tangible signs and of all support in 'this-worldly' realities, is not a blind and arbitrary decision; it is an act of acceptance, made with full awareness of what it involves.[1]

We can see from this that the *kerygma* itself forms part of the saving event, because it is created by God: it is the temporal proclamation of the liberating judgment. The New Testament itself declares it: in addition to the death of Christ which judges and liberates, God has established the 'ministry of reconciliation' and the 'Word of reconciliation' (II Cor. 5.18); it is this word which is added to the Cross,[2] and expresses the meaning of the saving event. 'As this word resounds, the Cross and the Resurrection become "present", the eschatological hope becomes the "Now" of the redemptive present'. The eschatological promise of Isaiah is fulfilled (49.8): 'Behold, now is the acceptable time; behold, now is the day of salvation' (II Cor. 6.2). Therefore, when the apostle preaches this 'Word', the divine judgment is at work, sifting the hearers' response: to some the preacher is 'a savour from death unto death', and to others, 'a savour from life unto life' (II Cor. 2.16). It is also through the mediation of the preacher that the power of the Resurrection is transmitted (II Cor. 4.12). Similarly, it is of the same preaching that we must understand the words of Christ in the Gospel of John: 'Verily, verily, I say unto you, he that heareth my word, and believeth him that sent me, hath eternal life, and cometh not into judgment, but hath passed out of death into life' (John 5.24ff.). The Risen Lord comes to us in the preached Word (and not in the process of historical research) and in it alone. 'So belief cometh of hearing, and hearing by the word of Christ' (Rom. 10.17). Here we observe that, as a typically Protestant theologian, in his theology Bultmann assigns to preaching an outstandingly soteriological *rôle*, which is far more important than that of worship and the sacraments, of which he simply says in passing, and rather vaguely, that in these

[1] B. I, p. 46, ET, *KM*, pp. 41-42.
[2] *hinzukommt*, B. I, p. 47, ET, *KM*, p. 42.

also, in some way or another, the eschatological presence is realized.[1]

Finally, like the Word, like the preacher, the Church also is integrated in the saving event—this Church in which the proclamation of the Christian message is transmitted without ceasing and where all those are assembled who, thanks to their faith, have a share in the eschatological existence. 'The community (ἐκκλησία) is an eschatological conception, and when it is described in terms of the "Body of Christ", it suggests its "cosmic" significance; it is not an historical phenomenon (*historisches Phänomen*) in the sense in which we speak of other events in world history (*im Sinne der Weltgeschichte*); it is a *geschichtlich* phenomenon, in this sense, that it is accomplished within (divine) history'; it denotes the divine event, accomplished within time.[2]

Having reached the climax of this theology of 'the event', Bultmann believes that he has succeeded in entirely demythologizing the New Testament presentation of the Gospel message.

But he is confronted by the objection: is there not a relic of mythology in the idea of God's action, and above all of his decisive intervention in time, of his eschatological action? Bultmann's answer is noteworthy: it is based entirely upon that narrower conception of myth which we have already distinguished from a more general notion.[3] Anyone is free, he says, equally, to call the action of God as we have presented it 'mythological'. But anyone who does so ought at least to concede that the saving event, understood in this way, 'no longer has anything in common with "mythology" in the older sense of the word', with this mythology which disappeared along with the disappearance of the mythological picture of the world.[4] Only a transcendent reality, which is supernatural, non-temporal, can be truly 'mythological'; a reality of this kind is said to manifest itself in its

[1] B. I, pp. 42, 43, ET, *KM*, p. 36.
[2] B. I, pp. 47, 48, ET, *KM*, p. 43.   [3] Cf. above, p. 64.
[4] '*Aber jedenfalls ist dann solche Mythologie nicht mehr Mythologie im alten Sinne, die mit dem Untergang des mythischen Weltbildes versunken wäre*' (B. I, p. 48, ET, *KM*, p. 43).

supernatural character within our terrestrial world, by means of forms and expressions which it borrows from it: e.g. miracles, spiritual gifts, etc. In the myth, Bultmann says, further, that the transcendence of God (*die Jenseitigkeit Gottes*) becomes immanence and reality within this world.[1] Now here, there is nothing like it: God's action, who is himself situated above time,[2] is certainly involved in man's history and transforms it into *Geschichte*; but it does not transform this history in a miraculous way in order to prove itself and bear witness to its reality. Understood in this way, the divine event is not unacceptable to modern man.

Further, we have seen that the New Testament itself, in its underlying intention, tends to suggest this conception of the event, a conception which is truly paradoxical, in that it does not recognize in God's messenger anything more than a concrete historical humanity (in his *Theology of the New Testament*, Bultmann, we may recall, insists on showing that the Jesus of the Fourth Gospel is not in any way presented as a $\theta\epsilon\hat{\iota}os$ $\dot{a}v\hat{\eta}\rho$); in this Gospel the eschatological action of God is achieved in the destiny of a purely human person, and no attempt is made to prove its eschatological character by means of 'this-worldly' forms. Look at these biblical passages: 'He emptied himself' (Phil. 2.7); 'though he was rich yet for your sakes he became poor' (II Cor. 8.9); 'God, sending his own son in the likeness of sinful flesh' (Rom. 8.3); 'manifested in the flesh' (I Tim. 3.16); and above all 'the Word was made flesh' (John 1.14): they all show that the New Testament has many different ways of stating the paradox of the divine event, and also that it refuses to try to prove its transcendence, in a mythological way, by the use of unusual phenomena.

We can even speak of a sort of divine 'modesty' of God in Christ: the one in whom God wills to realize his presence, and by whom he reconciles the world to himself, is a real man, living at a real date in history. There is the same 'modesty' in the Word of God and in the Christian message:

[1] *ist . . . zum Diesseits gemacht*, B. I, p. 48, ET, *KM*, p. 44.
[2] *jenseits der Zeit*, B. I, p. 42, ET, *KM*, p. 36.

it is not one of these oracles charged with mystery, as in the mythical religions, which aim at casting a spell upon us: here there is nothing but an extremely sober message which tells us about Jesus of Nazareth. On the one hand it shows the relevance and the saving significance (*heilsgeschichtlich*) of Christ; and this 'Word' claims to be the eschatological Word of God; but, on the other hand, it does not present Jesus of Nazareth, Bultmann might say, any differently than the Dialogues of Plato present Socrates: in both instances there is a spiritual reality which is simply human, a simple phenomenon of the history of the soul, and from the point of view of ideological content, the message does not offer us more than a possible *Weltanschauung*, like so many others: it is in this sense that we can speak of its modesty and restraint.

It is the same with the apostles and the Church: they form part of the eschatological event; nevertheless, these apostles are only men, intelligible in their historical humanity; and the Church is only a sociological phenomenon like so many others.

Thus everywhere there is discretion, paradox, and to some extent, scandal—scandal, precisely because the event, divine as it is, does not appeal to our senses, but only to bare faith. It is in this way that the Christian message has avoided mythology, and has escaped the danger of being compromised when the latter went to pieces.

(ii) *The Objective Interpretation of Demythologizing: based on the work entitled 'Zum Problem der Entmythologisierung'.*
(*1951*)[1]

Up to this point, in our exposition of Bultmann's theology concerning the act of God in Christ, we have drawn almost exclusively upon Bultmann's first essay: 'Neues Testament und Mythologie' (New Testament and Mythology) (1941). Ten years later, the author returned to the same subject. At present we are going to follow the course of his thought in

[1] An ET of part of this essay appears in *KM*, pp. 191-211, 'Bultmann Replies to His Critics'.

this later book;[1] this will inevitably involve a certain amount of repetition, but it will clarify some points in the earlier expression of his thought which are still obscure. Two features, especially, will be emphasized. The first is this: we are going to follow the author as he makes a more conscious effort to clarify his conception of *Geschichte*: he is going to try to assign to, or, if we prefer to put it so, to recognize in the divine *Geschichte*, in the divine saga of salvation, a reality, an objective character, which is proper to it, which is totally different from the objectivity of 'this-worldly phenomena'.

The second feature is not entirely distinct from the first one: Bultmann, we shall remember, claimed that the essentialist ontology was wholly unsuited to express the saving event; by the use of its concepts of 'Nature' and 'Substance', etc., it ends by 'mythologizing' it in a very crude way; on the other hand, he believes that in Heidegger's ontology he has discovered a possibility of a non-mythological expression of God's action; this ontology, he believes, could provide us with the means of understanding the reality, the real objectivity proper to the saving event, an objectivity totally different from the *Gegenständlichkeit* of representative thought;[2] but until now he had not explained his views on this particularly difficult point: precisely how does Heidegger's system of thought—and indeed, carried further, succeed in rendering this service? This is what he is now going to tell us: in a word, the objectivity (non-mythological) of the divine action will be that of 'existential' encounters.

1. In the eyes of certain critics, the most serious danger to which demythologizing exposes the very idea of the saving event in Christ appears to be the following: demythologizing implies the denial of God's action, at least of an action coming *objectively* to meet me; at the most it allows us to describe purely subjective experiences by means of the conception of the divine event.

---

[1] B. II, pp. 196-208, ET, *KM*, pp. 196-211.
[2] Cf. above, pp. 37 and 68.

Once more, Bultmann sets himself to refute this criticism. I certainly intend, he says, to conceive God's action as fully real and objective in character. But demythologizing of this character, and—this comes to the same thing—its existential interpretation, do not, in the slightest degree, endanger this 'objectivity'. All it means is this: God's action is not on the same plane as the other phenomena which constitute the world and are visible to ordinary human perception, without taking their existential meaning into account. So far as man is concerned, God's action, in its final form, comes to fulfilment in his personal encounter with God; now human life is essentially historical; it is situated in space and time; consequently, the divine action, the encounter with God, has no other reality than that of a fact situated here and now; it is the event in which someone, here and now, is summoned, questioned, judged, and blessed; but, because God's action thus becomes an inward, integral part of my existence it does not follow that I may not speak of it as of a real event, which confronts me.

Let us examine this explanation more thoroughly: the mythical conception of God's action represents the divine action as the violent irruption of a new element into the context of nature, of history, of the life of the soul, like a miracle. It is only that idea which we must reject: the divine action does not mingle with the phenomena of this world, nor does it manifest itself in the objective complex of our representations; it leaves the closed system of history unchanged; but this does not prevent it from existing as the action of a transcendent reality; only, withdrawn from our faculties of observation, we must admit that it only reveals itself to the eye of faith.[1] Some event which touches me like many others, and is part of the course of happenings in the spheres of nature and of history, may not appear to be distinctive, in any way, to the neutral and speculative observer, yet faith knows that it is the gift or the judgment

[1] *'Gottes (Handeln) ist verborgen für jedes andere Auge als das des Glaubens'* (B. II, p. 196, ET, *KM*, p. 197).

of God; faith asserts that a certain thought, or decision is wrought by God, although from the 'phenomenal' point of view, this thought or this decision is not distinct from other phenomena. Thus there is a divine event, an objective act, but it is for faith and in faith: the encounter with God only exists within the sphere of faith. We must add that it is in the Word of Jesus Christ (*im Wort von Jesus Christus*), in the preaching of the Christian message, that this encounter takes place. Further, the faith that comes into being in this way is never transformed into a knowledge which has been acquired once for all, nor into a system of ideas (*Weltanschauung*), nor into a general theory which can be taught to others; it always retains its character as an 'event'; it only remains living to the extent in which the believer seeks to know what God wishes to say to him here and now (*hier und jetzt*). What God is in general (that is to say, for speculative thought), in nature and in history, is hidden from the believer as much as from anyone else. His faith is limited to this conviction: that in this actual fact, God acts in a mysterious way, and what God does is only identical with the phenomenon against all appearance. To sum up: the vision of faith does not modify the closed system constructed by objectivizing thought by discovering within it a miraculous element which would disturb it; rather, it suppresses it as a whole (*als ganzes*) confronted by a fact which presents the characters of all the other facts, it declares: 'and yet' (*dennoch*): and yet, it is something quite different, in spite of the appearance of identity: it is the very action of God.

2. The objection, however, still holds good: in Bultmann's conception, it goes on to say, the fact remains that God's action does not possess this 'objectivity' which can be perceived by neutral observation and by objective scientific thought. Now, no other 'objectivity' can be imagined. Thus God's action remains enclosed within the subjective sphere, and faith is merely an *Erlebnis*, a psychological phenomenon, without reference to a reality which confronts it.

This statement causes Bultmann to make a twofold observation.

A. Certainly, let us repeat, only the man who knows that he has been addressed by God can speak of God, and this amounts to saying, we must admit, that the believer cannot speak of God without at the same time speaking of himself: but it does not follow from this that God has no other reality than that which the subject confers on him. We ought to see this clearly.

In the terminology of existential analysis, we remember that man achieves his authenticity in an existential and personal decision. But this is scarcely more than the statement of a formal law: what we need to know is the *content* of our decision, and to what reality it is related. Now, as we have seen, man is not a pure 'self' facing an object which is in every respect foreign to him: 'There is no "self" save by and in an actual relation with something other than myself'[1]—could we not now say in more precise terms: in a relation *with another person*? Yes, that may well be so: the human being, who is essentially social, realizes himself, and verifies the fullness of his interior life in meeting with others, and in 'inter-subjectivity'; he becomes 'personal' to the extent in which he is willing to go out of himself and to respond to the call of his neighbour. And if perchance it is God himself who comes to summon him in a wholly unexpected way, henceforth, no man can have any hope of personal and authentic life unless he accepts and welcomes this 'call' from his Lord. But, as we already know, the divine revelation cannot be presented in the form of a physical reality, of a world externally 'consecrated', or in the form of a miraculous phenomenon occurring in the visible universe: all this would be mythology. The whole question which remains to be answered—and it is precisely this which makes the objector so insistent—is this: 'Can God *really* come to us otherwise than under the form of myth?'

[1] A. De Waelhens, *La philosophie de Martin Heidegger*, Louvain, 1940, p. 36.

Is there for God another possible type of revelation than that—impossible—by which he might address us through the transformation of a world of objects.

Yes, this other kind of revelation is perfectly conceivable. Its character is suggested to us by certain characteristics of our human relationships. Let us analyse an existential encounter like that of love: the genuine love which a beloved being devotes to us, in its singular quality, in its unique and original elements, escapes entirely from the objective and neutral outlook of representative thought; seen from the outside, by one who is not the object of it, which does not touch him, nor address him, this love cannot be grasped in its concrete essence; for the outsider it is scarcely more than a psychical phenomenon, which offers a wide range of possible interpretations.[1] At the most he can only gain some knowledge of it by comparing it with similar experiences, and by gathering them up under a general heading, as a type; but in so doing, all that is new or novel in this kind of love escapes him. Thus true love only reveals itself to the person to whom it is given. Conceivably, the latter could meet it with ignorance or with contempt: the existential encounter can assume various forms; in all cases, the fact remains that love does not reveal itself save in the experience of this 'meeting'. But because it is not 'objectivized' by a speculative eye, which is not 'committed', are we to conclude that this love does not exist, that this singular quality has no objective reality? Evidently not.

Similarly, with God's action, his revelation, his summons, his love directed towards me: it is perfectly possible that it should be addressed to me, from the depth of my being, through history and the Christian message, without however becoming materialized in physical realities supernaturally transformed, and thus also without offering itself to the judgment of the speculative reason or to the confirmation of objectivizing thought; it will not be perceptible save in

---

[1] *'Ein geistesgeschichtliches oder psychisches Phänomen, das verschiedenen Möglichkëiten der Interpretation unterliegt'* (B. II, p. 199, cf. ET, *KM*, p. 200).

the existential encounter of faith. But this circumstance does not allow the one whom it touches to have any doubt of its reality. Certainly, the objectivity here verified will not be that of 'this-worldly' phenomena; hence in the eyes of representative thought the content of faith will always seem to be an illusion; on the plane proper to science, the believer could never refute the charge of being non-objective; but he can reassure himself: the content of his faith is not a pure *Erlebnis*, a purely subjective 'experience', unconnected with reality, on the contrary, it enjoys the most authentic objectivity.

Let us express this somewhat differently: 'Faith cannot be demonstrated in its relation to its object': it is precisely the transcendence of God in relation to the whole domain of objective knowledge which protects God against all human efforts to demonstrate its reality. Faith is the *'existentiel'* response to the message of grace addressed to some particular man, a message which has its origin and its justification in the New Testament. We can also define it simply thus: listening to Scripture as the Word of God. On one condition, however: we must not regard the Scriptures as a compendium of doctrine; nor even a document containing testimonies to the faith of other men, testimonies capable of awakening in us by the means of *Einfühlung*, by affective agreement, religious experiences like those of the men of the Bible. But we must understand the Scriptures as the Word of God, hidden, which cannot be grasped as we understand the 'objects' of this world speaking directly to us at the present moment, and only verifying its nature as a divine message at the moment, *'intra usum'*,[1] in the existential encounter of acceptance (or of rejection).

But, some may say, if God cannot be demonstrated, surely his action, the 'saving events' (*die Heilstatsachen*) can be proved. No—that too is impossible. They too are objects, but only in relation to faith, and in the existential encounter which defines it; and faith is not based upon these events as upon facts which have been previously recognized as such

---

[1] B. II, p. 200, ET, *KM*, p. 201.

by scientific objective study. Or if it be said that they are the basis of faith, it is because these events are grasped as such by faith itself. Here faith is like the confidence which exists between two friends: it does not seek the support of external, objective 'evidence'; both friends know that their mutual trust is based upon their deep intuitive knowledge of each other, expressed in the friendship itself. From the point of view of speculative and impersonal thought, it is quite true that such a friendship is not without risk, but what does this matter to existential thought? Here, too, it is the same between man and God, the foundation and the object of faith are one and the same thing.

B. Here is another observation, or another way of meeting the critic's objection: he seems to have been scandalized by Bultmann's insistence on presenting faith as a new knowledge of existence; this would mean that God's action (to which faith is supposed to relate us as to its object) would be limited to giving us a new knowledge of ourselves. Does not this imply that the event of revelation (*das Offenbarungsereignis*) is nothing more than a kind of psychological 'shock' which liberates within us the true understanding of our being? That it is not a fact introduced into the real order in order to transform it; or, at the most, that it affects nothing but man's consciousness? that the content of this real understanding would be, at bottom, a non-temporal truth whose discovery is subordinated to the shock of the so-called event, but whose possession, once obtained, remains within us quite independently of the historic fact which has quickened it into life?[1]

When the critic talks like this, he shows his misunderstanding of the *'existentiel'* knowledge of the self; or, to put it more precisely, he confuses it wrongly with the *'existential'* knowledge of the human being. This *'existential'* knowledge

[1] This is the way in which H. Thielicke expresses the criticism in 'Die Frage der Entmythologisierung des Neuen Testaments', B. I, pp. 184ff., ET, 'The Restatement of New Testament Mythology', *KM*, pp. 168ff. Cf. also B. II, p. 201, n. 1, ET, *KM*, p. 202, n. 3.

of oneself simply makes statements which express truths which are void of events, revealing nothing but existence 'in general'; but with *'existentiel'* knowledge it is different: this knowledge is gained only within the sphere of *'existentiel'* operation, that is to say, in concrete encounters, in which man faces another who comes forth to meet him, objectively. Here it does not matter whether this *'existentiel'* knowledge is always conscious of itself, by a process of reflection; often indeed it will be rather *lived* than known explicitly: for instance, think of the knowledge by which a child grasps his reality as a child faced by his parents: a knowledge which the child exercises without reflection in his filial affection, his confidence, and in his obedience. What does matter is to notice that in all these instances, it is due to the shock of an objective encounter: there is no knowledge of the self which is not at the same time knowledge of the other, no revelation of the self to itself, outside of the sphere of inter-subjectivity.

To this we should add that this objective encounter must be maintained and prolonged if the subject wants to conserve this new way of understanding himself. In other words: the coming into the presence of another is not confined to awakening within us a new comprehension of life, after which we can rest satisfied with this result, feeling that we now possess truths which are in some way non-temporal, about the essence of human existence; rather, this knowledge needs to be unceasingly renewed: the relation of friendship for instance, ought always to be strengthened and deepened if we want to preserve the revelation which has been given to us of the knowledge of ourselves. Why is this necessary? Because this relation is involved in the truth which it reveals: man is not himself, and does not verify his authentic existence, save in the spheres of personal encounter and community. Let us apply this to the knowledge of ourselves which faith gives to us: far from suppressing the objectivity of the fact which has awakened it to the reality of a non-temporal truth, this knowledge only remains authentic on condition that it is continually re-aligned to

the encounter with the Word of God; there man understands himself, it is true, but precisely what he understands
is that he is himself essentially response to the Word of God,
to that Word 'which proclaims the action of God in Christ
in such a way that it is always contemporary'. Once this
has been understood we shall no longer be open to the
charge of secularizing the Christian message, of reducing
the saving act of God in Christ to the immanence of human
existence.

But on the other hand, it is true, this argument emphasizes
another correlated truth: it is impossible for man to apprehend, in faith, the revelation of the objective love of God
if he remains what he is, refusing to acquire a new knowledge of himself; our impersonal and speculative knowledge
cannot grasp the event of our liberation in Christ; the latter
is not the object of a *Bericht*, of a doctrine, of a statement,
accessible to reason in general; we do not believe it or perceive it save in the act in which we consent to be set free from
ourselves and led into a new understanding of our existence.

3. 'Very well', says the critic: 'I am shown, it is true,
that in faith man is confronted by an objective act of God;
but the fact remains that this action is an event wrought
within me by God; Bultmann's conception leaves no room
for the truth of God's action in Christ, once for all, for the
whole world. And by this very fact he is untrue to the
biblical message; for his view eliminates the ἐφ᾽ἅπαξ of Rom.
6.10.' 'For the death that he died, he died unto sin once
for all.' (RV Marg.)[1]

Bultmann answers: this is a misunderstanding. Christ
exists as the Word of God and as a divine event *'ante me et
extra me'*.[2] God has acted, once for all, in Jesus Christ. We
say simply this: this divine action has not assumed human
features; it is not written, in the shape of miraculous facts,

[1] This is the view of E. Brunner: *Die christliche Lehre von Schöpfung
und Erlösung. Dogmatik*, II, Zürich, 1950, p. 314, ET, 'The Christian
Doctrine of Creation and Redemption', *Dogmatics*, Vol. 2, London,
1952, p. 267.
[2] B. II, p. 206, ET, *KM*, p. 208.

in history; Christ was not a θεῖος ἀνῆρ charged by his transcendent appearance to prove that he is a Saviour-God. All this would be mythology. Thus it follows that the divine action wrought in him cannot be discerned by history; we cannot date it as we can date—as the result of historical research—other historical events. From the point of view of the historian, and his 'objectivizing' attitude, Jesus of Nazareth has a merely human destiny, which is absolutely foreign to the very essence of the eschatological event. Where indeed is the latter to be found? Once again realized in Jesus Christ—in this sense that the revelation of salvation begins in Christ—it is prolonged in the preaching of the Church and in the Holy Scriptures; but in their turn, these two forms of revelation and of the Word of God elude all merely impersonal and speculative knowledge: the divine saving act cannot be grasped outside of faith, of the existential encounter at the 'moment', of this encounter which, as we have seen, does not reveal the saving act without at the same time conveying to us the new knowledge of ourselves.

Henceforth we see that we must say, finally, that strictly speaking, there is no divine event, no eschatological reality, save within a personal commitment at the present moment; not because no divine intervention—not discerned by 'science'—has occurred in history, but because there is no effective salvation apart from the man who is actually united to God by faith; before being received by the subject at the present moment, the preaching of the Church, the Scriptures, and Christ himself are at the most no more than objective conditions of the eschatological reality. 'The eschatological event, which is Christ, is never realized save in the concrete, here and now, where the Word is preached (II Cor. 6.2; John 5.24); or further, where it is received in faith, or rejected in unbelief.' (II Cor. 2.15; John 3.18; 9.39.)[1]

In a word, God and his saving action are not evident to the objective gaze. The saving event can only be believed against appearances. It is the same with the justification of

[1] B. II, pp. 205-206, ET, *KM*, pp. 208-209.

the sinner: that also cannot be believed save against the accusations of the guilty conscience. By this last remark, Bultmann wants us to understand that his theology as a whole is closely connected with the deep meaning of Luther's thought. We recall the Lutheran interpretation of the doctrine of St Paul on justification: justification by faith alone, apart from the works of the Law. Radical demythologizing is simply the logical application, on the plane of knowledge, of this interpretation. Just as the doctrine of justification destroys, in man, the false security of his own 'works', similarly and in a parallel way, demythologizing destroys our confidence in our 'objectivizing' knowledge (*konstatierendes Erkennen*). The man who wants to believe in God as his God, and in his saving action as an action truly proceeding from him alone, must know that history does not offer him anything on the basis of which he could believe, that his faith is as if in the air (*dass er gleichsam in die Luft gestellt ist*), that faith must not desire any proof for the truth of the Word which summons him. The foundation and the object of his faith are strictly identical. He alone finds security and certitude who renounces all desire for intellectual certainty, and is ready to plunge into that 'dark night' which constitutes faith. And even as his faith in justification refuses to invoke human 'works' which are supposed to be 'sanctifying', thus equally his faith in the creative (or re-creative) action of salvation cannot be based upon the existence of a 'sacred' sphere which God is supposed to have 'hollowed out' within history.

Have we indeed forgotten Luther's doctrine? Did he not insist that the world has no 'holy places', that the whole world is a 'secular' realm—without prejudice nevertheless to the fact that '*terra ubique Domini*': a divine ubiquity which is real, it is true, but which can only be believed against all appearances? What Luther thus declared in relation to the doctrine of justification, we have to apply to religious knowledge: there is nothing, in the system of Nature and of History, which manifests to any extent a sacredness, a consecration; doubtless the preached Word confers on certain events the character of an action of God and even of a miracle; but this character is not grasped save in faith, and against all the appearances of sense and of reason.

In this final remark, Bultmann reveals a new *motif* for his opposition to a mythological interpretation of the fact of Christianity. At the outset of his essay, this opposition was mainly inspired by the modern view of the world: the natural sciences, he said, have made it impossible for our minds to accept the mythical world-view of the Bible. Then, a second *motif*, no longer due to science, but to philosophy, has been introduced: the essentialist ontology and the theology which is based upon it, compare the action of God to a physical force, and 'mythologize' it; but by that very act they betray its true nature, for God is not on the side of 'objectivized existents' but on the side of Being.[1] Here then a third *motif* appears, a reason which is positively religious, and which Bultmann regards as immanent in the nature of the Christian Faith itself: faith, which is its very essence, aspires to free itself from all attachment to any particular 'world-view', whether it be the product of scientific or of mythical thought. Faith is darkness; it seeks no support outside itself. Possibly this conception of faith is inspired, in his mind, more or less consciously, by a point of view rather typically Protestant, according to which there exists a kind of incompatibility between God, his transcendence, his holiness, and the world created by sinful man: a world in which no manifestation of God can be found capable of forming a foundation for faith. But whatever the *motif* may be, do not let us seek to discover within history any kind of incarnation, any materialization of the divine and the sacred—meaning by this: that which can be materialized so that it can be discerned by our rational faculties—a myth, as if the invocation of a secular element, visibly transfigured, would not quench the obscure light of faith!

This is the objective interpretation of Bultmann's theology. According to it, Christ has realized the eschatological

[1] Cf. above, p. 40.

event in himself, at least in this sense, that, in the life of Christ and in his Cross, God has begun, for the view of faith, the announcement of the divine act which saves us. Such an interpretation consists in making Bultmann say, in spite of his desire for radical demythologizing, that in the divine act of salvation there is a certain objectivity manifested within history (the saving event has in some way taken place outside of man's sphere) or rather, it reconciles objectivity and absolute demythologizing, for however objective the event may be, still it no less absolutely excludes 'myth' in the strict sense of the word. In the course of this exposition we have noted, in the author's text, the statements on which it is based; in a word, this seems necessary, in order to explain Bultmann's refusal, explicitly stated, of an integral subjectivity. This treatment alone, we believe, fully respects his intentions. Besides, we find this interpretation explicitly stated by himself. The critics too often confine their reading of Bultmann to the two sources which we have been using up to the present (1941 and 1951). But there are other passages: the theologian Schniewind had expressed the fear that Bultmann's theology would sever all connexion between the Christian and the Cross of Jesus. Bultmann dispels this fear in such a way that it should remove all doubts about the 'objective' character of his conception of the event: 'To ignore the connexion between faith on the one hand and the Cross of Christ as a past event on the other, would certainly mean surrendering the *kerygma*. But that was not at all my intention. What I am concerned with is the permanent "historic" (*geschichtlich*) significance of the unique (*einmalig*) event of past history, in virtue of which, although it is a unique historical event, it is nevertheless the event of final eschatological significance. That is how the New Testament interprets that event, and it is for us theologians to decide whether this is a merely mythological proposition, or whether it is capable of (*existential*) interpretation.

'Now, it seems to me that the eschatological character of this event has to be explained by means of the following paradox: the unique event of past history is an ever-present reality (it is always "contemporary"). I do not mean that it is timeless, like an abstract idea, for that would make the Cross a bare symbol. I am seeking rather to give full weight to the intention of the New Testament, according to which the Cross is an ever-present reality, on the one hand in the *kerygma* and the sacraments (both of which are forms of personal encounter), and secondly in the concrete expression of faith in our life. Thus this unique event of the past is always "contemporary" for faith. I do not hesitate to speak of "history" (*Geschichte*) in the relation between God and man (especially in liturgical language): on condition that this expression, by its interpretation, is freed from its mythological associations; that is what I am trying to do. . . .

'It cannot be denied that simply as a past fact the Cross cannot be an event in our own lives. It is only through the preaching of the Word that the Cross can become a personal encounter, and so an ever-present reality. But this is not to deny the uniqueness (*Einmaligkeit*[3]) of Christ. On the contrary, I have given full weight to this uniqueness by my emphasis upon the "Word made flesh" in which alone the proclamation of the Word (*kerygma*) has its origin and its credentials' B. I, pp. 128, 129, ET, *KM*, pp. 110, 111.[1]

It is this objective interpretation which is emphasized by Gogarten, in his book, *Entmythologisierung und Kirche*[2]—a criticism full of sarcasm aimed at the gross misunderstandings which, according to Gogarten, many of Bultmann's readers, and especially the General Synod of the United Evangelical Lutheran Church of Germany have expressed. Here we will briefly outline the thought of Gogarten: not

[1] The document from which this page is derived ('Zu J. Schniewinds Thesen das Problem der Entmythologisierung betreffend', ET, 'A Reply to the Theses of J. Schniewind') is not dated in B. I, but it must be at the earliest from the end of 1943, since Schniewind's work to which he is responding, bears the date of 27 October 1943.

[2] Gogarten, *op. cit.*, p. 68 (cf. ET, *Demythologizing and History*, pp. 7 and 66ff.).

[3] *Einmaligkeit* = lit. 'once-for-allness'.

only will it confirm the interpretation which has been suggested above, but it will help to clarify Bultmann's conception of divine 'history' (*Geschichte*). In point of fact, here and there the actual thought of Gogarten is difficult, but the general sense is clear.[1]

Gogarten would prefer the phrase: 'realistic', rather than 'objective' interpretation. It is evident that in Bultmann's thought, the Christian Faith is the affirmation of a real divine *Geschichte*: the 'mighty acts' of God have a reality which is independent of human existence; they have been effectively achieved in Jesus of Nazareth; they are not, in his view, in spite of what most people think, simple subjective phenomena, any more than for him faith is the simple interpretation of facts awakened within man. What is true is that Bultmann's intention has been to give to this 'history' an expression appropriate to its reality, which is quite individual, quite specific: in many New Testament statements it is expressed in a mythical form, in which the body misrepresents the intention of the soul.

Precisely, in order to discern this appropriate expression, we must first of all give up terms like 'objective facticity' (*objektive Faktizität, objektive Tatsächlichkeit*)[2] and we must cease to conceive the reality and objectivity of this history in the sense of objective 'this-worldly' phenomena. Otherwise, we shall be 'mythologizing', we shall cheapen that transcendence which that divine history, and God himself, in his attitude to us, should always have for us. For the same reason, we shall cease to translate the relation of Jesus to God in terms of ancient Christology: concepts of the divine and human natures in their union in the unique Person of the Word: these concepts of 'nature' are borrowed from an ontology based on physical, 'this-worldly' realities:

[1] Here we are referring particularly to paragraph 8 in the work mentioned, under the heading 'Das geschichtliche Verständnis des Glaubens in der sogenannten "Theologie der Entmythologisierung"', *op. cit.*, pp. 41-67 (ET, 'The Historical View of the Faith in the "Theology of Demythologization"', Chapter VIII, pp. 48-81).

[2] Gogarten, *op. cit.*, pp. 56 and 67, ET, pp. 55 and 68.

whether they will or no, they too are 'mythologizing'.[1]

But, positively, what are we to say? What statement of the human-divine event could respect its mystery? Are there, in human thought and language, concepts and expressions which are not mythological, which could possibly be applied to a story of God becoming really involved, for our sakes, in our history?

We would say this: There is in God an eternal event, that of his *Zuwendung*, of his 'turning' towards us, and that is also his Word for us, the Word itself. Nevertheless, this 'turning' does not become true for us save in and through Jesus, who does not enter into our earthly history save at this point, chosen by God himself; and it is this encounter of the eternal event with our 'time' which constitutes *Geschichte*, which implies that it is an *einmaliges Geschehen*.[2] But—and here this is the decisive remark—Jesus is not this meeting-place in his human nature, as in the view of ancient Christology, but in his Word, in its proclamation: that the Word became incarnate—this means that the Divine Word is offered to us under the sign of the Word of Jesus of Nazareth: it is as a herald (κῆρυξ, from which the word κήρυγμα is derived) and as a messenger that Jesus is the expression of the eternal event, and of the mercy of God: to listen to him is to listen to God himself. We might also say that the divine event assumes a temporal form in the obedience of Jesus and in his death on the Cross; but in both cases, it is through the mediation of his message: Jesus shows his obedience to his God in his humble acceptance of the role of 'messenger' which God has given to him, in the οὐκ ἀφ' ἑαυτοῦ of the Gospel of St John; he does not speak in his own Name but in the Name of him who sent

---

[1] Bultmann himself (B. II, p. 184, n. 1) had expressed, as we have seen, his rejection of an anthropology of 'objectivizing' thought, 'which cannot understand the human being otherwise than as a world-phenomenon (*Weltphänomen*)', and, p. 206, n. 1, 'In my opinion, Christology ought finally to shake itself free from the toils of an ontology of "objectivizing" thought, and should make a fresh presentation in terms of a new ontology' (*in einer neuen ontologischen Begrifflichkeit*).

[2] An 'event' which happens 'once for all' (*Tr.*).

him. And so far as his death is concerned it achieved the divine event as far as it was interpreted in advance by Christ himself, in his discourses to his disciples, as the exposition all at once of the condemnation of our sin by God and of our liberation.

Now, another point: because the Christian message has assumed this form, we can well understand that this *Geschichte* may henceforth be equally 'present' at every moment in our history. To effect this, it is enough that the message of Christ should be continually proclaimed; that is what the first witnesses did, and that is what the Church is always doing: in the message of the Church the divine event is achieved to-day as it was yesterday, and the Word extends the Incarnation. 'Just as the word of Jesus is the Word of God, so that whoever hears him hears God, so too the proclamation of those whom Jesus sends as his messengers is his own proclamation, so that it can be said of them, that "he that heareth you heareth me"' (Luke 10.16).[1]

In short, God's 'turning' towards us is at work in the original *kerygma* of Jesus, and in this *kerygma*, presented by the Church; in both instances with equal force, save that we ought to add that it only receives its full actuality in the faith and obedience of those who hear.[2]

Thus Gogarten, following Bultmann, believes that he has attributed to the divine *Geschichte*, to the divine saving event, an authentic objectivity, or better, a reality independent of human consciousness, and yet quite different from all 'this-worldly' phenomena and a-mythological reality. It is a reality: for the Word of God has made itself really present under the symbols of human language and of the message of the historic man Jesus. It is, however, not a phenomenal kind of objectivity, for the divine Word, as divine, remains hidden beneath a veil; it does not reveal its transcendence; it is not an irruption of the divine into the human which

---

[1] Gogarten, *op. cit.*, p. 57, ET, pp. 68-69.
[2] Gogarten, *op. cit.*, p. 65 (ET, p. 69), '. . . dass sich diese Zuwendung Gottes zu uns im Kerygma ereignet, wo und wann immer es verkündigt und *gehört wird*'. (The italics are mine.)

can be *seen* as such. The Catholic theologian will here be reminded of the views of Dom Casel upon mystery: under the sacramental rite, the mystery of the Passion and the death of Christ is present in its substance, but according to a mode which is no longer the phenomenal mode of the historical death of Christ upon the Cross. It is a 'presence' of this kind that Bultmann and Gogarten ask us to conceive for the saving event under the species of the human message of Christ and the Church.

We see then that if *Geschichte* is such a peculiar reality, our understanding of it does not depend upon historical methods. Doubtless, Bultmann does not burn the bridge, as we have seen, between the concrete Jesus of history and the saving event; the human existence of this historic Jesus, as well as the fact of his message and of his death upon the Cross, can and should be submitted to the judgment of the historian, and the latter does in fact admit this. But the divine event itself, present under the phenomenal appearance of the message, completely eludes the historian. *Geschichte* is not a fact to which we look back, as we do to other past events. We are aware that without being non-temporal, it is not subject to the time-series, and knows no past: it is always *there* for us, equally new every morning. Hence in order to find it we need not examine the story for signs of transcendence in the Jesus of history. It only speaks to us as to bare faith, and within its mystery, it contains the reasons for the confidence we give to it.

We shall note that this interpretation coincides substantially with that which we have proposed. Doubtless, according to Gogarten, it is not the Cross as such, but it is the interpretation which Jesus gives to it in advance, which is the point at which the divine event is proclaimed; the saving event is in the Word of Christ, the *kerygma* precedes his death, and it is that which gives the Cross its significance of judgment and of divine liberation. For our part, in our exposition, we have refrained from laying much emphasis upon the *kerygma* of Jesus himself; this reserve seems necessary owing to the silence of Bultmann on this precise point. Thus there is a difference between our exposition and that of Gogarten. But it is not as important as it might seem at first sight, for, on the one hand, Gogarten would not deny, we believe, that in Bultmann's theology the death of Christ forms part of the saving event: the Word of Christ and his message, the anticipated interpretation of the Cross, are the *form* of the event, and the Cross, interpreted, is like its *material* element, and on the other hand, in that which concerns us, we have admitted that Bultmann integrated the life of Jesus, and thus also his message, into the structure of salvation. Above all, the two interpretations converge in the affirmation of an objective statement: whether this be in the message, or whether it be more particularly in the death (of Jesus), in both cases the Word of God is truly uttered and truly present in our history, independent of the subjective consciousness of those to whom it is addressed, and whom it seeks to win. By this common affirmation, which we have a right to regard as of capital importance, the two interpretations are really only one and are distinct from the subjective interpretation to which we must now turn.

2. THE SUBJECTIVE INTERPRETATION OF DEMYTHOLOGIZING

Although we believe that it is not true to the intention of Bultmann, we must admit that his own language often suggests this very forcibly, and we can well understand why so many critics are held up at this point. At the same time it is a great pity that they have not noticed the possibility of the objective interpretation; but their misunderstanding does not justify the severity of the strictures of Gogarten in this respect, as if they were blind to the evidence; the truth is, we must repeat, that Bultmann's language has given colour to their interpretation of his thought, and it is not even quite certain whether, in his first book of 1941, his thought can be clearly distinguished, in his own eyes, from the subjective interpretation; this first book provoked all kinds of attacks and questions; he was forced to go deeper in his thinking, and the result of his effort is that his more objective conception has emerged, and he has himself become far clearer about his aims and purposes.

The subjective interpretation differs from the previous one in this respect: according to it, neither in the life of Jesus, nor in his death, was there any divine event, not even to the eyes of faith. As has been said, 'in effect, nothing in this Christ event transcends its own time'. This seems to mean that in Jesus no saving act takes place, not even by way of a preliminary announcement. Again: 'according to the programme of demythologizing salvation is a sacred event, but it is subjective, to which there corresponds an objective fact which is not sacred, the death of Christ'.[1] Again, this seems to mean that the story of Jesus of Nazareth does not in any way form part of the divine history of salvation; the latter is wholly subjective. To sum up, the whole drama of the saving event takes place in the actual encounter of faith, in the new knowledge of ourselves which God's action gives us. Doubtless, this salvation is supposed to be transmitted to us through the method of external preaching, and particularly the preaching of the Cross of Christ: but first of all, this preaching is not to be considered as the prolongation of the preaching of Jesus himself (Gogarten): the New Testament *kerygma*— so it is said—was created after the death of Christ, by the faith of the disciples, as the fruit of their own interpretation of the new knowledge which had come to them and of their subjective faith;[2] and then, in addition, this apostolic

---

[1] We are here quoting from J. Hamer (article mentioned in our Introduction, p. 15), p. 645, who, it seems, has been influenced by R. Prenter, *op. cit.*

[2] *'Eine interpretierende Deutung von Bewusstseinsvorgängen'* (Gogarten, *op. cit.*, p. 62, ET, p. 67). Cf. also *ibid.*, p. 77: for Künneth (see the work ed. by E. Kinder: *Ein Wort lutherischer Theologie*, Munich, 1952, p. 87). The New Testament *kerygma*, according to Bultmann, only effects the subjective belief and the piety of the Church '. . . *nur eine subjektive Gläubigkeit und Frömmigkeit* der *Gemeinde* darstellt'. Bultmann has given more of a handle to this interpretation by his critics, since while he was working on *Formgeschichte* (*Geschichte der synoptischen Tradition*, second edition, Tübingen, 1931), he related the whole formation of the Gospel message to the faith of the Early Church.

kerygma itself as an objective reality, does not form part of
the constitution of the saving event; for Christians of the
present day it can only be the occasion of a divine event
which in itself is integrally subjective.

Thus, Bultmann should argue, according to these critics
that by the reading of the Scriptures, or better still, by the
hearing of the living Word, preached by the heralds of the
message, we are inwardly illuminated by the grace of God
which pardons us; now a speculative, impersonal, 'objectivizing' mode of thought would not see this at all; or rather,
it would not perceive the divine character of this encounter;
all it would perceive would be the *'existentiel'* attitude of
commitment or rejection; in the act of commitment
(based on our free decision, and not on the 'mythological'
activity of a divine Spirit?) we should raise ourselves
to the level of authentic existence. Understood in this way,
the saving event would be almost entirely 'subjective' in
character; the saving intervention of God would only take
place within 'my' inner existence; the phenomenal history
of Christ would have nothing to do with it; the believer,
however, would still be brought face to face with God, in
a real, objective, existential encounter, and to this extent,
the protagonists of the subjective interpretation cannot deny
that they can also speak of an 'objective' interpretation.

But in this interpretation, what exactly is the positive
rôle assigned to the Gospel story? For, in the intention of
Bultmann, this story ought to retain a certain eschatological
bearing, and this point should not be neglected or overlooked, if Bultmann is not to lose absolutely the idea and
the reality of a faith which is *distinctively Christian.* The critics
say that Bultmann's answer to this question is uncertain
and vague, and it cannot be made more definite save by
risking an hypothesis. The Crucifixion in the past would be
scarcely more than an 'example', or an 'indispensable inspiration', a stimulus required by our own *'existentiel'* decision. The whole encounter between God and the sinner
would be effected in the actual understanding of the message; once more, we must repeat, God's action in Christ

would not be 'present'; but we could only decide to accept the pardoning grace by looking to Christ as our example, by contemplating this acceptance in the prototype of the dying Christ.[1]

Having been thus defined, the subjective interpretation then marshals its evidence. We remember that Bultmann's notion of myth was left very vague: the irruption of the divine into the human, assimilated with a natural action: that is, 'myth' in the restricted sense; all irruption of the divine whatever it may be: that is 'myth' in the broad sense. Now, when Bultmann outlines his programme of absolute demythologization it seems that his claim extends, at least sometimes, to the exclusion of myth understood in the broad sense. It is here that the subjective interpretation comes in, for it alone satisfies the demand for absolute demythologization, to the exclusion of myth in any shape or form. In point of fact, even this is not evident: for, after all, this interpretation still preserves the idea of an act of God, at least within the subject, and we shall have to ask later on, if, by this very fact, it does not re-introduce surreptitiously, an idea like that of the Divine Spirit acting within the heart of man, an idea which, moreover, demythologization does not want to retain. But, at least, the subjective interpretation demythologizes more completely than the objective one: the latter certainly eliminates myth in the narrower sense of the word, but it retains the idea of an intervention of God in external history, in the historical fact of Christ, save that it adds that this intervention can only be grasped by faith; here, on the contrary, there is no longer any presence of God in the world of objects, neither of the kind that can be felt, nor even in a hidden way; the Christ is no longer in himself the act of God; certainly there is an encounter, a confrontation of man with God in the event of faith, but at least the phenomenal world is not in the least affected by it; there is nothing left but the gift of a new self-knowledge, of a victory over the despair of *Dasein* by the certitude of pardon; the mythical notion of a universe which is full of

[1] All this comes from R. Prenter, *op. cit.*, p. 61.

the supernatural has been eliminated; myth, in the broad sense, has been abolished.

Further, the subjective interpretation, as its second line of support, appeals to certain definite passages from Bultmann's works: the life and death of Christ have no saving meaning or value in themselves, they do not contain these values even in the message given by Christ's followers; objectively considered, we only receive this saving grace in our actual obedience, and in the response of our faith. 'The Cross', Bultmann writes, 'in its redemptive aspect is not an isolated incident which would have happened in Christ as in a mythical personage, it is owing to his significance that it acquires cosmic importance. (Its decisive, revolutionary significance is brought out by the eschatological framework in which it is set.) In other words, the Cross is not merely a past event which can be contemplated in detachment, but it is the eschatological event in, and beyond, time, for, so far as its meaning—that is, its meaning for faith—is concerned, it is an ever-present reality.'[1] In other words, when the believer accepts the Cross of Christ as his own, allows himself to be crucified with him, when he commits himself to the way of condemnation to death as to the way of life, when he says 'yes' to the divine Word, when he accepts the revelation of his nothingness and of his sin, then the believer finds that the Cross is the Act of God. According to the traditional interpretation of the New Testament, the Cross is an event which is significant in itself; the *kerygma* confines itself to announcing this intrinsic significance. According to Bultmann, the opposite would be true: it is in presenting it to us in the concreteness of preaching that God gives to the Cross the value of a divine gift, of a transcendent summons, of which by itself it is entirely void. And as a passage does not take life and meaning save in the mind of the one who reads it, and a word to the one who listens, preaching itself would not become the saving event save in the actual hearing, and in the mind and heart of the believer.

[1] B. I, p. 42, ET, *KM*, p. 36.

These arguments have their weight. But, in our opinion, they do not outweigh those which we have presented in favour of the objective interpretation. So far as myth in the broad sense is concerned, it would be difficult to prove its presence in the thought and writings of Bultmann; and so far as the passages which give colour to the subjective interpretation are concerned, the objective interpretation can come to terms with it: the objective elements enter into the structure of the saving event, but the fact remains that the latter does not receive its full actuality save in the acceptance of faith; there is no effective salvation apart from subjects who open their minds and hearts to receive it: it is in this sense that, in Bultmann's thought, the message and the death of Christ do not acquire their saving significance save in the heart of man.

Finally, we note that the second, subjective, interpretation does not succeed, so it seems, in defining itself completely without returning to the first one. According to it, Bultmann would admit that the historic death of Christ is an indispensable inspiration for 'my' '*existentiel*' decision. But why is it necessary to refer to the Cross? If, in order to receive salvation, I am obliged to refer to Christ as the great example, must that not be because God himself has expressed the type of my authentic existence in the death of Christ? If God saves me in attaching me in some way to the Cross of Jesus, is it not because he himself has spoken to me from the Cross? Then on Calvary there must have been an objective divine manifestation of the elements of salvation; and it is for this reason—one cannot see any other —that my actual liberation is attached to the remembrance of the past as to a necessary inspiration.

In coming down strongly on the side of the objective interpretation, it is plain that we believe that Bultmann's thought, and his theology, does more justice to the fact of Christianity than other critics would admit. Cullmann has written that Bultmann's theology does not do justice to the Gospel story, and that 'he strips the Christian proclamation of its time-setting in redemptive history'.[1] The charge is unjustified: the earthly story of Jesus, or at least of his death, and the message which followed it, dates 'once for all' the intervention of God in our history: there is accomplished the objective declaration of salvation, in consequence of which our time has become a new time. Thus the historic Christ remains, in Bultmann's view, the place of, and the decisive moment for, our encounter with God.

On the other hand, it is true, in Bultmann's teaching, this same Christ has no other part to play than that of proclaiming salvation by his message and by his death; he is, we do not know why, the human organ of the Word of God; that is all; his Person lacks mystery, and has no peculiar relation to the God who sends him; his Resurrection or his survival are not important for our salvation. How can the Christian reader of Bultmann help exclaiming in his surprise: 'They have taken away my Lord and I know not where they have laid him?'

[1] *Christ and Time*, ET, London, 1951, p. 30.

V

THE VERDICT OF TRADITION

HAS Bultmann's theology something to contribute to Christian thought?

I. 1. Bultmann, in his essay, offers us a theology of revelation. Whether it be sound or not, it has at least the merit of drawing the Christian's attention to the very heart of a central theme, the theme of revelation and of the Word of God, and of its incorporation into history. We might express Bultmann's thought in the following way: God has brought man out of his solitude. He has come to meet us, he addresses us: by his call he speaks to us, in the most profound depths of our *Dasein*, in that sacred region where, left to ourselves, we are limited, to making the experience of being (Heidegger).[1] However, this divine initiative is not wholly interior; it has achieved something within history, and to speak more precisely, in Christian history; the Christian Fact is attached in some way or another to the interior divine revelation. But, and this is precisely the question: How does this take place? We might say that all Bultmann's writings are an attempt to answer this question. In a word, this is his answer: God has created within history, in the Christ, a Word which is both human and divine, human by the conceptions it uses, divine by the action to which it has given rise. It is through this Word that we recognize the revelation which he utters at the heart of *Dasein*; the historic message enables us to interpret the interior message, and to proclaim its content. We may certainly question

---

[1] On this point, see below, pp. 145, 146, and, above all, the illuminating words of Max Müller, *op. cit.*, pp. 59-66.

the correctness of this theology of revelation; especially we may consider that although it may present his teaching in the right light, it does not do justice to his Person, his being; we may argue that it almost entirely eliminates the mystery of the God-Man, replacing it by a message, which, though it is derived from Christ, ends by being detached from it, and is supposed to have an independent validity, apart from the One who first proclaimed it. We shall certainly bring this charge against Bultmann. But, precisely, the very inadequacy of his attempt forces us to re-investigate the theme with which his theology deals; it invites us to deepen the Christian theology of revelation, and to strive to gain further light upon this central encounter, which is infinitely mysterious. This is the problem: how can the Jesus of history—who approaches us from the outside, and the 'Christ within'—through the Holy Spirit working in our hearts, combine to form *One* Word? How are both integrated in the indivisible unity of our meeting with God?

2. Then there is Bultmann's concern for a formulation of the Christian message which will make it easier for modern man to understand: here too, Bultmann confronts the theologian with a task which he cannot evade. Protestants are not alone in recognizing this necessity. A Catholic theologian has said, very rightly, that Christian thought cannot avoid the obligation of trying to 'communicate' with modern man, and that the 'will to get into contact with the thought and the needs of our own day, should characterize every genuine theological effort; this is all the more necessary, because it is so easy to fall into the error of thinking that we *are* "in touch" when we take a fundamentalist or ultra-biblical line of approach. It is not sufficient simply to repeat the *kerygma* in its biblical form; on the contrary, we ought to transpose it into the key which will make it intelligible to the people of our own day.'[1]

The expression of this concern is all the more noteworthy in Bultmann's thought since his specialized knowledge as an

[1] J. Hamer, art. cit., pp. 645, 646.

exegete had scarcely prepared him for its formulation: like other historians of Christian origins, he could have confined his studies to the sphere of biblical archaeology, and could have been content to formulate what has been called the '*kerygma* of erudition'. Study of the primary Christian sources, so dear to modern theologians, must resist the temptation to fall back on the simple formulas of a past age, ignoring the task which is incumbent upon them at the present time, namely: to labour, both in heart and mind, to reach the true understanding of the Christian Faith (*fides quaerens intellectum*); patristic and scholastic theology never ignored this task, and thus each succeeding generation was able to attack it, with added resources. Among these resources we shall reckon to-day not merely methods (we are thinking here of the methods of historical research), but definite results: modern science has given us a new insight into the world of bodies, of space, of duration, of the universe, of the world, and also of man himself, insights which seem to offer some definite results; the Christian message should face these results, and present itself in a form which will succeed in integrating them, or at least in respecting their value; between it and them, no conflict, no incompatibility is possible. The preservation of the Christian Faith is at the price of this ever-renewed labour.

3. It is also to the credit of Bultmann's theology that he lays so much emphasis upon the existential interpretation of the Christian message. Doubtless, on this point we must be on our guard: sometimes, Bultmann conceives this principle as scarcely more than the positive expression of the negative principle of demythologizing: to give an existential interpretation is to 'demythologize' and, in its turn, to 'demythologize' amounts to a denial of all divine intervention, recognizable as such in history; thus understood, we shall show later on, the principle in question shakes Christianity to its very foundations. Again, Bultmann gives an exclusive significance to the principle of existential interpretation: all that the Christian message can retain are the

elements which relate to the knowledge of ourselves (more-over, of ourselves in the situation of the *hic et nunc*, in 'to-day'), to the exclusion of all objective doctrine concerning God and our future and eternal destiny (because such a doctrine is always mythological in character): here again, these claims are disastrous. Finally, in Bultmann's thought the existential interpretation of the biblical *kerygma* has to be formulated in terms of the existential philosophy of Heidegger; here too, we must refuse to follow him; we have quoted the remark of Jaspers; the analysis of Heidegger, to the extent in which it sees in *Dasein* a sense of despair, is very dubious, and it cannot claim universal value; it does not express the truth of man as a whole, it is simply a cer-tain view of man, in which some minds, and possibly many to-day, but certainly not all, see themselves.[1]

But, in itself, the principle of the existential interpreta-tion of the Christian message need not involve these un-fortunate extremes. It can be formulated in the following way: to be acceptable to the modern mind, the Christian message must show that it has an affinity with certain human hopes and longings, revealed by an existential ana-lysis which has not necessarily anything to do with the philosophy of Heidegger. Understood in this sense we do not believe that it is possible to refuse this interpretation. The theologian and the preacher ought to be able to relate human concerns to Christian doctrine, and to show how its message challenges us, takes us to task, and helps us to understand ourselves. In the depths of our concrete *Dasein*, in man, in his situation in history, there is, inscribed by God himself, a longing for the possession of God in Christ, and of his revelation, under the species of faith, which is a point of contact with the supernatural. This need to relate human life and Christian doctrine to each other, not only applies to the Christian message as a whole, but also to particular points of doctrine: we ought to examine each doctrine in particular in order to try to discover how much it can help us to live well. As has been said, the New Testament

[1] K. Jaspers, art. cit. (B. III, p. 42).

itself is full of this concern: St Paul does not speak of
the death and resurrection of Christ without at the same
time pointing out their bearing upon the destiny of man, and
of the Church, without questioning the existence of man, to
whom he speaks.[1] Surely this affinity between human existence and the message has a certain value for apologetics,
although it is not sufficient to prove the truth of the Christian message.

In formulating this claim, Bultmann, having at the same
time fortunately severed his connexion with Barth, cleared
the way for his own particular message, which has made a
deep impression upon Protestant theology. Of course, Bultmann did not mean to make a complete break with Barthi-
anism. We know the contribution that Barth has made to
theology;[2] when Liberal Christianity was at its height, the
subject of 'religion' was predominant: Christianity was believed to be a system of timeless religious truths, regarded
as immanent, and contained in the anthropological function
of religion, regarded as idealistic sentiment or as *a priori*
argument. Barth set himself to overcome the subjectivism
of Schleiermacher, this mistaken religion of 'experience', and
he re-awakened in the Protestant Christian consciousness
the sense of the objective divine event, the revelation of
God in Jesus Christ: a revelation which man cannot measure,
but which on the contrary, measures man and all his dimensions by its truth and sovereign demands. In this reaction
against immanental theology, as a whole, however, Barth
did not hesitate to deny to the human subject all legitimate
intervention in the act of appropriation of the objective act
of salvation: between man and God, and his Word in
Christ, there was no preparation,[3] no 'point of contact'

[1] J. Hamer, art. cit., p. 649.
[2] For the bearing of Bultmann's effort on the development of Protestant theology we may read with profit E. Brunner: *Das Ewige als
Zukunft und Gegenwart*, pp. 231-235, ET, *Eternal Hope*, pp. 217-220, on
which this passage is based.
[3] No *pierre d'attente*: 'toothing', i.e. stones left at the end of a wall,
projecting, in order that they may be built into the wall when the
building is being extended (*Tr.*).

(*Anknüpfungspunkt*) between the supernatural and the natural; God himself, by a vertical and absolute miracle, creates within us all the psychological and critical conditions required for us to make the response of faith.

This 'objectivity' was so extreme in its devaluation of the human element, that its inevitable consequence was to increase the isolation of the Church and of theology from a world which, in spite of the disaster of two world wars, had remained attached to its own values.

This is the precise point at which Bultmann's protest arises. As we have seen, he does not intend to return to Liberalism. He wishes to retain those elements in the Barthian theology which emphasize the objective act of God, as a unique and decisive event accomplished by God within history. But at the same time he believes it is necessary to face this theme of objectivity with the claims of contemporary thought, and the picture of the world which modern man has painted. In other words, according to Bultmann, the data of faith must have an affinity with the natural knowledge which man possesses of himself; in achieving this the actual truth of these data is established. Thus while Bultmann rejected the absolute fideism of Barth he brought the Christian message into relation with man— in his situation—and faith with reason, and thus protected the Church against the threat of isolation. There is no doubt that it is this salutary reaction which explains the shattering effect of his teaching upon Protestant theologians.

II. But it remains to be seen whether his insistence on demythologizing and on the integral existential interpretation of the Christian message, has not overreached itself, and has even become a threat to that truth which Bultmann wishes to defend. We shall see that this is the case. In a general way we shall try to enumerate the main errors in Bultmann's effort to reinterpret the Christian message.

1. We have already made it clear that the first charge the Christian will bring against Bultmann is that he has

taken away his Lord. Even supposing that Bultmann's theology should succeed in proving its fundamental integrity, it would substitute, in the Christian consciousness, the presence of the *kerygma* for the adoration of 'God-made-man'. Not that it would eliminate all the elements of the living Presence of God, nor that it would replace the confrontation of the Christian with God by the acceptance of a doctrine, or by the hearing of an impersonal message; on the contrary, Bultmann means that in the message, and through it, it is the living God who comes to meet us, who summons us, and sets in motion the dialogue between God and man; it is his Word, which is given to us under this veil. Still, the fact remains that this is not the mystery of the God-Man: we are no longer confronted either by the ontological reality or the spiritual presence of the ever-living Christ. For Bultmann the nature of the historic Christ has nothing to do with our salvation—all that concerns us is the message, of which he is the instrument, so also he believes that the Resurrection of Christ, if it ever happened, does not in any way form part of the saving event: we are not united with him, even by the mediation of the Spirit, as the One who pours upon us 'grace upon grace'.

For the Christian such a negative view would be equivalent to the ruin of Christianity itself. In certain disputes between the Jews and Paul, Festus explained to the king Agrippa: 'they had certain questions against him of their own religion, and of one Jesus, who was dead, whom Paul affirmed to be alive' (Acts 25.19): this brief statement by Porcius Festus expresses very well what Christians, from the days of Paul down to the present day, have always held to be the essence of their faith: the confession of Jesus as Lord, life, and the source of life, 'raised for our justification' (Rom. 4.25).

Here, I am aware, Bultmann rejects the mythological character of such a presentation of Christianity, which he regards as unacceptable to the modern world; he goes further, he declares that very early in the history of Christianity at least St Paul and St John saw that this mythology (which

is not of Christian but of Gnostic and Hellenistic origin)
was a purely mythological covering of the Christian message,
from which, they realized, they had to strip off the extraneous
elements; the proof of this is that in their work we see the
first attempts at demythologizing. But, not to speak of St
John, what an allegation to make against St Paul! Far from
eliminating the mystery of the God-Man, the source of
salvation not only in his Word, but primarily in his Being
and in his resurrection, was not St Paul the first, not to
have formulated it, but at least to have made it an integral
element in an already well-developed theology? Bultmann
may indeed, if he chooses to do so, consider this mystery
to be 'mythological': the fact remains that Christians have
always regarded it as essential to their faith. He cannot
escape the charge of having made an attack upon the very
substance of Christianity. Or, if his 'demythologizing' at
last reveals to us the essence of Christianity, then in this
case there have never been any Christians before Bultmann
(or at least before Luther). This is a new religion which
is being proclaimed to us, which represents a break with
the past, and this religion has the purely human authority
of its author.

2. The fact remains that in the eyes of Bultmann, traditional Christianity should be classed with the creations of
mythical thought, creations which are manifestly incompatible with *contemporary scientific thought*. Can this 'incompatibility' be taken for granted? Bultmann has certainly not
proved it.

Here we must begin by defining the point at issue. The
principle which governs Bultmann's thought might, at first
sight, be held to be the following: to modern scholars,
whether they are historians or students of the philosophy
of religion, religious myths, at least so far as their body is
concerned, are simply fictions, produced by the faculty
which creates fables; now the Fact of Christianity, as the
Churches present it, is obviously mythological (and indeed
its mythology is not in the least original; it seems to be

derived from Jewish Apocalyptic and from Gnosticism); it is therefore pure fiction, a collection of religious fables, and, as such, it cannot possibly be reconciled with rational modern thought.

Those who believe that Bultmann follows such a line of thought—some of his critics seem to understand him in this way—place great emphasis, in their discussion with him, on the study of the idea of myth; in their eyes, there are two major questions: is Bultmann's notion of myth correct, does it correspond to the religious realities which it is supposed to cover? And: is it true that mythical thought creates nothing but fictions? On the contrary, ought we not to admit, that the language of myth, symbolical and figurative as it is, is an absolute necessity for authentic religious thought, which needs the human sense of mystery in order to bring out its content?

In reality, Bultmann's line of thought is quite different: emphasis on the mythical character of the Christian traditional fact is not his first line of argument; it is secondary; it is derived from a primary fundamental statement. This is his argument: the traditional presentation of the Christian fact cannot be reconciled with the picture of the world and of man which science gives us to-day; *hence it follows* that it belongs to the human faculty for creating symbols, often in the form of fables, or to the fictions of mythical thought. In this instance, in a discussion with Bultmann, we must realize that these questions about the nature of myth do not matter very much; nor shall we spend too much time on trying to find out whether, very wrongly, he has actually said that the traditional Christian fact is 'mythical'.[1] All that really matters is the criticism of the

[1] We fully agree with Bultmann when he writes: 'I do not think the concept of myth is one of the most important questions. Rather, the discussion of this question seems to me to divert our attention from the point at issue in the problem of demythologizing' (B. II, p. 180). Precisely because this is only a secondary question I am dealing with the idea of myth in Bultmann's thought and its comparison with the current conception among historians of philosophies of religion in Appendix I.

central part of his argument. This is how he expresses the heart of his contention: the preaching of the Churches conceives the divine *Geschichte* (history) as a supernatural intervention in Nature and in History; furthermore, a supernatural intervention which claims to be recognizable as such, for instance, in the miracles of Jesus, in which the divine becomes transparent in the human sphere. This, says Bultmann, is the point at which we must protest: such a conception of the redemptive event is incompatible with scientific thought; the modern picture of the world, of a world which science conceives as ruled by an empirical causality which is strictly determinist, has no room for discontinuity, for the rupture which miracle would cause, or, more generally, for the manifestation of the divine in the world of objects; likewise the modern view of man attributes to the human being an independent unity which excludes all intervention from the outside, whether demonic or divine. This challenging statement of Bultmann is the only one which concerns us here.

Karl Jaspers has challenged Bultmann with a remark whose sense we will try to reproduce: By what right, asks Jaspers, does Bultmann speak in the name of modern scientific thought?[1] Everything suggests that, like most of the rest of us, he either ignores or does not understand its fundamental statements. If there is something of which we can be quite certain, for us all, it is this, that in the form which it has assumed during recent decades, science has given up the attempt to make any picture of the world at all, because it knows that such a picture cannot possibly be created. Doubtless, by its very nature, it tries to make an orderly scheme of knowledge which is universally valid; but it is aware of its limitations; it knows that at present it has only begun to understand some of the phenomena of this world and that the profound mystery of being eludes it entirely. This is Bultmann's first misunderstanding.

Then there is a second misunderstanding: Bultmann thinks that the form of scientific thought was born in Greece, when man put the question of the $\dot{\alpha}\rho\chi\dot{\eta}$, the primal

[1] K. Jaspers, *op. cit.* (B. III, pp. 12, 13).

THE CHRISTIAN MESSAGE AND MYTH

principle, of the One, the source and the foundation of the many. This is quite wrong: this question has always been a philosophical question, which scientific thought, governed by its own method, and by simple fidelity to its own laws, has refused to ask, or to try to answer. Doubtless science has constructed what we may call 'systems': simple hypothetical classifications of the phenomenal world, which do not pretend to cover the whole of being, and which do not remain 'scientific' save on condition that they provide points of departure for new methods of investigation.

Modern science, therefore, in so far as it is both scientific and contemporary, does not lead to the disintegrating results—where the mythical idea of supernatural intervention is concerned—for which it is supposed to be responsible; we may even say that, *as scientific contemporary thought*, it is no more incompatible with mythical thought, in the sense in which Bultmann uses the word, than it was with prescientific thought. Are we to conclude that Bultmann has not shown any real incompatibility between mythical thought and another kind of thought, which without being fundamentally scientific is none the less a form of rational thought? No. But the incompatibility which he does assert is that which exists, from time immemorial, between mythical thought and ordinary rationalism. The mental attitude which tends to reject miracle, and the irruption of the divine into the human sphere in general, is very ancient. It was as active in the past as it is to-day; it was this which made the Greeks of the Areopagus smile, when Paul spoke to them of the idea of resurrection: 'Now when they heard of the resurrection of the dead, some mocked, but others said, We will hear thee concerning this yet again!' (Acts 17.32). Thus Bultmann has unduly exaggerated the difference between ancient and modern thought; or, and this comes to the same thing, he has not grasped the identity of their fundamental outlook: there is the same materialism to-day as yesterday, and also the same credulity, the same facility for believing the absurd, the same interest in astrology or theosophy; we hardly notice much difference between one generation and another, save in a certain superficial difference in the content of their philosophies.

These observations by Jaspers are interesting: but they are not decisive. If it be true that Bultmann has exaggerated the differences between these periods in human thought, the fact remains that the modern mind has other objections to traditional Christianity which were not felt to the same degree in antiquity.

One objection seems to be derived from a large use of the historical method. On the one hand, this method, applied to the history of religions, has revealed the existence of so many collections of religious fables which more than formerly are described as 'mythical', in the sense of being fictitious; on the other hand, applied to the history of Christian origins and Christian dogma in general, analogies to the Christian mystery are found in the aforesaid fables; for instance, the analogy of the mystery of redemption with the myths of gods who die and rise again. We know very well that this analogy is quite superficial, but it was inevitable that its statement awakened in the minds of modern people—who were already detached from Christianity—a question which would not have occurred to people at an earlier period: is Christian doctrine derived from the same source which created the ancient myths? Bultmann, it is true, has not dealt with this first objection in his essay, and this is rather surprising when we remember that he is himself an historian and not a scientist; probably, however, this objection has implicitly influenced his own choice; if he has so easily equated traditional mythical Christianity with myth, it is undoubtedly due to the fact that his knowledge of history suggested to him (wrongly of course) this similarity. However, precisely because he does not argue expressly from the point of view of this similarity we need not discuss it here.

A second modern objection to the Christianity of the Church springs incontestably, whatever Jaspers may say about it, from the widespread use of the methods of natural science. In vain did the soul of antiquity profess to hold an

authentic rationalism, in the person of some of its out-
standing men, like Celsus for instance; nevertheless, it remained very generally largely open to the idea of supernatural
forces at work within the world of phenomena. It is not the
same to-day; many of our contemporaries loathe this idea;
this repugnance is partly due to the influence of a scientific
education of a popular kind; the average western man has
not himself practised the methods of positive science, but
he possesses enough of the spirit of it to be inclined to assign
an absolutely naturalistic explanation to everything. These
methods, and the triumph of technics, have aroused a general
mistrust of 'other-worldly' explanations, a distrust unknown
to the ancient world, and which the Church herself maintains to some extent when she puts the faithful on their guard
against too great a credulity with regard to certain facts
which are so-called 'supernatural' and 'marvellous'.

Thus in a discussion with Bultmann we cannot entirely
evade the question: is it true that the experimental modern
sciences, as such, exclude the possibility of a supernatural
intervention in history? Now it is easy to see that this is
not the case.

Here we must distinguish between two types of supernatural intervention, equally represented in Christian doctrine: according to one type, God is said to have introduced
a real being into our immanent world, although the transcendence of this being was not integrated, in a tangible
way, into the phenomenal order; such as, for instance, the
assumption of human nature by a divine person, or the
mystery of transubstantiation in the Eucharist. What we
mean is this: we do not say that the Incarnation of the Son
of God has not caused certain phenomenal manifestations,
by which this mystery became, to a certain extent, transparent: e.g. the sublime character of Christ's life, the unique
influence of his teaching and his healing power. But precisely, these were only the visible consequences of a divine
intervention which in itself remained invisible; the relation
which unites the human nature of Christ to the Word in
person does not manifest itself in its real nature: it is a purely

intelligible and metaphysical reality, which is not in any way revealed to our senses, nor to be attained by any conceivable process of experiment; this reality is open to faith alone. What right then has modern science to refuse these forms? Its competence is confined to the definition of order in the sequence of phenomena—now, the reality here considered does not belong to phenomena. In point of fact, Bultmann's negations are not due to the knowledge of scientific method; rather, they are inspired, though this is not recognized, by this 'ordinary rationalism' which Jaspers has just described.

Now, this is not to say that, however, 'ordinary' it may be, this rationalism is not asking a legitimate question: is not the philosophical reason (rightly) opposed, *a priori*, and in principle, to the idea of a non-phenomenal intervention of God in nature and in history? But this question is not the object of scientific reasoning, I mean, of reason applied to the knowledge of phenomena and the constitution of the experimental sciences. Bultmann has not seen this; thus he has not even succeeded in stating the true problem correctly, nor has he put the only question which it would have been profitable to discuss.[1]

This first statement already takes us a long way in our discussion with him. In this first type of supernatural intervention we must include not only the two terms already mentioned: the Incarnation and the Eucharistic mystery, but the very substance of the Christian message of the Churches; this substance, as Bultmann himself admits, consists in the affirmation of man's salvation by the death of Christ on the Cross; God intervened at this point in our history in order

[1] The answer to this question will follow a remark that we shall be making further on (pp. 135-6): we shall see that reason, far from refusing, *a priori*, to accept the idea of a possible divine intervention in the phenomenal world, says the opposite; from which it will follow, by a kind of *a fortiori* reasoning, that it also declares the possibility of a non-phenomenal, non-revelational divine intervention of transcendence. Further, if our 'objectivized' interpretation of Bultmann's thought is correct, he himself admits the existence of these non-phenomenal divine interventions in history: in the *kerygma* there is a certain presence of the mystery of God and of his Word.

to reconcile and unite us with himself; this is a supernatural intervention which is wholly meta-empirical, beyond the reach of all experimental investigation. We have just seen that—contrary to Bultmann's thought—the scientist has no right to object to an intervention of this kind, since it does not belong to the sphere with which his work is concerned.

But Christian dogma offers a second type of supernatural intervention in Nature and in History, an intervention of which it declares that it sets its mark upon our immanent world, and there creates phenomenal realities; these will not always be necessarily, and in all cases, obviously a 'revelation' of their supernatural source: (such as, for instance, many of the 'graces' of 'light' and of 'will', fruits of the Spirit, but of which the one who possesses them is not aware of the divine principle), but sometimes, to a certain extent, they will betray the transcendent cause from which they proceed: in the latter case, we shall be in the presence of a phenomenon which is properly speaking 'miraculous' (and we shall meet also that which corresponds to Bultmann's notion of 'myth' in the narrower sense of the word: a supernatural intervention which is recognized as such, the transparence of the divine in the human).

Thus the question which confronts us is that of knowing whether modern science has any right to reject the idea of such an intervention. Speaking broadly, it is also the question of the possibility of miracle versus modern science. We cannot dream of treating this question here in all its fulness: others have done so recently, to whom we must refer the reader.[1] A few remarks must suffice.

[1] Cf. L. de Grandmaison, *Jésus-Christ*. Paris, 1928, Vol. II, pp. 225-255; J. Mouroux: 'Discernement et discernibilité du miracle' in the *Revue Apologétique*, Vol. LX, 1935, pp. 538-562; E. Pfeifer, *Das Wunder als Erkenntnismittel der Glaubwürdigkeit der göttlichen Offenbarung in der katholischen und protestantischen Apologetik*, Aschaffenburg, 1936. On the Protestant side, see Ph. H. Menoud, 'La signification du miracle selon le nouveau Testament' in *Revue d'Histoire et de Philosophie religieuse*, Vols. XXVIII-XXIX, 1948-1949, pp. 173-192; G. Crespy, *La guérison par la foi*, Neuchâtel, 1952; in this last work *miraculous* healing is not treated explicitly; the author seems to question whether miracle can even be *proved* (p. 8); but he is very far from Bultmann's attitude of

From the Christian point of view, miracle fulfils three major conditions: it is a prodigy, an unusual event, a phenomenon in the physical world, effected *praetur cursum ordinarium naturae*; further, it is of the essence of this event to depend upon a special divine intervention, and so to transcend the causality of creatures; finally, this direct relation with God ought to be manifest as such, since apart from this the miracle would never be formally acknowledged.

It is the second condition which interests us here. Frequently (but not necessarily, as we shall see in a moment), the Christian theologian tends to regard the transcendent intervention as a breach in the laws of nature: the divine causality, he will say, does not interfere with the phenomenal series without causing a disturbance which constitutes an exception to the natural laws of created existence. It is indeed this idea of a 'breach', an 'exception' in the laws of nature to which Bultmann is opposed, believing that in so doing he is interpreting the mind of the scientist. But his refusal is completely useless. What right has a scholar to claim that a breach in the laws of nature is impossible? or, and this comes to the same thing, that nature does not remain absolutely obedient to the call of him who has created it?

A primary reason which Bultmann could invoke, and which he actually does invoke, is the scientific postulate of determinism: for modern science the world is rigorously determined, governed by immutable laws; thus any breach in the course of phenomena, even one provoked by a transcendent agent, is, properly speaking, inconceivable.

We might be tempted to try to refute this statement by appealing to the conceptions of atomic physics[1] and Heisenberg's Uncertainty Principle. But this argument would soon

point-blank, over-simplified, refusal to believe in the *possibility* of miraculous healing. In our own work we have received much light and inspiration from an unpublished lecture, 'De Miraculo', by our colleague, Ed. Dhanis, to whom we are glad to acknowledge our indebtedness here.

[1] If we read him aright, A. Oepke, in 'Entmythologisierung des Christentums' (B. III, pp. 171, 172), tends to do this when he reproaches Bultmann for having misunderstood recent developments in physics.

break down. For what, after all, is the legitimate conclusion to be drawn from atomic physics? At the most, it has established the impossibility of determining exactly the position of particles at the same time as their momentum. Many physicists regard this 'ignorance' as final. They therefore give up the hope of constructing a synthetic picture of the world: if the scientist decides to fix the position of the particles more precisely, he will treat the phenomenon as a case of elastic collision between particles; if, on the other hand, he wants to know more exactly the momentum, he will deal with the same phenomenon as an interference effect between waves. He will even use these two images, since the one corrects the other: the image of the corpuscle represents that which is erroneous in the image of the waves; and inversely, the latter corrects the image of the corpuscle. But he will use them alternately and not synthetically; how can he make a synthesis since they are incompatible? This amounts to saying that the atomic reality does not correspond to any of our imaginative schemes, or if you wish, that it is a *mystery for our imagination*, and that atomic physics has shaken to its very foundations the picture of the world which we associate with physics of the classical type.[1] But this does not mean that contemporary science henceforth considers that physical reality is open to the action of agents which are not within it. It is impossible to draw any conclusion from the Heisenberg Uncertainty Principle in favour of a possible breach in the determinism of phenomena by means of a transcendent intervention: it is quite mistaken to invoke this principle against Bultmann's allegation.

This, however, is his error: he has not seen that science has no authority to set up the principle of determinism as a necessary principle in physical reality. The scientist cannot see positively, as we have just said, that this reality is obedient to free agents which act on it from the outside; but, on the other hand, neither can he declare that it is

[1] See, on this subject, A. Grégoire, S.J., *Lecons de philosophie des sciences expérimentales*, Namur, 1850, in Chapter V, 'Nécessité de la science. La légitimité', revised by G. Isaye, S.J., pp. 227, 228.

closed to them, he cannot say that his own strict determinism is a condition of understanding this reality. Doubtless,
the scholar, very rightly, as a method and as an hypothesis
of research accepts the supposition of an external world
determined and controlled by strict laws. His task is to seek
in all honesty to know the laws of nature in their continuity,
and, to this end, he has to accept the idea of a certain determinism, since apart from this he would despair of ever
establishing any continuity, any universality of law. But he
can only accept this idea as a norm for discovery, as the
necessary means for his inductions and his generalizations;
if he goes further, sets it up as a necessary principle of
physical reality, and asserts that the physical world is not
intelligible save on the condition of being conceived as a
strictly closed system, then he is going further than he has
any right to do; he has left his own sphere, and now claims
to be a metaphysician and the whole question now is: what
is the value of this metaphysics? It is easy to see that it has
none. Not only, in the eyes of the Christian, does it flatly
contradict the great biblical affirmations of the omnipotence
of God in the world which has come from his hands, but it
is also condemned by the affirmations of reason applied to
the conception of reality: for reason, the world of bodies
and minds is the creation of God; now the very notion of
creation implies the idea of the obedience of created being
to the call and the command of his Creator.[1]

There is another reason which Bultmann could produce
in support of the idea of a breach of the laws of nature: it
is inconceivable that a phenomenon should abstract itself
from the order of nature, because, by definition, the phenomenon can only be the partial expression and manifestation
of this order; in its actual terms, the idea of a phenomenal
exception, of a rupture in the connexion of phenomena, is
contradictory. To this we would reply that in point of fact
a phenomenon is inconceivable save as part of a whole,

[1] St Thomas, in *S.Th.*, I. q. *105*, a. *6*, ad *1*: '*Deus enim potest agere
praeter ordinem naturae creatae, et cum hoc facit, non agit contra naturam, sed
secundum potentiam oboedientialem, qua quaelibet creatura apta est oboedire Deo
ad accipiendum quidquid ipse voluerit.*'

like a chord in a vast concert; let us also admit that usually the order of which the phenomenon ought to be the revelation, is the order established by the laws of nature. But let us suppose that this order of nature has itself been integrated by God into an order which transcends it by encompassing it—the order of these free supernatural relations which God has decreed to form the link between himself and the universe of spirits—to start from there, we then see that the idea of an exception in the laws of nature ceases to be contradictory: in this instance, the phenomenon which makes the breach would be a miracle produced by God in order to signify to the spirits this superior order to which he has assumed them: there is then no disorder in the fact of miracle, and consequently no longer any impossibility; on the contrary, it will be both the manifestation and the expression of the supernatural order, and thus it will rediscover all the intelligibility that can be desired. Now that is indeed the conception which the Christian has of miracle. It is not in his eyes an extraordinary exhibition, fantastic, arbitrary, gratuitous, given for nothing, without reference to a spiritual reality, it is a surprising cosmological event whose meaning is that it signifies the gift, wholly inward, unheard, and unexpected, of a love which is both mysterious and overwhelming.

Finally, a third objection to the idea of miracle could urge, not the impossibility of a breach in the laws of nature, but rather the impossibility of stating that such a breach should take place. As we have said, in his idea of miracle the Christian admits the idea that it might be proved to be possible: the special intervention of God should be discernable as such, otherwise the miracle would not be formally recognized; on the other hand, we have admitted implicitly that it was the breach in the laws of nature which should attest this divine intervention: thus the breach should itself be evident. But it is precisely this that is said to be impossible: in order to recognize the breach, the exception, it would be necessary first of all to know, with absolute certitude, the laws of nature; but this certitude is not our concern. After all, the scientist does not measure nature. Scientific laws in relation to the world of phenomena are only provisional formulas, needing constant revision; further, the modern physicist only sees, in the laws of the natural macroscopic order, laws which are purely statistical, which do not state necessities, but simple probabilities, which are also highly probable. Do we need more than this in order to deny the possibility of miracle? Such a phenomenon may indeed break through scientific laws as at present formulated: we have not sufficient reason to declare that it breaks the laws of being, that it does not proceed from a natural power which is still hidden, nor that it thus attests a divine intervention.

The answer to this last objection calls for a distinction; the Christian will concede that where certain surprising events are concerned, veritable exceptions to the laws of science, it is not possible to prove that they are also breaches in the laws of nature; after all, it is true, it is not impossible that they are due to latent forces of which we are not yet aware; however, in his eyes they will still have the value of authentic miracles; they would attest the presence of the transcendence and the intervention of God, because it would appear from their religious context that these latent forces in nature act instrumentally through the working of God responding to our prayers: veritable miracles, but of the second order, so to speak, a transcendence which does not manifest itself as an exception within the laws of nature: there is no need to say more on this point. But there are other surprising events of which we may say with reason that as exceptions to the laws of nature they are also exceptions to the laws of being. As has been said,[1] the laws established by science doubtless only express one part of the laws of nature, but a part which is certain: it follows from this that a strange fact cannot be without doubt antecedently declared to be mathematically improbable; but its probability can be treated as a negligible quantity: to such an

[1] L. de Grandmaison, *op. cit.*, pp. 236-239, to which the following pages refer.

extent that it can be affirmed that we shall never observe scientifically the spontaneous elevation of a brick to the first storey by the Brownian movement. So there is a regular course of things, and we do know at least, quite certainly, what we cannot do. As we also know there are sequences in irreversible phenomena, whose course can never be reversed by any natural force; certain physiological changes, for instance, put an organ into such a disturbed state that no one can remedy it. The inertia or the weakness of the powers of action erect a limit to natural forces: the latter cannot pass beyond them; if they do over-pass them it is precisely because the Creator has intervened, beyond themselves, in order to increase their efficacy.

Up to this point, Bultmann's objection to 'mythical thought' in the name of science was inspired by the principle of determinism: a *formal* objection, so to speak, founded rather upon the *methods* of contemporary science than upon their content; and at the same time, what he objects to in the Christian myth is not its mythical content proper, but the very *form* of the myth as a whole, with which it clothed the message. We may even say that, in his explicit formulation, this alone is the point of his objection. But without any clear explanation this objection is also inspired, in part, by considerations which relate the *matter*, the *content*, both of science and of the Christian myth, that which he calls the picture of the scientific world, with the mythical image of the world of the Bible.

Modern astronomy has vastly enlarged the dimensions of our universe; situated in its exact place in the spatial and temporal immensity of its galaxies, the earthly adventure of the human race risks being regarded by the scientist as a rather mediocre story; or rather, it may be granted that in relation to matter it holds the primacy of spiritual realities; but its importance, however real it may be, still seems to be something quite relative; the scientist and the philosopher surprise each other by renewing the hypothesis of the plurality of inhabited worlds. It is difficult to admit that our minute planet, situated at some point or another, but not in the least in the centre of the universe of space, can be the unique theatre, actual and possible, of the life of the spirit.[1] Now the Christian message in its traditional form contests this notion; or rather, let us say that it confers on man a spiritual primacy which is higher than any other spiritual order. For, it says first of all, it is our human nature that the Word of the Eternal God assumed; and then above all, it lays emphasis upon the entire subordination of the universe to man, as thus divinized: all things have been created in Christ, 'Things visible and things invisible, . . . and in him all things cohere' (Col. 1.16-17); in such a way that the humanity of Christ and ours in him are truly the *raison d'être* and the final cause of the universe. This then explains Bultmann's temptation: in his view, biblical anthropocentricism is not in accordance with the modern picture of the universe; if not all irruption of the divine into the human, at least that which ends in making man the lord of the whole creation, from the point of view of the present day, seems to be incompatible with science; and thus in order to protect us in advance against all future conflict between faith and reason, we will do well to renounce, from this moment, the whole idea of an irruption of the divine into the human sphere; let us offer an exclusively existential interpretation of the Christian message.

But here Bultmann has exaggerated the value of a simple hypothesis. The traditional doctrine of the Incarnation is perfectly reconcilable with the supposition of other spiritual lives created by God in the vastness of the material universe; God was made man, that is what we are taught by revelation; but this tells us nothing about the relations made by him with other hypothetical materio-spiritual beings. It is true, some Pauline texts, which refer to the Incarnation, seem to suggest the idea of anthropocentricism;[2] but if the critic believes that this is the necessary meaning, the believer

[1] Cf. A. S. Eddington: *The Nature of the Physical World*, Cambridge, 1929, p. 177.
[2] I.e. in presenting Jesus Christ, the God-Man, as the head of the universe.

does not find here any insurmountable conflict between his science and his faith. After all, neither science nor philosophy can bring any decisive objection against the possibility of a certain sovereignty of humanity, in Jesus Christ, over any inhabited world which might really exist. But this very existence is only a hypothetical one; it cannot provide any actual proof of it by experiment; at the most it can be based on nothing more than a vague hypothesis: the human spiritual drama hardly gives meaning to the vastness of the universe. How can the Christian believer reasonably allow these doubtful extrapolations to prevail against the traditional forms of his faith?[1]

In conclusion, in the name of the principle of determinism Bultmann has not stated anything valid against the idea of a possible intervention of the transcendent in nature and in history; nor in the name of the scientific picture of the world has he proved the impossibility of the traditional interpretation of the message, in the elements which it doubtless offers, to the assent of our faith.

But even when, in principle, this general affirmation has been accepted, other questions remain on particular points which are no less serious; for instance, as Christians are we obliged to accept all accounts of 'miracles' at their face value, even if they are drawn from some legends of the saints, included by the preacher in his morning sermon? Again, what are the criteria which enable us to be sure when a 'miracle' is due to genuine divine intervention? Similarly, how are we to judge certain conceptions of the world which are now and again presented in the New Testament or in the Creeds?

Let us take one of the examples chosen by Bultmann himself: *descendit ad inferos, ascendit ad cælos*:[2] the truth

[1] This confrontation of the hypothetical plurality of worlds with the theology of the Incarnation has just been done in terms which are both subtle and profound by Jean Guitton in his book, *Dialogues avec Monsieur Pouget sur le pluralité des mondes, le Christ des Evangiles, l'avenir de notre espèce*, Paris, 1954.

[2] B. I, p. 17, ET, *KM*, p. 4.

presented by these propositions for the Christian's acceptance is expressed in spatial terms—the images of ascent and descent—which seems to suggest that the Ascension of Christ took place in a celestial region bordering on Palestine. In a Ptolemaic view of the world it would not have been absolutely impossible to think that it was actually this particular region of the universe which the Exalted Christ would henceforward inhabit, and whence he would one day return. But what of a Copernican picture? Would the Christian, in order to remain loyal to his faith, be forced to hold to the Ptolemaic system? It is evident that a faith which has to be associated so closely with ancient cosmology cannot be reconciled with the modern picture of the universe. But the real object of the message of the Ascension is independent of these images, whether of the ancient or of the modern world. While the Ascension affirms the final exaltation of Christ to the right hand of God, it also proclaims the end of an epoch, and the beginning of a new age: henceforth, Christ is withdrawn from our 'felt' experience; he no longer manifests himself save to a pure faith which is happy to believe without 'seeing'. *Beati qui non viderunt*. . . . Thus, we may admit, the progress of scientific thought—the obligation to abandon the Ptolemaic system—has helped Christian thought to explain its true content at a particular point, and to separate it from images and representations which surrounded its first formulation, but which were not themselves proposed to belief. We would then understand that the question, put by Bultmann, of making a distinction of this kind between the content of faith and the terms in which it is expressed, could be applied equally well to other points in the Christian message, and we would then be able to have a profitable discussion with him on his final views on these subjects. But, as we have seen, his denial of this possibility has been absolute: he rejects, in the name of science, any idea that the transcendent could be represented in our immanent world. Here we must confine our efforts to testing the validity of this allegation as a whole. Now, as we have seen, it has no foundation. The biblical message would lose its whole point if the whole idea of supernatural divine intervention were eliminated, and especially that which Christians call 'resurrection': but we can retain this element with a good conscience: scientific honesty does not in the very least oblige us either to reject or to deny it.

3. Rejected by Bultmann on account of its supposed incompatibility with scientific thought, the idea of a possible irruption of the divine into the human sphere is opposed by him for another reason, which is actually *philosophical*: the expression of the saving event in terms of physical realities and natural forces, a statement which the classical theology takes for granted, is the fruit of an essentialist ontology; but we have seen that this ontology, incapable of expressing being, is equally incapable of expressing God in himself and in his action, for God remains on the side of Being. An authentic philosophy, a metaphysic worthy of the name, will refrain from attributing to divine history and the redemptive event the objectivity of 'this-worldly existence', as is done in essentialist theology. Since this 'objectivity' or 'mythologizing process', according to Bultmann, cannot be defended, he claims that the only 'objectivity' which is acceptable to the philosopher is existential objectivity; here, the divine action only takes place within the existential encounter of faith; here there is no materialization of the divine in 'things', no supernatural physical reality presented to our observation or to our methods of induction; nothing but the presence of God in *Dasein*, to the extent in which *Dasein* accepts God in faith. Further, we would point out that when it is said that the divine act of salvation is known only by existential knowledge, we do not mean that it is the creation of the believer, in the way in which the content of thought, generally speaking, is created or produced by the self (pure) according to idealist philosophers; the Word of God addressed to us has to be compared with the love which a beloved being cherishes for us; this love, in its peculiar quality, only exists for the subject which it touches: is this

a reason to question its reality? It is the same with the act of God: although only existing in the light of faith, it is none the less a reality which constrains and controls it.

Having thus compared the two kinds of objectivity in their respective interpretation of the saving event *in general*, Bultmann then compares them *in detail* in their application to the two major aspects of the Christian event.

(a) *Comparison of Christologies:* traditional Christology, by its doctrine of the Word (*Verbe*) assuming the physical reality of a single human nature, mythologizes the theology of the Incarnate Word; on the contrary, the Christology of Bultmann does not mythologize; for here the Word is limited to a human word (*parole*), which it communicates in a message; now, a word has no meaning save in the intelligence of those who listen; there is no Incarnation, therefore, in the physical world; no full actuality of the event outside the existential encounter with the believer.

(b) *Comparison of the doctrines of the Spirit:* traditional theology, by its conception of a *pneuma* acting upon the soul, mythologizes the divine Spirit by comparing it with a phenomenal cause, or a force of nature;[1] but it is not so in Bultmann's theology: here the Spirit means nothing more than the presence of the event to faith, or, to put it better, it is the act by which the believer grasps the meaning of this event, and the light which it throws upon his sinful existence.

Accepting this distinction between these two aspects of the event, let us ask first of all what we are to think of the incompatibility of traditional Christology with authentic philosophy.

Let us begin by recognizing that the distinction between the two forms of objectivity here are of some service to Bultmann: it permits him to lay the foundation of a Christology which is different from the traditional Christology. Doubtless, as we have already seen, the latter teaches that the relation of the human nature of Christ to the Word is not manifest in the phenomenal order; despite the fact that

[1] *Kraftstoff,* B. I, p. 204, n. 1.

the Incarnation posits a real being in our immanent world; this being is not revealed in its precise transcendence to any human experiment; it is only affirmed by faith;[1] owing to this fact, traditional Christology is nearer to Bultmann's Christology than he is willing to admit. Nevertheless, there is one notable difference between them: the former predicates a kind of exterior objectivity to the union of God and man, entirely independent of the faith which he professes; in Bultmann's theology, on the contrary, the Word of God may indeed be clothed, objectively, in a human 'word', and the message may indeed become part of human history, and thus transform it into *Geschichte* (Gogarten), but, none the less it does not receive its full reality as a message save in the '*existential*' (*existentiel*) *hic et nunc* of actual faith: the meaning of a phrase only exists in the mind which welcomes it.

But even if Bultmann has succeeded in evolving a Christology regulated by his own ideas, does this mean that it proves the philosophical impossibility of the classical Christology? Far from it! Bultmann evidently thinks so; in his view, the language of traditional Christology uses and implies (*implicitly*, in the conciliar formularies, *explicitly*, in the treatises of theologians) the concepts of essentialist ontology; now the essentialist ontology is a false ontology.

What wild statements!

First of all, can we take for granted that the older ontology is so mistaken? Certainly, the proper object of ontology is Being. But precisely, has it been proved that the older ontology, that of St Thomas for instance, has overlooked the question of Being, Existence, and deserves to be called 'essentialist' in the bad sense of the word, in the way in which this word could be applied to the ontology of Wolff? The severe strictures of Heidegger are very unjust, if it be true (as has been claimed by a recent writer) that the Thomist metaphysic has wished to be, and above all succeeded in being, a metaphysic of existence.[2] Henceforth, it

[1] See pp. 130-1 above.
[2] Cf. É. Gilson, *L'Être et L'essence*, Paris, 1948, pp. 78-120.

is argued, traditional Christology, expressed in terms of this metaphysic, would there find the guarantee of its compatibility with the true philosophy.

Here, however, we cannot enter into a critical examination of the older ontology and its value. Let us argue rather *ad hominem*: even supposing that the ontology of Heidegger should succeed in influencing certain minds, the claim that this puts traditional Christology out of court would still have to be proved. Bultmann has not done this, and indeed he is unable to do so.

And, actually, Heidegger's critics seem to agree to-day in refusing to accept the nihilist interpretation of his *Sein und Zeit*: doubtless 'that which causes anxiety' is, for Heidegger, Nothingness: but it is the nothingness of existence (*étant*) of determined forms; 'the indetermination however of that of which, and of that on account of which, we are in anguish is not a simple absence of determination, but the essential impossibility of all determination'.[1] In other words, nothingness is *Being* (*être*) itself: if Being manifests itself *for us* in the phenomena of nothingness, or *of that which is fathomless*, it is because it is *we* who there lose all support.[2] Thus that which *Dasein*, in anxiety, experiences under the form of nothingness, is the ontological reality itself 'inexpressible in words and which covers all with its shadow'.[3] 'This nothingness is Being (*être*) in the way in which it unveils itself originally for us.'[4] Heidegger himself has written: 'thought holds itself attentive to the voice of Being (*être*) and beyond that to the echoes of this voice, which summons man in his essence (*das den Menschen in seinem Wesen in Anspruch nimmt*), in order that he may learn to experience Being (*être*) in nothingness'.[5]

Now, some interpreters (Welte, J. B. Lotz) have appeared to identify this Being, thus experienced, with God, 'the

---

[1] M. Heidegger, *Was ist Metaphysik?*, Frankfurt, fourth edition, 1943, pp. 12-13, quoted by B. Welte, 'Remarques sur l'ontologie de Heidegger' in the *Revue des sciences philosophiques et theologiques*, Vol. 31, 1947, p. 386.

[2] B. Welte, art. cit., p. 389.   [3] *Ibid.*, p. 385.

[4] *Ibid.*, p. 389.

[5] M. Heidegger, *Was ist Metaphysik?*, Epilogue, p. 26.

Christian God of revelation'.[1] We may agree that this identification does not correspond with the intentions of Heidegger: the Being of which he speaks does not exist without limited form or essence, 'its actuality consists uniquely in *that which* is rendered possible by it, and in the act of rendering *that* possible'; 'it is not pure act, but it is like the possibility which makes everything possible'; 'it does not become actual save in the act of founding'; or again: 'being supposes the "being-there" of man and of existence. This relation belongs to it intrinsically.' Thus in the fundamental experience of 'essential thought', it is not the pure act nor the transcendent which manifests itself. But it has been pointed out that if Heidegger has not made any definite pronouncement about the Christian God, neither has he excluded the possibility of knowing God by a revelation in the very heart of *Dasein*: if Being is united with existence, and only exists as its foundation, may it not be 'the indication of a transcendence which is possible, probable or certain';[2] and the reflex sense of anxiety, the recollection of our spirit in itself, right up to that point where it apprehends Being in nothingness, should prepare us for the fact that 'we are open (but uniquely in a revelation) to the dimension of the sacred, of holiness, in which alone "the Holy" can speak to us'?[3]

If this were so, if the *Dasein* of Heidegger's philosophy were susceptible of this extension into authentic transcendence, then, *the philosophy of Heidegger would prepare us both for traditional Christology and for the revelation of the true God*. Certainly, it would never permit us to conceive the positive possibility of the Incarnation; but when the message came to tell us: 'God has become incarnate', that is to say, 'has united himself hypostatically with a humanly determined *Dasein*' it would not, *a priori*, refuse to admit this. If *Dasein* is susceptible, at its deepest point to a revelation, a communication from the true God, it does not seem impossible for a particular *Dasein* to receive this communication in the

---

[1] This, at least is as Max Müller understands them, *La crise de la Métaphysique*, p. 62, n. 1.
[2] Max Müller, *op. cit.*, p. 65.   [3] *Ibid.*, p. 66.

shape of a union in the unity of the divine Person. Bultmann's objection to the traditional conception of the Incarnation would find the ground cut away from under its
feet and there would no longer be any incompatibility between this conception and the ontology which he regards
as the only authentic one. He could still refuse to admit the
fact of the Incarnation: but *he could no longer object to the idea
of incarnation, against its possibility, in the name of philosophy,*
nor could he insist on calling it 'mythological'.

Secondly, what are we to think of the incompatibility of the
traditional theology of the Spirit with philosophical thought?
Here it is important to note that the distinction made by
Bultmann between the two forms of objectivity, useful to
him as we have seen, in Christology, is of no use at all in
the theology of the Spirit. Firmly decided, on the one hand,
to maintain the reality of the divine event and the saving
act, Bultmann declares, on the other hand, that this reality
only exists in the sphere of faith; it is not part of the phenomena which reveal it: thus by reducing the notion of the
Spirit to the presence of the event in faith, he flatters himself that he has given a totally different interpretation of
the work of the Spirit from that of traditional theology. But
his misunderstanding is complete. The traditional theology
of the Spirit holds that the Spirit, to whom it attributes the
divine movements and interior graces, does not disclose itself
to our methods of experiment; doubtless, he acts within us:
the effects of his power are seen in our lives, but his actual
power is still hidden from our eyes, we do not grasp the
interior grace in the principle which creates it; the supernatural and transcendent nature of the cause are hidden
from us; we, like Bultmann, declare that we only affirm
this, 'work of the Spirit' in faith. Further, and this is still
more noteworthy, we speak, it is true, of the action of the
Spirit, of its efficacy, and this language tends to suggest that
we are comparing it with a natural force. But that is only
the inevitable translation on to the plane of human discourse
of the relation which unites the working of grace with God,

its author, a relation which is the *creation* of this grace, and of which the metaphysical reality is quite different from the empirical causality which in the phenomenal order relates a phenomenon which follows to one which precedes it. Bultmann himself is indeed obliged to say that the divine event is made known to the believer, since, otherwise, there would be no 'event' at all: the saving act consists in the *Offenbarung*, in the revelation of the divine forgiveness; Bultmann ought to go even further; he ought to recognize that this event calls out the free will of the believer, since apart from such a summons, the existential act of faith would not be conceivable: the act of God, he has told us, ought to appear to us as coming to complete and bring to perfection the natural knowledge which we have of ourselves; otherwise, the 'yes' which we give would not be an enlightened assent; in other words, it ought to reveal its suitability, and its goodness, and by this means it should attract our will. But when he speaks like this, saying that the event is a 'message' addressed to our spirit, a summons addressed to our will, is he saying anything different from what is always said, in traditional language, about the work of the Holy Spirit? Does he not reintroduce, in other words, the realities of grace, the 'lights', the inspirations, the gifts of the Spirit? Actually, from the point of view of objectivity, Bultmann's theology of the event is no different from the older theology; from the moment that Bultmann admits a 'presence' and a 'statement' of the event to the mind and heart of the believer, he attributes to this event the same objectivity which we attribute to the Master of our inward life.

This leads to a conclusion, easy to follow, on the question of the relation between the traditional theology of the Spirit and philosophy. Bultmann believes that his own conception of the objectivity of the event, and of the presence of the Spirit, is in complete agreement with genuine ontology. But then he ought to admit that this agreement is no less between ontology and the traditional theology of the Spirit, this latter being, as we have just seen, fully equivalent to the Bultmann theology so far as objectivity is concerned. Or if the older theology 'mythologizes' with its doctrine of the Spirit acting inwardly in man, the theology of Bultmann also mythologizes, and to the same extent.

To sum up: Bultmann has not succeeded in proving the incompatibility of the tradition with philosophy; he has not shown that the traditional theology of the two major elements of the Christian event are in conflict with the authentic ontology.

The remarks with which we have just concluded the examination of the theology of the Spirit, naturally raise the following question: has Bultmann's theology been as successful in achieving absolute demythologization as it flatters itself it has done? Bultmann wants to purify Christian theology from all mythology, in the interest of a purely existential interpretation; but by his belief in a divine event making itself known to *Dasein*, and in all this behaving exactly like the Spirit working inwardly, a tenet which, however, Bultmann wants to reject, and, above all, by his doctrine of the divine message present in some way under the veil of human words (the objective interpretation), has he not re-opened the door to myth, and re-introduced the very thing which he thinks he has expelled? If this question were answered in the affirmative, we might as well say that Bultmann's theology contains an intrinsic inconsistency: it could not very well conceal a contradiction at its very heart.

Certain critics have indeed taken this view. One of them has written that 'the idea that man only receives his own existence by a gift is just as mythological as that of breathing a *pneuma* into the depths of the soul'.[1] Jaspers says something very similar: 'the preaching of the redemptive event implies a myth'.[2]

To some of them the contradiction has seemed so evident, and Bultmann's incapacity to eliminate the myth so blatant —so long as he insists on retaining the divine saving act, that

[1] R. Prenter, art. cit., p. 60.   [2] K. Jaspers, art. cit., p. 101.

they have not hesitated to go further than Bultmann on the path of negation. This is the case with Fritz Buri, for whom the *kerygma* is a final relic of a mythology which is arbitrarily maintained (*inkonsequenter Weise*): there is no longer a divine redemptive event, neither in the story of Christ, nor even in the message addressed, *here and now*, by the preacher to the listener; or, even more precisely, there is no longer any message, any revelation at all. Further, Buri continues, Christian theology should no longer be distinguished from philosophy, by an appeal—belonging to it alone—to a saving act wrought within history; it shares, with philosophy, a common task: that of helping man to understand himself; that is all; it retains one privilege alone: in the richness of its tradition, and above all in the formulations of the first Christian epoch (in its conception of humanity), indications and lights which can scarcely be found anywhere else, at least with an equal power of evocation, or which philosophers who are not well acquainted with the sources of Christian thought would find it difficult to understand.[1]

So far as we are concerned, we would not dare to say that Bultmann has not succeeded in expressing his thought in terms of a radical demythologizing; if the act of God in which he believes, still retains the notion of myth, it is, so it seems to us, solely the notion of myth in the broad sense of the word. Now, we have said more than once, that in our view, for Bultmann, myth in the broad sense of the word was not the true myth, which he felt must be eliminated. In consequence we would hesitate to say that his theology contains an inner contradiction. Let us confine ourselves to this one criticism: admitting that the theology of Bultmann does succeed in demythologizing the divine act; but, as we have seen, traditional theology, in the expression of the two major aspects of the Christian event, does not involve, in the theology of the Incarnation or in that of the Spirit, categories and concepts which could be shown to be unacceptable to authentic philosophical thought. In other words,

[1] F. Buri, 'Entmythologisierung oder Entkerygmatisierung der Theologie' (B. II, p. 96).

the traditional theology of the Incarnation and of the Spirit is no more mythological than the theology of Bultmann. Under these conditions is it worth while trying to substitute for tradition new views which are inwardly no better than the older ones?

4. Bultmann objects to the idea of the possible irruption of the divine into the human sphere for a third reason, which is a religious one, a reason which we might call a high sense of transcendence. In his thought Bultmann here manifests what has been called the 'essence of Protestantism', that is, 'purity', or the refusal to compromise in any shape or form: here it comes out as hostility to all ideas of a divine 'condescension', to any 'adaptation to our imperfect use of language', to any idea that God will 'inhabit tabernacles made by human hands'[1]: God is so high, and the world of humanity has fallen so low, that the very idea of divine action being blended with the course of human existence cannot be conceived. And, he adds, this theology alone is able to ensure the necessary purity of our faith: thus there is no revelation of God in the world of our objects, nor, in consequence, no 'signs' offered for our rational interpretation; but precisely, this night, these shadows, in which God leaves the reason, permit faith to be founded on nothing other than itself, without appealing to any other alien elements.

This same dualistic conception of God and of the world explains Bultmann's opposition to the idea of an interior action of the Spirit. Without doubt, this opposition first of all invokes a 'scientific' reason: to submit the spirit of man to a divine power acting inwardly, alienating him from himself by handing him over to the impulsion of a mysterious *pneuma*, this is to misunderstand the most sure certainties of contemporary anthropology, according to which the most accomplished man is one whose action has the maximum of autonomy. But there is certainly another *motif*

[1] All these phrases are taken from J. Guitton, *Difficultés de Croire*, Paris, 1948, pp. 231, 239.

151

here, which is specifically Protestant: sinful man is wholly separated from God; therefore his justification remains relatively extrinsic; there is no spiritual union between him and God, no mystical communion in one life, since such a communion would impinge upon the holiness and the purity of God.

Here, however, we cannot help remarking that if the Bible proposes a very pure idea of transcendence, no less does it present us with what we may call an authentic presence of God, even in fallen man. It is enough to recall the Epistle to the Romans and the description which it gives of the pagan who does not know God and the Mosaic Law: without any positive revelation this pagan does possess the manifestation of God in the creation, and in the voice of his conscience; and he has sufficient light for his misconduct eventually to be judged inexcusable in the sight of Jesus Christ, by whom God will judge all men (Rom. 1 and 2, especially 2.14-17). It is the remembrance of these words of the Apostle which causes many Catholic theologians to found on them their doctrine of the natural desire for God: God, they say, disquiets the heart of man, and this disquiet has such deep roots within him that one can see there an 'existential' element in man, as he actually is, an element of the ontological structure of our *Dasein* in its situation in history. Further, when Bultmann tries to analyse *Dasein* existentially, he is led to reproduce the words of St Augustine: *Fecisti nos ad te, Deus, et irrequietum est cor nostrum, donec requiescat in te?*[1] But since man, a sinner, is thus tormented by God, this means that God is already present with him to a certain extent, in the way in which an end is always present as the incentive which urges one towards it by an interior imperative. Bultmann is thus constrained, in spite of himself, to confess a certain immanence of God in fallen man. It is this immanence which makes the interior action of the Spirit possible. If God were not in some way inhabiting the heart of man, we could not understand how he could ever succeed in acting upon him; we concede to Bultmann that the

[1] B. II, p. 192, ET, *KM*, p. 192.

action in our spirit of a Spirit which would be in all respects
entirely outside of us would amount to an alienation from
ourselves, and would make us 'schizophrenics'; here then
in our inward life, there would be certain phenomena which
would have their principle in us, while others would proceed
from a principle foreign to our deepest self; far from persona-
lizing and completing us, such an intrusion of the Spirit
would end in the destruction and division of our internal
unity. But the reality is quite different. The Christian admits
that in the man who is still a sinner, but who is moving
towards conversion, God creates within him, by grace, light
for his conscience, and strength for his will; in so far as these
experiences are divine movements, gifts of God, these intui-
tions and these aspirations are not derived from a preceding
'phenomenon'; they thus represent a rupture in the tissue
of our psychological determinism; but we would be wrong
to regard them as a rupture in every respect; for the God
from whom they proceed is already installed at the heart of
Being, and has created a mysterious relation with him; indeed, that is why this interior grace, springing from a God
who is already present, unifies us, integrates us, makes us
one with our higher self; thus, as St Paul and St Augustine
have taught us, the interior grace of the Spirit is a liberating
grace: by this we understand that by helping us to break
away from the determinism of our instincts it gives us our
authentic liberty, our true personality; far from alienating
us from ourselves, it gives us back to ourselves; but it only
succeeds in doing this because its Author is already within
us. In truth, God enters only those in whom he dwells.
Only those who are his can receive him; they can doubtless refuse to admit him—*sui eum non receperunt*—but if they
welcome him it is because they recognize that he was
already within them, and that in receiving him they also
fulfil themselves.

In the same way we can explain the possibility of satanic
action in man, even in the Christian as he is, or as he seeks
to become. Bultmann wants to get rid of all this. Indeed,
in a spiritual being, free from every taint of evil—as in

Christ or in his Holy Mother—it is inconceivable that Satan should find an entrance into such a heart; for this would mean—in a wholly innocent being, such a 'divided self', such a breach in his personality, that it would be incompatible with the perfect unification of his freedom to be good. But it is not the same for the sinner, nor for the imperfect Christian. Here, there are still points of contact, more or less numerous and deep, with the forces of evil and sin; in fact, the latter are still as it were 'at home' within the heart; it is precisely because they *are* still within that they can still influence man; and when he gives way and listens to their tempting voices, the sinner, even the Christian, is true to his sinful self; he still agrees with himself—with that self which, in him, still remains an accomplice of sin; he is unified in evil.[1]

5. We must now deal with the points at which Bultmann's thought impoverishes the Christian Faith.[2]

Here, Bultmann, it is true, has his answer ready: if it is regarded as an 'impoverishment' of the message to purify it from its mythological elements, for which credulity, of a certain kind, even at the present day, is always eager, then indeed, he says, I have 'impoverished' it. I would even go further: I express the message in terms which are a positive scandal; I emphasize the feature which is most offensive to man and his self-sufficiency; the Easter faith adjures man not to depend upon himself, to commit himself to God

---

[1] St Gregory the Great gives the following explanation of demonic action, which makes it possible to distinguish the 'exterior' temptation which Christ endured from the temptation which Christians endure:
'Sciendum nobis est, quia tribus modis tentatio agitur: suggestione, delectatione et consensu. Et nos cum tentamur, plerumque in delectationem, aut etiam in consensum labimur: *quia de carnis peccato propagati, in nobis ipsis etiam gerimus, unde certamina toleramus. Deus vero*, qui in utero Virginis incarnatus, in mundum sine peccato venerat, *nihil contradictionis in semetipso tolerabat.* Tentari ergo per suggestionem potuit: sed eius mentem peccati delectatio non momordit. Atque ideo omnis diabolica illa tentatio foris, non intus fuit' (*Hom.* 16 *in Evang.*, P.L., 76, 1,135).
[2] Cf. on this subject R. Marlé (the critical bulletin quoted in our Introduction, p. 15), pp. 628ff.

alone, for the achievement of his authentic existence. But this very 'impoverishment' is a compensation, if my conception of Christianity succeeds in saving it from the shipwreck which menaces it, by giving it an expression acceptable to modern reason (whereas the 'very richness' of the mythical conception compromises it with regard to this reason); and as for the 'offence' of the Cross, I ought, as a Christian preacher, to count on the immanent power of the Word of God: it will triumph over all human resistance and will sweep away all that hinders us from full Christian life; it will certainly gather large numbers—re-grouped—into the Christian Church, to the extent in which the heralds of the message have eliminated the needless 'offence' of the mythological conception.

However, Bultmann would get out of his difficulties too easily by such a simple answer. First of all, to have confidence in the power of the Word to overcome the resistance put up by the listener to an impoverished and scandalous message is very much like an act of faith, which can only be described as 'mythological': does demythologizing entitle Bultmann to invoke the possible 'miracle' of the Spirit? And then above all, the power of God which is invoked, certainly resides, at least partially, in the content of the message, in its intrinsic richness: if the *kerygma* is, in itself, extremely poor if it does not give man any light upon God himself, or on our destiny after death, or on sacramental realities, which are holy and sanctifying, we may well think that it is destined to defeat, and that it will not evoke any loyalty or even any interest, in any school of thought, ancient or modern.

Now the Christianity of Bultmann suffers precisely from this cruel poverty. It is reduced to preaching: there is no worship; no real sacrament, and the preaching itself is reduced to this mediocre theme: you are forgiven sinners; it is confined to giving us a certain self-knowledge of our present condition, without any firm prospects for the future; also it puts the listener on his guard against any rational justification; his affirmation of the act of God is quite gratuitous; it refuses to give any signs of it, or even to accept any kind of foundation in history; at the most it makes us observe that this knowledge of man which is offered to us prolongs and completes a certain 'natural' self-knowledge which is immanent in existence itself. But that God acts effectively, that is to say, that he pardons us, the very fact requires to be believed without proof: it is offered to us for our free decision. How can we seriously think that a Christianity understood in this sense could have any attraction for the modern mind? Here there is even a certain contradiction in Bultmann's thought: he believes it is in the interest of reason to demythologize the message; but then how can we explain the fact that he imposes silence upon this same reason when it asks for the least light on the foundations of belief?

Let us consider a little more closely some of these attacks which Bultmann has made upon the richness of the biblical message. The first one is on the revelation of God, against the light which he has given us about himself. Bultmann justifies this by the positive principle of the existential interpretation, and by the negative principle of demythologizing. He thinks that the only elements we should retain in the message are those which apply to our knowledge of ourselves; we ought to sacrifice all the doctrines relating to God because, being formulated by human intelligence, they introduce the transcendent to the world of objects, they 'mythologize' them.[1] His theology is thus absolutely silent about the God whom it urges us to worship; there is nothing about his nature or his attributes; nothing remains of the doctrine of the Trinity; God forgives us, that is all, in a mysterious act of mercy and love. The only valid elements in the idea of God are those which proclaim his action upon us, his participation in our concrete *Dasein*. God illuminates our existence, but he himself remains veiled.

Now let us look at this anthropocentricism in the light of the Bible. Its point of view is quite different. Certainly, we can agree that the main statements of the Christian creed

[1] Cf. above, p. 26.

all concern human existence in some way or another; they make the Christian knowledge of man possible, and constitute the basis of the Christian doctrine of man: thus, we are permitted to examine them for light upon our condition and upon our history. But, as Barth has observed, the Bible does not present them first of all from this point of view.[1] That which interests the man of the Bible most of all in its message, is the light it throws upon the Being and action of him who is *not* man, who is, on the contrary, the Lord of man and of the universe, and who controls both by his sovereign command. The Bible is not primarily a treatise on anthropology: its whole aim is the knowledge of God, and the contemplation of God; it points towards a 'theology' which is its own end; this is the source of the abundance of statements in the Old Testament about the intimate life of God, of his thoughts and his designs; and in the New Testament *'haec est autem vita aeterna'* . . . : there is no activity higher for man than to know God in himself, and to love him for his own splendour.

This is what the Bible teaches. And to do Bultmann justice he would not deny this. But it remains to be seen, he adds, whether this ought not to be disavowed; he thinks it should; for the biblical doctrine of God mythologizes it by the very fact that it expresses it by means of concepts borrowed from the world of objects; it betrays its transcendence and compares it to the realities of our immanent world.

What are we to say about this, save to point out the principle which contradicts and denies his agnostic outlook? Like many modern people, Bultmann has forgotten that our spirit is drawn towards its objects by the inner compulsion of a desire for God, by an 'intellectual appetite' which is a veritable dynamic possession of the transcendent (and leads to self-knowledge in the form of a sense of mystery); our 'objective ideas' are the terms which our intelligence constructs in order, by their means, to give a partial satisfaction to the infinite breadth of its love of the Absolute Being. It is this origin of the concepts which is the basis

[1] K. Barth, *Dogmatik*, III, 2, p. 534 (reproduced in B. II, p. 106).

of their theological value. Doubtless we do not forget that these same concepts are elaborated by an intellectual function connected with the exercise of our senses; they bear within themselves the trace and the remembrance of this connexion: beyond their relation to God, due to the infinite spiritual dynamism from which they emanate, they contract a relation to matter and quantity due to the sense-data from which the mind has constructed them; that is why when God is compared with our concepts a certain reserve is justified, and should be maintained: our 'objective ideas' are not applied to transcendence according to the manner which is fitting for the quantity with which our understanding cannot help investing them. But none the less, the fact remains that these same ideas are indeed the fruit of an intelligence in love with God; this is why their transcendental usage, their 'analogical' application to God, becomes legitimate and necessary; owing to the fact that they are moved by our longing for the infinite, and carried by it beyond themselves, they indicate and signify, with truth, the transcendent Being. That is why the Christian theologian, sure of a certain theological value of our mind, protests against the negations of Bultmann; he takes the biblical doctrine (and tradition) of God seriously, of his nature, and of his intimate life, and refuses to sacrifice this to an unfounded agnosticism.

The point of our reproach should be carefully considered. We do not confine ourselves to saying to Bultmann: it is impossible to sacrifice all conceptual expression of God, all imagination of the divine in human terms; the sense of mystery cannot do without symbols and images; a complete demythologization would atrophy all our mystical faculties. Thus formulated, the reproach would indeed declare a sort of psychological necessity for images and theological concepts for the expansion of the religious life, but it would not yet risk anything for the value and the truth of these concepts. Now it is indeed their truth that we mean to affirm here: our concepts of God are truly bearers of transcendent significance; through them and by them, it is the transcendent that we attain in its Being. After that, a certain criticism of our concepts has to be instituted; that only some of them can be applied to God, in their proper sense (God knows, God loves), that others, on the contrary, are not applicable save in a figurative sense (God sees, God hears), in other words, that we must distinguish the concepts of simple perfections from those of mixed ones; that, thus, if we wish it, a certain demythologizing is necessary, although this word, owing to its connexion with the idea of something fictional or fabulous is, in this case, rather awkward, we would not disagree on this point: Christian theology has always known it. But when all these considerations have been taken into account, the fact remains that it is possible to have a valid knowledge of transcendence and of mystery.

Another weakness in Bultmann's theology is this: the doctrine of the Last Things. It is of course true that Bultmann does not explicitly deny the reality of a realm beyond death into which man can enter, but his silence on this subject is disquieting; a silence which some writers take to be the sign of an unavowed denial.[1] Certainly these critics ascribe to Bultmann the following dialectic: all the New Testament representations relating to the judgment of God in the beyond involve the idea of the irruption of the divine into the world of man, into the physical world which this irruption transfigures and controls: an idea which is essentially mythological. For Bultmann, there is only one eschatological reality, while if not acceptable, is at least certain: the decision taken by man for or against God in history, in the present. Man reaches the final realities at the present time, when he ranges himself for, or against, the Word which summons him; that is all; we cannot say more than this. Damnation and salvation can only be known in an

---

[1] H. Sauter, B. I, pp. 204-205; W. G. Kümmel, B. II, p. 158; and, above all, E. Brunner, *Das Ewige als Zukunft und Gegenwart*, p. 147 (here Brunner is referring to Bultmann, B. II, p. 205, ET, *KM*, p. 207) and p. 232.

historical sense: to be 'lost', means that under the pressure of anxiety we try to secure our existence by our own efforts, and thus make it impossible to be 'open' to the future, which means that, here and now, we are unable to enter into our authentic existence; to be 'saved', is to accept, *here and now*, the Word of grace which helps us to break away from the past, and liberates us for our true life, which consists in the renunciation of our own works, and in surrender to God.

For our part, we hesitate to ascribe to Bultmann the denial, even virtual, of the beyond. Already, in connexion with the resurrection of Christ, we had noted an uncertainty: does Bultmann deny the fact of the Resurrection? Ought he to deny it in order to remain loyal to the exigencies of demythologizing? The same uncertainty seems to affect the doctrine of our own survival. But if our hesitation is unjustified, and if others were right to overcome it, in this case we ought to say that Christian preaching inspired by Bultmann's thought, denying the reality of the life beyond, would extinguish in the heart of the Christian every ray of hope: there would no longer be any message of a happy immortality; but by this very fact, we can foretell with certainty, there would be no more interest in Christianity, no more ears open to listen to its message.

Finally, there is another defect which is no less serious: an absence of objective, holy, and sanctifying reality. Though perhaps this absence is not absolute: after all, Bultmann could speak of the decision of the believer for God, and of his authentic existence, in terms of sanctity and inward justification; now, the message, the preached word, is the objective witness that the believer gives of his subjective faith, and the sum of these acts of witness, gathers believers into the Church; preaching, Church: two phenomena in which we can see sanctifying realities, and of which Bultmann himself has said that they are integrated in the saving act. However, we must say that they are rarely considered excepting on certain occasions: as we have been given to understand, for Bultmann, the Church is no more than an 'occasion for me, by its preaching, to hear the Word of God in converting me existentially (*existentiel*)'.[1] In other words, the Church, being simply a space in which the Word resounds, remains in itself a wholly secular entity; its liturgical and sacramental institutions do not form a consecrated whole, in which God gives himself into our hands (we think here of the Catholic conception of the Eucharistic Presence): to Bultmann this is an ecclesiology which is mythical and even magical, wholly opposed to the exigencies of demythologization. Here, of course, Bultmann seems to be simply faithful to the general line of Protestant theology. He himself has reminded us of Luther's protests against the existence of 'holy places' in the world: 'the whole world is a secular realm'.[2] And we have been, very rightly, reminded of the general Protestant tendency 'to reduce, in the conception of the relation of man with God, the mediation of the objective, given indissolubly in the dogmatic edifice, the ecclesiastical and sacramental institution'. For this mediation Protestantism tends to substitute 'the direct, though paradoxical, relation of the Word heard personally in faith',[3] and in the actuality of the *here and now*. Thus, this sacrifice of consecrated 'objectivity' could well be part of Protestantism as a whole; but it is allowable to consider that, commanded, as it is here, by the claims of demythologizing, it constitutes for the Christian an authentic impoverishment.

And now, in conclusion, we are in a position to make a judgment as a whole upon Bultmann's enterprise. It is inspired, at the outset, by the view of man common to very many of our contemporaries: the consciousness of our desperate condition. The distress of *Dasein*, 'thrown-into-the-world', is vast; philosophy does not even begin to sound the depths of the distress of man, left to himself; for, crushed as he is by his evils, he still flatters himself that he can find, within himself, a principle of interior liberation; let him courageously accept his destiny: in this acceptance, starting

---

[1] R. Marlé, *op. cit.*, p. 629.   [2] See above, p. 103.
[3] R. Marlé, *op. cit.*, p. 630.

from himself, he will reach authentic existence, he will save himself from himself. 'No', says Bultmann: 'the Fall of Man is total.' See, this is what the message tells him, but this same message assures him, at the same time, of the possibility of his salvation from God; he must renounce, to the last ounce, his pride, and trust in the free grace which liberates and pardons; a grace which we have not to wait for, towards which we do not go as to an uncertain future: it has already been proclaimed to us in Jesus Christ. The whole significance of the Christ event is summed up in this command, or rather in this summons: 'accept your cross and your desperate condition; confess your impotence to tear yourself away from all your self-will, your self-indulgence, your "inauthentic" existence; trust in the love of God; if you make this confession and this act of trust and surrender, you will reach the truth of your being and you will be set free for the love of men. That is all; the message does not ask more than this.' Everything else, all the theology of the Word of God personally united to a human nature, all the *mystique* of a Saviour risen from the dead, and acting supernaturally by his Spirit—all this is mythology, which is not acceptable to an enlightened mind; but also all this has nothing to do with the authentic Word of God, and even the first hearers of the message understood this and tried to demythologize it.

A Christianity thus presented might sometimes attract, and lead astray, a mind which is not very thoughtful or observant. In fact, it will not stand the test of *thought*, whether for the believer or the unbeliever. The believer will not be satisfied with it: on the one hand it takes away from him the Person of his Saviour and his living presence, and on the other hand, it asks him to confess the presence of the Christ event in his faith. But this demand, coming on top of the denial of Christ his Saviour, will astonish him: as we have seen, whatever it does, the theology of the event, and more generally the theology of revelation, reproduces even that which it believed it had effaced, namely, the idea of a Spirit taking hold of the heart of man, illuminating him with his light, and leading him into the ways of God. Henceforward, the believer will ask: why should I give up the belief in my Saviour, living to-day, and conforming me to himself by his Spirit? This belief has always been that of the Church. Shall I substitute for it a creed, which, curiously enough, on the one hand asks from me the affirmation of the interior divine action, but, on the other hand, suppresses the agent of this action, at least the agent who has been traditionally so designated, the Risen Christ? But the unbelieving reason will also be disconcerted. At bottom, by his programme of demythologizing Bultmann wishes to give satisfaction to the old rationalistic exigencies of the Enlightenment; but on the other hand, he asks the reason to make a violent act of commitment: the act of God, the divine intervention in history, is to be imposed upon it without proof and without support. Bultmann has sought for a position midway between faith and rationalism, between the theology of revelation and Liberal theology. It is an illusory enterprise. On the way on which he has entered, Liberalism alone is possible, and a philosophy which is self-sufficient, closed to the idea of an historical intervention of God, will always have the last word over the thought of Bultmann by its frankness and its clarity.

THE IDEA OF MYTH IN THE THOUGHT OF BULTMANN AND IN THAT OF HISTORIANS OF RELIGION

AMONG our contemporaries, the idea of myth means a great deal more than its connexion with religion.

The following definition has been suggested: 'myths are traditional tales, derived from a collective source, which are attempts to explain every kind of reality, whether supernatural or natural; essentially they are dynamic, irrational, and they transcend ordinary experience'.[1] This definition emphasizes certain negative elements: 'the myth does not confine itself to tales about gods or heroes; however deeply it may be penetrated with religious ideas or feelings, religion is not its unique object'. It also mentions certain positive elements: 'myth constantly appeals to the supernatural —it is the product of a collective creation and the object of a collective belief; it bears the marks of an irrational inspiration, ignoring the boundaries of ordinary experience, it is mystical, and full of deep feeling.' This idea of myth 'applies equally well to the sacred myth of the *Alcheringa*, held by the Arunta tribes in Australia, as to the political myths of the Divine Right of Kings, or to certain social myths of modern times';[2] we can think for instance of the myth of blood, or *Lebensraum*, so dear to the theorists of the Third Reich.

We note that, in this sense of the word, the word 'myth', in the view of those who use it, always acquires a depreciatory meaning: we have just seen how the myth is accused of being irrational, indifferent to experience, and its critics also

[1] V. Larock, *La pensée mythique*, Brussels, 1945, p. 5.
[2] V. Larock, *ibid.*, pp. 7, 8.

speak of a 'doctrinal fiction' or of a 'social or political Utopia'; further, they remind us of the Bergsonian idea of the genesis of myth: it is the gregarious instinct 'which, in order to conserve intact and living all that the intelligence menaces, creates intuitive fictions, which are myths'. '. . . Since the intelligence works by means of mental images, instinct will create "imaginary ones" which will resist the representation of the real, and will succeed, by way of the intelligence itself, in counteracting the intellectual process. This would explain the origin of fables.'[1]

In the works of historians of religion, the concept of myth, although already much more restricted, is still rather indefinite. For some, it means all 'the narratives in which the gods (taking the word in the broadest sense) play one or several of all the principal parts.'[2] For others, a myth is a 'story expressing mysterious relations between man and the divine'.[3] The latter definition is certainly more happily expressed, though it needs to be made more precise; a 'legend' also expresses the relations between man and the divine; nevertheless, it is not a myth; it tells an edifying story, besides amplifying it, it heightens the marvellous features of the story; this is done in order to strengthen the effect of edification or of admiration for the hero, but at least its proper object, its content is essentially human and earthly; even when it transforms it supernaturally, it does not seek to express the divine in itself; and that is why it always places its content at a particular moment in time, or at a certain point in space.

The myth, on the contrary, is inspired above all by a certain perception of divinity, by a *Gotteserlebnis* (experience of God) which it wishes to communicate to its listeners; doubtless, it mediates this perception by means of sensible forms, by means of a narrative in which a divine intervention occurs in Nature and in History; but its aim is the

[1] V. Larock, *op. cit.*, p. 7, here quotes H. Bergson, *Les deux sources de la morale et de la religion*, Paris, 1932, p. 124.
[2] A. H. Krappe, *La genèse des mythes*, Paris, 1952, p. 15.
[3] K. Beth, in the *Handwörterbuch des deutschen Aberglaubens*, ed. E. Hoffman-Krayer, 1927-1936, Vol. VI, p. 719, quoted by Krappe, *ibid.*, p. 15, n. 1.

revelation of the divine (among primitive peoples its intention is to ensure the communion, the participation of a group of human beings with their supernatural ancestors) ; and that is why the actual content of the story, the features of the earthly history which it narrates generally remain very indefinite, so far as circumstances of time and place are concerned, in which the divine intervention is supposed to have taken place.

To sum up: the myth is a representation of the divine itself, in its relation with the world of men: whether it relates the origin of a natural phenomenon like solar myths, for instance, or whether it tries to explain the origin of God, or evil, or death, primarily, it seeks to interest the listener in the nature of the divine, in the mysterious power from which earthly realities are derived; but because it contemplates this power in its action upon the world, it clothes it with attributes which assimilate it strangely to the action of man himself, or at least it often happens that it makes God in the image of man, attributing to him our ways of thinking, our instincts, our passions, thus menacing the character of transcendence, of mystery, of the wholly other, of the sacred reality, to which it was its profound intention to lead us.

Finally, we note that modern historians of religion seem to agree in giving a bad sense to the notion of myth: here, it seems that the rather general idea of myth—expounded above—has influenced the more exact sense of 'myth' as 'religious' in the proper sense of the word; whatever may be the anthropological function which these historians regard as the creative source of these myths—for they hold different views about their origin in man—at least, very generally, they guard against ascribing their origin to a divine revelation, and they even ascribe it to a human faculty of invention, totally unrelated to the perception of reality; or, perhaps it would be better to say that the historian or the philosopher of religion does not necessarily deny that a sense of mystery may be at work in the constitution of the myth, and may truly lead to the divine itself; through myth, we may come into real touch with the divine; and as the language of myth, which consists of symbols and images, remains indispensable, even to-day, for this perception of the divine, it would be a mistake to wish to suppress this language itself.

But the fact remains that it is the power to create fables which gives the myth its tangible design, its form; the divine is really attained, let us repeat, but the features which describe its intervention in Nature or in History, the cosmic or historical rôle which it plays, are not real: 'as a rule the myth only offers pseudo-history';[1] all its material elements, its 'body', is the product of fiction.

With the exception of a criticism of the sense of mystery (is it true that in mythical thought a sense of the divine is at work and to what extent does it attain its object?), the Catholic Christian will have no objection to this conception of myth. Without doubt, for him both the story of Christ and the conceptual expression of transcendence have the value of truth; but that is precisely the reason why he refuses to class them with mythological tales.

We do not charge Bultmann with having used the notion of myth in a quite different sense from that which we have just described. If the reader takes the trouble to refer to the definition which Bultmann gives of myth in the narrow sense of the word (the only one which he considers to be truly mythical), he will see that this reproach does not apply to him. But even if Bultmann had departed from the common use of the word, there is no need, as we have already shown,[2] to attribute any importance to this 'departure' in a discussion with him. But the fact that he applies the term 'mythical' to traditional Christianity is serious: in so doing, Bultmann suggests that in his eyes the story of the God-Man, and of Christian theology, are scarcely more than fictions. That he has erred in so doing, we have tried to show by refuting the affirmation that traditional Christianity is incompatible with scientific thought.

[1] '. . . while as a rule myth is wrapped in a pseudo-historical garment' (K. Goldammer, 'Die Frage der Entmythologisierung im Lichte der Religionsgeschichte und in der Problemstellung der Missionsreligionen' in the *Theologische Literaturzeitung*, Vol. 78, 1953, p. 254).

[2] Cf. above, p. 126.

BIBLICAL EXEGESIS AND PHILOSOPHY: TWO OPPOSED CONCEPTIONS OF THEIR RELATIONSHIP: R. BULTMANN AND K. BARTH[1]

OUR purpose here is to make a contribution to the under-standing of the relationship between intellect and faith and, more precisely, of that between philosophy and scriptural exegesis. This contribution will take the form of an *exposé* of the thought of R. Bultmann and K. Barth concerning this relationship, of a confrontation of their points of view, and of an appreciation.[2] It would be wrong to think that the biblical hermeneutics of these two authors form no more than a minor or secondary chapter of their theology. On the contrary, it is their preoccupation, or at least it is the heart of their differences. Bultmann especially has stressed its gravity: 'The real problem is the hermeneutic problem —that is, the problem of interpreting the Bible,'[3] and it is the one which has always governed his research and whose solution has brought him, if not to 'demythologize' the scriptural message, at least to interpret it existentially.[4]

[1] From *Nouvelle Revue Théologique*, Vol. 78, November and December 1956, pp. 897-914 and 1027-1042.
[2] For a comparison with bearing on the general theology of Bultmann and Barth, see H. Fries, *Bultmann-Barth und die katholische Theologie* (Stuttgart, 1955). Apart from pp. 120-127 and p. 129, there is little direct comparison of their respective hermeneutics, but the author well emphasizes the primary importance, especially for Bultmann, of her-meneutic problems.
[3] B. III, p. 51; B. II, p. 191, ET, *KM*, pp. 191-192.
[4] For an introduction to Bultmann's thought on demythologization and the existential interpretation of the message we would refer the reader to our work, *The Christian Message and Myth*, pp. 10-167, above.

I

Biblical hermeneutics is for Bultmann a special case of general hermeneutics. It is therefore proper and in his interest that he should first of all explain to us his way of understanding the general term.[1]

The interpretation of a text should of course, as occasion arises, call upon all the techniques of philology. But they are not enough. The interpreter must from the very beginning be conscious of having some vital relation with the object expressed in the text; he must belong to some extent to the same world as the author, must share the same problems, the same joys, sufferings and anxieties, must already possess a precomprehension of the text and of the realities of which it tells. I cannot for example understand anything of a text in some way relating to music unless I have some prior understanding of music, some means of entry into the particular world into which this text wishes to introduce me. Sometimes such prior relationship and communion may of course be simply 'ingrown' and in no way 'considered', but their presence, whether naïve or reflective, is so necessary that without them I would have no interest in the text or in the matter treated therein; and their extent, or rather their specific content, will govern the direction of my inquiry and determine the *woraufhin*, the 'about what' I shall interrogate the text—in other words, the object of interest and investigation will vary in accordance with the nature of my vital relation to the content of the document.

In a given text certain things are directly enunciated,

For the study of the same thought as expressed in Bultmann's exegesis proper (above all in *Theologie des Neuen Testaments*, Tübingen, third edition, 1955, ET, *Theology of the New Testament*, London, Vol. I, 1952, Vol. 2, 1955), see the remarkably well documented work of R. Marlé, *Bultmann et l'interprétation du Nouveau Testament*, Paris, 1956, to which we shall certainly have more than one occasion to refer.

[1] For the most part the following *exposé* is modelled on 'Das Problem der Hermeneutik', *Glauben und Verstehen*, Vol. II, Tübingen, 1952, pp. 221-235, ET, 'The Problem of Hermeneutics', *Essays*, London, 1955, pp. 234-261. From now on we shall refer to *Glauben und Verstehen* as *GV*.

others indirectly. The first are the object of the author's explicit affirmation. The others are of two kinds: in the first the author reports them consciously and deliberately, but without making them the intention of his narrative— for example Homer interests historians to-day by his unintentional supplying of information about Greek arms at the time of the *Iliad*. In the second certain things are the object of the author's intention, but he conceals them, or at least he cloaks them under the express formulation of other realities—for example the novelist, beyond the things directly presented in his narrative, seeks to disclose to me the world of human passions in general and, in particular, my own passions, my own humanity. Let me offer another example in the works of a great philosopher, Plato. In the course of passing to me information about fifth-century Athenian culture he has really the intention of demonstrating to me the human being 'in its divers possibilities' and of revealing these to me as my own; consequently, the reader of to-day who opens the *Dialogues* merely as documents on ancient civilization will miss their authentic sense. Only a person who thinks philosophically with Plato, and who 'raises him to contemporaneity' by striving to assimilate to himself Plato's conception of man, will understand him.

Now to these texts, which reveal human realities indirectly, though intentionally, the above law of interpretation applies *par excellence*; nothing of their message may be understood without a certain at least provisional pre-intelligence of the human being and its possibilities; before I may grasp the true intentions of Plato there must awaken within me certain categories called the sense of personal life, the sense of humanity, the sense of the ethical norms of action and even the sense of salvation. Thanks to them—and thanks only to them—I shall lend an attentive ear to the message addressed to me in the written work; thereby I will lie open to myself in a manner richer and more profound; the naïve and sub-critical understanding of my human being, by whose dim light I have been living, will rise assisted by the text to the level of conscious reflection. Did not the author write his work precisely in the hope and purpose of helping me discover the possibilities of man? And yet he must find in me from the outset a presentiment of these possibilities.

Giving a more general significance to this first remark, Bultmann is of the opinion that not only a text but any historical reality whatever, no matter how it is communicated, is incomprehensible to the neutral observer (*Zuschauer*) who does not deploy, in his interpretation of the fact communicated, the conception of man already at his disposal.[1] For the understanding of historical facts a certain type of objectivity is unthinkable: we mean objectivity as understood and practised by the natural sciences (and even here it is recognized that objectivity, from the simple delimitation of the fact to be considered, entails a certain *a priori* assumption on the part of the subject).[2] Historical phenomena acquire a significance only through the activity of the person contemplating them. Let us consider for example the murder of Caesar: in itself and as raw material it is scarcely more than a casual datum presented to our susceptibility; is it not evident that before it may appear in its political significance—and there lies its only interest for the historian—the interpreter must already possess an acquaintance, either explicit or experiential, with political reality, and must bring that acquaintance to bear on the object he is considering? So it is with the death of Socrates: if I am to discover its universally human interest I must as I reflect upon it bring into action a philosophy, or at least a virtual philosophy, of my own—the one for example which is latent under my anxious interrogation of the sense of human life. Thus the events of the past may rise to the status of historical phenomena only in the eyes of the subject who himself has his place and rôle in history: they take on meaning only for one playing his part in the drama of human history. Naturally a single historical phenomenon may present a multiplicity of aspects: it may arouse the interest of the philosopher,

[1] *GV* II, p. 226.   [2] *GV* II, p. 229.

the art historian, the sociologist. In this case one might say that its significance has been determined by the choice of each interpreter in turn, by which would be meant not that each interpreter had imposed a meaning from mere arbitrary predilection but that he had distinguished, among the various objectively presented aspects of the phenomenon, the one which bore upon his personal interest and competence. However, it will still be true that the sense of each of these objective aspects will elude the observer who has no '*existentiel*'[1] link with them.

One should therefore refrain from demanding that the interpreter should suppress his subjectivity. Certainly, let us repeat, his attitude towards the phenomenon should be appropriated to its objective aspects; in this sense objectivity is rightly demanded of him. Similarly, and more importantly, one would insist on his being objective in the other sense of suppressing all his personal desires with regard to the *result* of the interpretation. But one should not expect of him an absolute neutrality wherein the sense of the phenomenon is not prejudged even in the form of interrogation. On the contrary, the following principle should be formulated: the historian will succeed in his interpretation of history to the extent that he himself has vitality and richness of endowment. The more extensive is the interpreter's experience in political or social matters, the more likely he is to interpret correctly a political or social phenomenon. As for the seeker in (philosophical or religious) texts for the 'possibilities of the human being', the more lively, if not more reflective, is his consciousness of disquiet and of the problematic nature of his experience, the more he will succeed in grasping the message which these texts address to him. 'The monuments of the past speak to us out of the depth of the reality which gave them birth only if (and to the extent that) we are informed by our own experience of the problematicality, the indigence and, in the last resort, insurmountable

---

[1] '*Existential*' and '*existentiel*': in the translation of this article the French terminations have been preserved, as in *The Christian Message and Myth*. See p. 185 note 2 below, on this distinction.—Tr.

insecurity which constitute the floor and abyss of our being in this world.'[1]

The significance of these views from the relatively recent past (1950) will be better appreciated if they are compared with earlier views of the same author. In a study published in 1925,[2] Bultmann was already making the observation that the historian, if he wishes to understand a philosophical or religious doctrine, cannot confine himself to the purely historical domain: he must envisage the question whether the doctrine held true by the author is effectively so in itself and absolutely. The so-called neutrality of many modern historians with respect to this question is governed by an inadmissible assumption: they appear to maintain that the historian is in a position to understand the idea expressed in a text *immediately* and without examination, provided only that he has established 'exactly in what circumstances and under what influences the text was written, and what is the character of the author'; thus the historian is 'deemed already to have at his command the thing which forms the very substance of the text'.[3] There they are mistaken. For documents from the past may very well contain ideas which are new for the reader of to-day, and in such a case the critic who would make them his own must step outside 'the historical domain at a given moment, in order to grasp this novelty according to its objective essence and in separation from its historical form'.[4] But on what conditions will this very grasp of the 'object' be possible? All the evidence goes to show that the critic must first abandon consideration of the object at arm's length and withdraw into himself: the

[1] *GV* II, p. 230, *Essays*, p. 256. Bultmann reproduces certain lines of F. Kaufmann, *Geschichtsphilosophie der Gegenwart* (*Philosophische Forschungsberichte*, 10), 1931, p. 41.

[2] 'Das Problem einer theologischen Exegese des Neuen Testaments' in the review *Zwischen den Zeiten*, Vol. III, 1925, pp. 334 *et seq.* O. Cullman gave a résumé in 'Les Problèmes posés par la méthode exégétique de l'école de Karl Barth' (*Revue d'Histoire et de Philosophie religieuses*, published by the Faculty of Protestant Theology at the University of Strasbourg, Vol. 8, 1928, pp. 70-83).

[3] Cullman, *loc. cit.*, p. 72.   [4] *Ibid.*

world of ideas has no reality outside the conscious mind; it is therein that the author found the ideas he is proposing to us, and there too we shall have to seek them, with a personal effort of concentration. Thus the critic, the historian, must himself approach truth along the same *subjective* path which led the author to its discovery. To understand a philosophical text of antiquity he will have to resort to philosophical knowledge, and for the understanding of a religious text he will have need of the cognitive act of a religious experience.

Thus far, if we read aright, extend the principles of historical criticism for Bultmann in 1925. But in his more recent writings (those whose views we have reproduced at the beginning of this article) these principles receive a more detailed exposition, if not an amplification. In 1925 we are told that it is in the historian's own conscious mind, and there alone, that he can discover and, as it were, verify the objective 'truth' communicated by the document; to-day it is clear that this way of talking is insufficient: if the new object furnished by a (philosophical or religious) author can be grasped only in the subject, this supposes that the novelty is not total but is to be found prefigured and, so to speak, pre-sensed in the latent possibilities and potentialities of our Self. Hence the grasping and understanding of the new object will consist in rendering explicit, via the action of the text, tendencies which already form, dimly, a part of our lives; in other words it will consist—to return to the actual expressions of those recent texts—in bringing to bear on the interpretation of a document our experiential pre-intelligence of its content and the vital relation which already links us with it.

We may now address ourselves to the question of biblical hermeneutics.[1] Bultmann considers that it is self-evidently no more than an application of hermeneutics in general, more particularly of the hermeneutics of religious texts. Concerning these we have just seen that they are not limited,

[1] *GV* II, pp. 231ff., ET, *Essays*, pp. 256ff.

as the current representatives of historical criticism would have it, to reflecting 'a state of mind expressed in intellectual categories' but that they propound an *'objective truth'* which is 'comprehensible only through the cognitive act of religious meditation, which postulates faith',[1] whence it followed that their reader should be led to discover the essence of the proposed doctrine in his own conscious mind. This law applies very closely to the religious book known as the Bible: here too, if one would understand, one must in exegesis possess a certain pre-comprehension of the object and a pre-existent vital relation to the reality of which the pages tell.

But at this point Bultmann hastens to forestall an objection which Barth will raise. To the question, 'What then is the reality of which the Scriptures tell?' Bultmann answers (no less firmly than Barth), 'It is the action and intervention of God in history, bringing judgment, grace and mercy to concrete man, to the believer to whom these things are revealed.' The text of the Scriptures are the testimony of that divine action; its intention is to enlighten man and his existence on the subject of the divine event accomplished for his benefit. Hence it follows, if the above law of hermeneutics is valid, that it is impossible for me to understand anything of the Scriptures unless in my reading I bring to bear not only my precomprehension of human *Dasein* in its relation to God but something further: a pre-intelligence of what the action of God may signify in general and wherein it is distinct from the action of man or the events of nature. It is just here that Barth raises an objection: natural man enjoys no relation with God; there is in his mind no pre-comprehension of a divine action to come; he cannot attain the slightest knowledge of God and God's action save through revelation, save, that is, through that very action. It is a supremely pernicious error to rank the Bible among religious texts, for these never deal only with 'him who bears the name of God in the symbol of the apostles, but always with one or other of the simulacra which we ourselves invent or create, whether it be Spirit, Nature, Destiny or Idea'.[2] There

[1] Cullman, *loc. cit.*, p. 77.   [2] Karl Barth, *Credo*, Paris, 1936, p. 21.

lies the reason why the Bible demands a technique of interpretation proper to it alone, a technique whose most important rule is as follows: the Bible is its own light—in
other words, discernment of its divine meaning proceeds
only from a pure gift of grace bestowed by the Spirit.

To this Bultmann replies by denying so absolute an ex-
trinsicality. He claims the support of Augustine's *irrequietum
est cor nostrum donec requiescat in te.*[1] And he adds this com-
mentary: there is in *Dasein* as such an *existentiel* knowledge
of God which is experienced and exercised *in the question of
happiness*, of salvation, of the meaning of the world and of
history, of the authenticity of the human being. Of course
the question about God is incapable of supplying its own
answer: man, anxious for God, proceeds to give shape to
the God he senses obscurely in his very disquiet—thus it is
that natural mythologies and perhaps all religions come into
being—and this shape remains, however varied, an illusion
and a fiction; in the terms of Christian faith the right answer
can only be the fruit of an entirely undeserved revelation
—God is not manifested to our natural reason either in
nature or in history.[2] Let us make still further concessions,
let us acknowledge with the objector that it is only in the
light of Christian revelation that we can designate the question as one with bearing on *God*; before we receive this
enlightenment our *existentiel* knowledge will scarcely be able
to give any other legitimate expression to its content than
that which expresses it in terms of questions about happiness or about the meaning of life. Yet none of these limitations will prevent this experiential question of happiness
from in fact constituting for the man who feels it an effective relation to God, to his revelation and action in time:
in the disquiet which torments him his *Dasein* is really, in
an ontological sense, turned towards God, even while he

[1] *GV* II, p. 232, ET, *Essays*, p. 257. Bultmann devotes a passage to
this text of Augustine's in 'Zum Problem der Entmythologisierung'
(1951), B. II, p. 192, ET, *KM*, p. 192.
[2] On this point cf. 'Die Frage der natürlichen Offenbarung' (1941)
in *GV* II, pp. 79-104 (especially p. 86), ET, *Essays*, pp. 90-118 (especially
p. 98).

fails to name him. It must be so. If God were not secretly troubling our existence, never 'would man recognize God as God in any revelation of God'.[1] Of course, whoever comes to hear God's Word must be ready to correct the first representation of God which he acquired vaguely in formulating his disquiet; furthermore, this correction will, as we have recognized, be necessary; the God of revelation will never be the God of our own thoughts. Therefore the reader of the Bible will endeavour with unceasing vigilance to keep his mind in a state of the greatest docility towards biblical teachings;[2] nevertheless he would not be able to carry out the correction demanded of him if 'the basic intention of the question comprised in the concept of happiness (or salvation) did not coincide with the intention of the reply given by the New Testament'.[3]

Thus by justifying the idea of a certain immanence of God in the *existentiel* subject Bultmann persuades himself that he has at the same time justified the application of general hermeneutics to Scripture; and he considers himself authorized to formulate the rule of biblical hermeneutics, which one might call the rule of the vital relation. While others, Barth in particular, consider the dispositions of readers of the Bible to be indifferent and interchangeable, the Holy Spirit taking it upon himself, if he wishes, to accomplish within them the pure miracle of understanding the scriptural Word, Bultmann believes that only he who approaches the text in a certain internal tension will open himself to the action of the Spirit, and since the text speaks to him of condemnation and pardon he must feel his dereliction and sorry state; he must, in a word, bring his passionate subjectivity to bear upon the task of interpretation. The more keenly we are aware of the wretchedness of our existence (and aware through that existence of the God which

---

[1] *GV* II, p. 232, ET, *Essays*, p. 257; *GV* I, p. 126.

[2] *Ibid.*, 'Die an das Neue Testament gerichtete Frage muss im Hören auf das Wort des Neuen Testaments zur Korrektur der mitgebrachten Vorstellung bereit sein.' Here Bultmann forestalls the objection Barth was to raise in *Rudolf Bultmann, Ein Versuch ihn zu verstehen*, Zürich, 1953, p. 49.

[3] *GV* II, p. 232, ET, *Essays*, p. 258.

troubles it), the better will be our position for hearing the voice of the God who forgives.

If Bultmann's hermeneutics went no farther, the rule which it states would scarcely have more than a *psychological* significance: to understand the Bible, preserve the frame of mind which might be called awareness of human disquiet. But now Bultmann proceeds to give his rule of interpretation a significance which is in the true sense *critical*: human disquiet becomes a criterion allowing one to distinguish within the message the assertions which faith should accept from those which it ought to reject. The only elements of the Word which should be retained as divine are those which throw light upon our disquiet and on our human condition in general.

The rule thus formulated is the fruit of long reflection upon the only possible conception of the Word, of God's activity. We must first give our account of that conception.

We have been told that the reality the Scriptures offer the believer is the very action of God and his intervention in history in order to announce to man simultaneously his condemnation and his pardon. Now Bultmann adds that the annunciatory action, or Word, of God has and can have nothing in common with the revelation of a doctrine, with the communication of eternal truths for the benefit of an impersonal and contemplative reason: it is a summons addressed to the concrete man, a summons whose acceptance through faith makes the believer a new creature, by raising him to his authentic existence.

That much arises in the first place from a faithful reading of both the Old and the New Testaments. While the Greco-hellenistic practice is to consider in the oracle, the inspired logos, above all the content of the thought it expresses and its non-temporal meaning (to the neglect of its character as an *Anrede*, a historical and personal summons or interpellation), Scripture, taken as a whole, sees the Word as a force, as a creative event: 'The Word of God is God, not

God in his inaccessible majesty but God making himself
sensible and present to man, God calling man to the existence before him and limiting him with his sovereign im-
peratives. The Word of God is not a theology, neither a
doctrine of God and the world nor a θεωρία, a contemplation of the divine in detachment from the external world;
but it is God's restoration of man to his rightful setting and
man's taking-up of his position before God; it is a divine
order and summons, raising human "existence" up out of
the void—in isolation from this order man does not "exist",
he collapses. To obey this Word is to live; not to heed it is
to be already dead.'[1]

But in Bultmann this conception of the Word is also inspired by certain *a priori* principles relatively foreign to
biblical reading.[2] He is of the opinion that one should reject any speculative doctrine of God, whether of his activity
or of his intrinsic entity, for the reason that any such doctrine, in its objectivized and universal form, betrays its
object, reducing the God of whom it speaks to a reality of
this world. Bultmann seems to think that speculative reason
has no other valid function than the scientific interpretation of the universe. Hence, if it is to this reason that you
entrust the development of theology, if you allot it the task
of expressing for example the divine omnipotence or omniscience, it will give you a concept of these 'attributes' of
God which no longer makes any qualitative difference between them and merely human power and wisdom—there
would seem to remain nothing but a purely quantitative

[1] Passage quoted from 'Der Begriff des Wortes Gottes im Neuen
Testament' (1933) in *GV* I, pp. 268-293.

[2] Speaking very generally, Bultmann's thought makes a simultaneous
advance along two lines, scriptural exegesis and the *philosophical* study
of the human being's theological demands. It is his constant concern
that the substantial identity of their results should be apparent, and
he fortifies one with the other, as we have occasion to see with respect
to his conception of the Word. This situation renders it difficult not
merely to criticize but even to give an exposition of Bultmann's theology, as R. Marlé, *op. cit.*, p. 77, and H. Fries, *op. cit.*, p. 129, have
already remarked. It is impossible in a brief survey not to emphasize
one element at the expense of the other.

difference between God and man.[1] Generally speaking, no sooner does speculative reason take hold of the transcendent than it degrades it to the immanent and constructs a system of purely this-worldly representations of God both in his essence and in his activity.

Alternatively, Bultmann adds in support of his rejection of a speculative theology the following (philosophical) argument: 'Where the idea of God is effectively thought, it signifies that God is the All-powerful, that is to say the reality which determines all things. Now this idea is not effectively thought . . . if I envisage God as an object of thought before which it would be legitimate to take the point of view of an impartial observer . . .'.[2]

This means that from the moment man adopts towards God a neutral, detached attitude, divorced from the obedience of faith, from the moment he judges this to be a legitimate attitude, he ceases by reason of that very judgment to confess and know the divine omnipotence—he removes himself from its domain. Moreover, any formulation of universal propositions concerning a reality presupposes the possibility of a viewpoint external to that reality. But there could never be a viewpoint external to God: can one conceive a region of being which would be alien to him and from which it would be legitimate to contemplate him?

While refusing to be subsumed under the categories of speculative reason, God's activity declines no less firmly to be classed with the phenomena of nature and history. At this point Bultmann condemns the theory whereby the supernatural is presumed to make an incursion into our terrestrial world and there to produce sensible effects (miracles) in order to render itself accessible to our powers of observation, or to raise up heroes or saints through whom its own divine essence shines as through a transparency. Many are the religions which make use of such a mythical interpretation of God's activity, and Christianity itself succumbs over and over again to the temptation of conferring

[1] B. II, pp. 184, 185, n. 1.
[2] Cf. 'Welchen Sinn hat es von Gott zu reden?' (1925) in *GV* I, p. 26.

a similar mythologizing significance on the fact of Christ. But we ought to understand once and for all that by so doing we again degrade the transcendent to the level of the immanent and that by assimilating it to natural forces we have ceased to conceive it in its purity. Moreover, by persisting in the desire to impose these conceptions of the miraculous and of God's alleged supernatural action in the phenomenal world, Christianity incurs the just refusal of the man of to-day, the man in whom scientific thought has definitively inculcated the idea of a world governed exclusively by its own laws.[1]

After all these negations how then, positively, are we to conceive the action of God? If God withholds communication from 'reason in general', it follows that he will reveal himself only to the concrete and *existentiel* subject: his Word will take the form of an interpellation, i.e. a supreme summons addressed to our free-will and personal choice. God calls upon us to accept, in the obscurity of faith and with no proofs valid for an impersonal reason, his absolute sovereignty over our life. At the same time he gives us to understand that in that acceptance, in that decision in his favour—and only therein—we lift ourselves up to our authentic existence. And we see at once that God will not reveal himself to us in that way without at the same time revealing ourselves to ourselves: not only acknowledging God as Lord, do we thereby acknowledge our absolute dependence, but learning that there is neither truth nor authenticity for us outside our receiving of God in faith, we see simultaneously disclosed to us our condition as inauthentic beings, as creatures condemned to sin so long as they fail to heed the call of God, and thus also our condition as creatures forgiven in responding to that call. This all amounts to saying that in revealing himself as Lord, God reveals himself also as our judge and liberator and reveals us to ourselves as creatures at once lost and saved. That explains Bultmann's

[1] The foregoing is a résumé of Bultmann's objection to the mythologizing conception of Christianity. See B. I, pp. 16ff.; cf. ET, *KM*, pp. 3ff., and B. II, pp. 180ff.

insistence on the necessarily existential and anthropological character of any possible divine revelation: over and over again he asserts that God cannot be comprehended save within a relation throwing light on my own condition, that the believer cannot talk of God without at the same time talking of himself, and that finally the divine action cannot be effectively accomplished within me without bringing me a new understanding of myself.[1]

This positive conception of the action of God involves several consequences. First of all it re-affirms Bultmann's condemnation of speculative theology. If I can know God only in his manner of being towards me, that is as judge and liberator, it is as much as to say that God cannot reveal himself in his essence and intrinsicality; herein lies yet another condemnation of the vanity and illusion of theoretical theology—that false Christian theology, of Greek inspiration, which discourses of the essence and attributes of God as if God could be reached outside his relation to the creature he condemns and yet graciously pardons.[2]

But the most important thing is that this view of the divine action permits us, in Bultmann's opinion, fully to accomplish our purpose of establishing, let us remember,

[1] *GV*, I, p. 28. In his *Jesus* (1926), pp. 89 and 90, Bultmann writes: 'It is not in the enunciation of abstract truths or doctrinal maxims that Jesus speaks of God, but solely in speaking of the ways of God to man, his action towards man. . . . Thus Jesus does not bring knowledge of a new concept of God, any more than revelations concerning his essence, but he brings the message of the will of God and of his coming kingdom. He speaks of God by speaking of man and by showing man that he has come to the eleventh hour, confronted by the decisive choice, and that God is addressing to his will a supreme summons.' Cf. also B. I, p. 27, ET, *KM*, p. 16; B. II, p. 200, ET, *KM*, pp. 201-202.

[2] Here one might make a profitable juxtaposition of Bultmann's thought and a study by Father K. Rahner, S.J., 'Theos im Neuen Testament' (*Schriften zur Theologie*, I, 1954, pp. 91-169). Father Rahner shows that in reality the decisive question about God to which the New Testament provides an answer is the following: How does God conduct himself towards man—what are the attitudes (*Haltungen*) to man which he chooses to adopt? But the author takes care to add that even so the Scriptures do not pass over the metaphysical properties of God: they are manifested to man in the freely-chosen history of the salvation.

the critical rule of biblical hermeneutics: since God can reveal himself only in his relation to our human condition, the only propositions of the Bible's message which may be accepted as divine are those which, while making statements about God, make statements also about ourselves and enlighten our understanding of our existence. These too will alone oblige faith to accept them: the believer will therefore retain, from his reading of the Scriptures, only the 'possibilities' they offer him of coming to a better understanding of himself before God. All the rest will be in his eyes no more than vain speculation or outworn mythology.[1]

To sum up: Bultmann's rule of biblical hermeneutics seems to present two aspects. One must meet the text halfway with a certain natural understanding of the condition of man before God (the psychological aspect), and one must retain only those elements of the scriptural message which help us to deepen and amplify that primary understanding (the critical aspect).

This rule is intended to govern all reading of the Bible, whether of an everyday or of a scientific kind.

Let us first consider everyday reading. The following is equally true for the simple hearing of the Christian Word. Both assume in the reader or auditor the wish to gain through faith a certain understanding of his existence. Since for the auditor it is a question of confessing, under the impact of the Word, his sin and God's pardoning grace, he must possess beforehand a kind of confused awareness of his plight and dereliction, lacking which awareness he would fail to see in God's Word revealing his sinful condition the answer to an expectation formed in the depth of his being. He would fail to understand that the confession demanded of him corresponds to certain possibilities of his existence; he would fail to grasp its force and human truth. In consequence therefore the Word would not distress him, not disturb him, and he would not in rejecting it be guilty of

[1] *GV* I, p. 28; II, p. 233, ET, *Essays*, p. 259; B. II, p. 196, ET, *KM*, pp. 196-197.

disloyalty.[1] In saying this Bultmann is doing no more than summing up the proof of his psychological rule. But, he adds, every man carries within himself this awareness of the wretchedness of existence, as is requisite for any hearing of the Word (thus for any 'faithwise' reading of Scripture, even if pre-scientific);[2] there is an understanding of existence (*Existenzverständnis*) which is given with existence itself;[3] of course, it is not given in a reflective or analytic but only in an experiential sense—this circumstance certainly impedes a little the *facility* of the act of faith; thus the preacher of the Word will do well to arouse in the auditor a reflective consciousness of his human condition, to help him to feel reflectively his wretchedness, thus putting him in a position to discern within himself the point of entry of the divine forgiveness and of the Resurrection; however, the mere exercise of the primary understanding of existence will, strictly speaking, suffice to render faith *possible*, as it will suffice to enable the Bible to be read 'pre-scientifically' with profit by a believer.[4]

Scientific reading or exegesis is governed by the same rule, with the proviso that the prerequisite understanding should here be analytic and reflective. In other words the exegetic scholar should read texts in the light of the concepts and categories furnished by existential analytics.[5] Or to put it another way, the exegete should call upon the resources of a previously elaborated existential analytics and translate the content of the message into the explicit categories of existence. This point is easily demonstrated: by definition scientific differs from everyday exegesis in that it sifts out with the utmost rigour and precision those biblical propositions which enlighten us about our own existence, in that it shows in a considered manner how these propositions help us towards an understanding of our human condition. But how could this task be attempted if we did not possess

[1] B. I, p. 124.
[2] B. II, p. 189: 'ein vorwissenschaftliches Verständnis der Schrift'.
[3] B. II, pp. 189, 191, 192.
[4] GV II, p. 232, ET, *Essays*, p. 258; B. II, p. 189.
[5] B. III, p. 53.

beforehand a certain already elaborated understanding of ourselves, if we had not the benefit of all the illumination which an existential analytics can throw upon the fundamental structures of *Dasein*? A certain considered interpretation of existence is therefore indispensable to the exegete from the very beginning of his investigation. And the aim of his investigation will be precisely to show that the message of the Bible extends the natural structures of existence or, much more exactly, that whatever is novel in this message may successfully be translated and formulated in the categories, the expressive concepts, of our existence.[1] For we must accept that the message does offer something novel, presents, that is to say, a content which biblical hermeneutics in no way expects from existential analytics: the saving act of God through Christ. The only service which the exegete asks of existential analytics is this, that it should provide him with the categories of existence, devoid of any speculative or mythological element, without which the expression of the biblical message would not be worthy of our faith.

Hereby, it must be admitted, exegesis, and therewith Christian theology, is placed in dependence on a philosophy. But this is in no way unacceptable. For the philosophy in question is not a system, not an organized ensemble of answers given by reason as to the meaning of existence. It is not even a doctrine defining a content, a material ideal. Being nothing more than the clear and methodical rendering explicit of the understanding of existence exercised in existence itself, existential analytics does not teach us how we ought to exist (i.e. it propounds no ethics), it offers us no more than a form, no more than the categories exercised by *Dasein* in its own self-contained position.[2]

[1] *GV* II, p. 232, ET, *Essays*, p. 258; B. II, p. 194, ET, *KM*, p. 195.
[2] B. II, pp. 189 and 192, ET, *KM*, p. 193. See also the article 'Die Geschichtlichkeit des Daseins und der Glaube' in *Zeitschrift für Theologie und Kirche*, Vol. XI, 1930, pp. 339-364 (not reproduced in *GV*). The first part of this article is of special interest: Bultmann sets out his views on the relations between philosophy and theology, and distinguishes between the *existential* and the *existentiel*: philosophy knows only the formal structures of *Dasein* and not the materials which may fill

We must now proceed to ask Bultmann what, according to him, are these fundamental structures of *Dasein* revealed by existential analytics. For our present limited purpose, which is to set forth the conditions on which Bultmann would have biblical hermeneutics practised, it will suffice to draw attention to two elements of his answer. One of

them; of course philosophy determines whether and on what conditions there may appear in *Dasein* something such as a love, its acceptance or rejection, or even something such as a faith, but for all that it does not take as an object of inquiry a concrete, specific affirmation of love. Similarly it is philosophy which provides the conceptual equipment necessary for the rational expression of relations such as 'message', 'word', 'summons', but it is unable to elucidate for us the meaning of a given message, hence of the Christian message. Theology on the other hand presupposes the fact of a precise and concrete summons and is addressed only to those who hear God's Word, whose significance it develops for them. This distinction may be translated into conventional language by saying that the theme of philosophy is what is *existential* or ontological, while that of theology is what is *existentiel* or ontic. But this distinction does not prevent the *existentiel* attention to God's Word from being related to philosophy's *existential* structures in exactly the same way as matter is related to form; in a general way every basic Christian concept must correspond to an ontologically definable constituent of *Dasein*. For example, the Christian concept of sin (*aversio a Deo*) corresponds to our Being's dereliction and sickness-unto-death as evinced in Heidegger's existential analytics, and if the first elucidates the second, since it determines it, it must be said that the second in turn throws light upon the first, for without an awareness of the existential character of our sorry plight, we could not see that confession of fault (as demanded by Christian faith) is rightly demanded of us—we could reject it without disloyalty to man, without any culpable infidelity. Here we rediscover the two functions of the rule of hermeneutics: 1. The clearer my perception of the structures of *Dasein* (e.g. Heidegger's *Verfallenheit*), the more penetrating will be my understanding of Christian concepts—this is the psychological function; 2. The touchstone of a Christian concept's authenticity will be its correspondence with some existential structure of *Dasein*; any concept devoid of correspondence is certainly not the Word of God, not that Word which, since it calls upon man, can only concern in him what constitutes him existentially. One may go so far as to say that Bultmann's whole exegetic and theological effort is directed to this end: to show how and wherein Christian theology corresponds to the existential structures of *Dasein*. He does not consider there is anything blasphemous in this endeavour, for to demonstrate the correspondence of the divine event is not to deduce it rationally.

(The author refers the reader to a French translation of Bultmann's article in O. Laffoucrière, *Bultmann, L'Interprétation du Nouveau Testament*, Paris, 1955, pp. 114-138.)

them is stressed by the existential analytics of Heidegger's school, which is where Bultmann derives his results:[1] among the Greeks man used to understand himself as one nature (φύσις) among others, as a part of the grand cosmos, organically incorporated into the objective totality of the world, and as objectively offered to his own (speculative) contemplation, exactly like the other objects of nature. But this manner of objectifying *Dasein*, of likening it to 'beings', of taking it to be a '*Vorhandensein*', a 'some kind of being-present', and of referring to it in terms of an essentialist philosophy, embodied a misconception of one of the characteristics which existential analytics (a pure application of phenomenological method to the interpretation of existence) reveals in *Dasein* with the utmost clarity: openness to the totality of being, the constant anticipation which leads to a venturing beyond every particular object, the 'capacity for asking oneself the question of total being'—in a word, transcendence: the process whereby *Dasein* 'raises itself above the chaos of primitive existents' (by uniting them in the totality of the world) and at the same time asserts itself as an 'ipseity'.[2]

In referring us to this first result of existential analytics and in opposing it to the Greek conception, Bultmann has the special intention of putting us on our guard against the tendency to 'thingism' ('*chosisme*'), the tendency 'to think of *Dasein* as a closed reality, one blocked up within itself'[3] and to express it in terms of stable and permanent substantiality. In this way he prepares us to accept the second feature of his conception of *Dasein*, a feature which he is most anxious to emphasize: man's being is essentially historical, the 'historically existing *I*'.

---

[1] Cf. 'Das Verständnis von Welt und Mensch im Neuen Testament und im Griechentum' (1940), *GV* II, pp. 59-78, especially p. 63; ET, 'The Understanding of Man and the World in the New Testament and the Greek World', *Essays*, pp. 67-89, especially p. 74. See also *GV* I, pp. 129ff.; *GV* II, p. 243, ET, pp. 269-270.

[2] Expressions borrowed from A. De Waelhens, *La Philosophie de Martin Heidegger*, Louvain, 1940, p. 255.

[3] *Ibid.*, p. 40.

'Historical' here is a translation not of *historisch* but of *geschichtlich*. Heidegger's analytics distinguishes a double history and a double reality: there is one history (*Historie*) which sets forth and expounds objects (*Gegenstände*) in the same way as nature—objects interlinked in phenomenal causality and ascertainable by impartial and scientific observation, which they precede and to which they are given. But there is another quite different history, *Geschichte*: in this we are concerned with *Dasein*, with that human Being about which we already know that it is not to be ranked with 'beings', with 'objects', and of which we mean to say, when we call it essentially *geschichtlich*, that since it has nothing in common with a nature, a given, ready-made thing, it exists only through making itself in a free decision.[1] This decision is taken in confrontation of the Being which encounters the human Being existentielly: the human Being personalizes itself only in intersubjectivity and in responding to the challenge of a second person: this second person comes to him not in the mode of natural objects (which address only our rational, neutral and speculative faculties, only scientific or 'general' reason) but in the very special mode of objectivity of *existentiel* encounters, as in appeals of love, friendship, trust. . . .[2] It would be difficult to exaggerate the exclusively act-wise character of the decision. One may go so far as to say that man realizes himself in action, and even in will, on condition, however, that by the latter word is meant not 'a faculty of the soul which rules its choices . . . in terms of dispositions supposedly anterior to it',[3] but solely the choice made at a given instant in total independence of a past determining it in any degree. Neither is the authen-

[1] *GV* I, pp. 117ff.; pp. 129ff. See, on this distinction between *Historie* and *Geschichte*, A. Vogtle, 'Die Entmythologisierung des Neuen Testaments als Forderung einer zeitgemässen Theologie und Verkündigung' in *Die geistige Situation unserer Zeit in den Einzelwissenschaften* (*Freiburger Dies Universitatis*, Vol. 4), 1956, pp. 24ff.

[2] On Bultmann's view of intersubjectivity, see the article 'Das christliche Gebot der Nächstenliebe' (1930), *GV* I, pp. 229-244, especially pp. 231 and 235. Cf. also B. II, pp. 199-201, ET, *KM*, pp. 202-203. On the objectivity proper to *existentiel* encounters, cf. pp. 97ff. above.

[3] R. Marlé, *op. cit.*, p. 95.

ticity of man to be found in the sum of the constituents of his psychological personality. In describing the essential features of Kierkegaard's notion of existence, it has been said that this notion is characterized 'by the absolute refusal to see in man *a reality susceptible of definition*'; 'the essence of human existence is to be entirely in the hands of him who exists by that existence. Man's being will be what man makes it, and it will be that alone.' 'Existence is not only free, subjective and able to choose, it is *freedom, subjectivity, ability to choose*. Thereby we know already that subjective existence could not be a state, a stable situation furnished with a definite constitution, but that it must establish itself as a discontinuous *succession* of acts.'[1] These words, the last especially, render exactly the thought of Bultmann himself:[2] for him too there is no human substantiality, no nature, not even any continuity in authentic existence. He also believes that to express *Dasein* one must abandon all the categories of essentialist ontology; one must say of the historical human Being, in conformity with the determinations of *existential* ontology, which alone are adapted to its expression, that it is verified only in the instantaneous present reality of *existentiel* decisions.[3]

[1] De Waelhens, *op. cit.*, pp. 331, 332.

[2] There is nothing surprising in this resemblance to Kierkegaard: Bultmann underwent the influence of the Danish philosopher, at least via works of dialectical theology, which he at one time supported. Cf. the Note at the end of this article.

[3] *GV* I, p. 132: 'The self is not considered (by St Paul) as something isolated and isolable, first given, then touched by the summons of God, but it is what it is, a self, only within that summons of God which reaches out to touch it. Man's unity therefore does not consist in a substance, nor in the organized totality of a psychic process (of a soul) intelligible to psychology, nor in the continuity of a rationally intelligible development (of a mind or spirit, in the Hegelian sense). Rather it must be considered as a *geschichtlich* unity, i.e. one established by the fact that man is claimed by a Thou (*von einem Du beansprucht*) (is summoned by God as by its Lord). Man's Being is (therefore) not envisaged (by St Paul) under the categories of a nature or a substance, but it is realized in accordance with its conduct in relation to God's summons; one can say that it is realized in its *action*, provided that this "action" is understood not as a process worked out in time, like the functioning of a mechanism, but as the fruit of a responsible

And so it is into these structures of existence, and the other Heideggerian structures derived therefrom, that Bultmann will attempt to introduce the expression of the act of God and, in more general terms, the relation of man to God in Christ, as it is conveyed to us through the message of the Bible.

The outcome of such a re-interpretation will be to remove from the event of Christ, in its aspect of salvation, any character as an event in nature, in the world of objects, and of conferring on it that kind of objectivity which only *existentiel* encounters possess: God does not approach us through consecrated physical realities nor through signs or miracles woven into the texture of our phenomenal world; he simply summons from within us, when we are listening to the Christian Word, the purely *existentiel* decision of faith. For such an interpretation the Johannine and Pauline realities, for example, of *sarx* and *pneuma* will assume a concrete form as follows: When John writes 'what is born of flesh is flesh; what is born of spirit is spirit', we shall take care not to interpret these two terms in categories of physical matter (in the case of flesh), and of divine substance or force acting in the manner of a natural force (in the case of spirit); moreover John himself, who has already begun the process of demythologization, does not understand them in this way, for '*sarx* designates rather the nothingness of the total human Being, the condition of a man grown to complete alienation from both his destiny and his own action, a man who, in his present situation, is not in his authentic Being, quite apart from whether he is aware of it or hides the fact from himself. Likewise *pneuma* designates the miraculous manner of Being of a man who finds himself to be

decision. And thereby one sees that man's Being is not at his disposal (like a thing), since that Being is (entirely) at risk in every "present moment", since, according to Paul, it is (at every instant) subject to the possibility of being determined either by God or by sin.' Bultmann claims to find this way of regarding man in St Paul, but it is easy to see that it was inspired in him by Heidegger's philosophy, whose influence, in 1928, the date of the text, he was beginning to accept, and that in this case St Paul is being read through Heidegger's spectacles.

authentic, who understands himself and knows he is no longer threatened with nothingness.'[1]

For the rest, it is not our purpose here to garner the results of applying existential analytics to the interpretation of the Christian message. Since it has been our aim to do no more than set out Bultmann's ideas on the principles of biblical hermeneutics, it is enough that we have shown how he justifies the use of existential analytics in scientific scriptural exegesis and what major categories this analytics places at his disposal at the outset of his exegetic work. In conformity with the above-noted distinction between the psychological and critical aspects of the rule of hermeneutics, these categories of existence will perform a double duty for the exegete: by rendering explicit the natural understanding of the human condition they will place him in a better position to grasp the meaning of the divine message addressed to man (the psychological function); but they will also permit him to determine with great precision which biblical propositions are of value for faith: only those who succeed in finding expression within the Heideggerian categories of existence will deserve the acceptance of belief (this is the critical function).

This, then, is how Bultmann's hermeneutics appears to us. And even at this stage we feel that if serious criticisms may be levelled against this hermeneutics, they will apply less to the principle of existential analytics (and the very general assertion of its necessity in scriptural exegesis) than to the inadequacy of the human structures at which this—specifically Heideggerian—analytics has arrived.

Nevertheless, this is not the opinion of Karl Barth, with which we have now to deal. It will be seen that Barth confronts Bultmann's hermeneutics with a criticism striking at its roots, since it rejects the very idea that a philosophy of any kind can underlie exegesis as an absolute norm.[2]

[1] *Das Evangelium des Johannes*, Göttingen, 1952, p. 100.
[2] Barth's most explicit criticism of Bultmann's hermeneutics is contained within *Rudolf Bultmann, Ein Versuch ihn zu verstehen*, Zürich, 1953.

II

If we are to gauge the full extent and depth of Barth's criticism of Bultmann, we must take as the starting-point for our comprehension Barth's fundamental intuition, which completely explains this criticism. As is generally known, Barth's theology is dominated by the idea of the absolute lordship of Christ. This lordship is more than merely ontic (Jesus being the alpha and omega, the origin and end of all reality): if Barth's Christocentricity were limited to this affirmation it would agree in substance with Catholic Christocentric theologies. But it is intended to affirm considerably more: it claims that Christ's lordship is just as much noetic, and perhaps is principally so. This is the feature we have to stress. 'All the treasures of wisdom and knowledge are hidden in him' (Col. 2.3): in him alone are we enlightened concerning God and our condition in relation to God; there is no revelation save that of the Word of God incarnate in Jesus. 'Our only possibility of knowing God resides in the fact that he is ready to make himself known and that he reveals himself personally to us in Christ.'[1] What if we spoke differently? What if we stopped thinking that faith began with the Holy Spirit, that therein lay our only possibility of receiving and responding to Jesus Christ, and what if we were to say, with Roman Catholic and neo-Protestant theology—and with Bultmann himself—that there exists a source of knowing God which is independent of his Word, and that God is given to us somewhere else in feelings, in consciousness or in history? Suppose our next step were to ascribe to this natural theology some kind of rôle as a *Vorverständnis* in the genesis of faith? Then by the same token we would have set man up as master of truth and criterion of the Word itself; by incorporating the

[1] J. de Senarclens, 'La Concentration christologique' in *Antwort, Karl Barth: Zum siebzigsten Geburtstag am 10 Mai, 1956*, Zürich, 1956, p. 203. Offprints of this article have appeared under the title *Remède de cheval*, Geneva, 1956 (this quotation from p. 34). It contains quotations or *résumés* of those passages in Barth's *Dogmatik* which most emphasize the Christocentricity of his theology.

Word into a more or less balanced religious system we
would have deprived it of its character, so plainly attested
in the Bible, as a free, great and, above all, sovereign principle. Just as Jesus Christ is the source and end of all creation, so he is also the absolute master of our thought: he
calls on us to admit the total poverty of our mind, to submit
unconditionally our judgments to his judgments and pro-
mises, and to refuse to interpret or supplement his Word
with elements borrowed from any other source.

It is in the light of this fundamental principle of his theology that Barth takes Bultmann to task. One feels in advance that his indignant criticism will have more bearing
on the very principles of Bultmann's hermeneutics than on
its results. Naturally Barth will not neglect to express his
explicit opposition to a number of theses in Bultmann's
theology, notably the demand for total demythologization
and the Bultmannian interpretation of the Resurrection.
But it is Barth's opinion that these individual theses are implicit in their originator's hermeneutics, that they arise as
its inevitable consequences. Not without reason, he sees the
first problem set by Bultmann's theology to be in fact that
of hermeneutics. The first thing to be disputed, he declares,
is the demand which Bultmann makes of the Word: the
demand that it should correspond to, in general, a *Vorverständnis* and, in particular, to the Heideggerian view of
existence; thence it is, as from a disobedience to God's
Word, that a theology has arisen which is gravely compromised and in which the message is no longer recognizable.

In his work, *Rudolf Bultmann, Ein Versuch ihn zu verstehen*,
Barth gives this criticism of principle, thus baldly stated,
the following elaborated form: The problem of hermeneutics
is a problem of understanding, of comprehension of a text;
and for the believer, the problem of biblical hermeneutics is
the problem of understanding the texts of the New Testament wherein the content of his faith is set forth. Now can
one really think, as Bultmann does, that the understanding
of these texts is conditional upon some hypothesis of an
immutable representation (*Vorstellung*), to be considered as

a norm of faith; upon the presence in the reader of an infused image (*eines gegossenen Bildes*) of what is in itself possible, exact, important, intelligible; upon the possession of some consecrated *Vorverständnis*?[1] If my reasoning powers cannot lead me to belief, how could they lead me to understanding? Let us not forget that to understand the message of the New Testament is to understand the Word of God attested in that message. But this Word is fundamentally alien to man and man's thoughts; there is no hope of comprehension through elements not furnished by the illumination of the Holy Spirit.

But, one might protest, there does exist a rational understanding subsequent to revelation and faith. Of course, replies Barth,—but this understanding is always inadequate, and to the extent of its inadequacy is moreover always a setback.

But surely, one might protest again, when we are confronted with the texts of the New Testament it is impossible for us not to apply to them certain *Vorverständnisse*: we are obliged to read them in the light of a certain notion of the limits of what is 'possible' and 'intelligible', and we cannot but reject anything presented which transgresses these limits and require the texts to comply with the demands of our *a priori* assumptions.[2]

To this Barth had already replied in the *Dogmatik*, in a context external to the Bultmann controversy. At that time Barth acknowledged—and he continues to acknowledge it to-day—that it is not in fact possible to approach the Scriptures without 'assuming them subjectively', without bringing to bear a certain philosophy, a certain way of comprehending divine and human realities, in however 'commonplace, eclectic and superficial' a way.[3] 'When we read the Bible, we make use—as on any occasion—of a certain intellectual schema, which serves as a key.' 'There is no one of whom

[1] *Rudolf Bultmann, Ein Versuch ihn zu verstehen*, p. 48.
[2] *Ibid.*, p. 49.
[3] The quotation, and those that follow, are taken from Barth's *Die kirchliche Dogmatik*, I, 2, Zürich, 1945, pp. 816ff., ET, *Church Dogmatics*, I, 2, Edinburgh, 1956, pp. 728ff.

it can be said that he does not adulterate the Gospel with some philosophy, for there is no one of whom it can be said that he is here and now free of all sin otherwise than through faith.' And as if speaking to himself, Barth adds: 'We must also recognize that we ourselves are in subjection to our own ideas and that we are therefore in a poor position to throw stones. Let us beware of taking up arms in a conflict where one philosophy will be opposed only by another, a conflict which as such will have not the slightest connexion with the quest for a right understanding of the Scriptures. Let us begin by paying heed to what our supposed adversaries, making use of their *a priori* understandings, believe they may affirm objectively—that is, as scriptural commentators.'[1]

But if it is inevitable and normal that we should read the Scriptures through the medium of a philosophical prism, it is none the less necessary that the use of the prism should be subject to strict rules. In the first place we will not forget for a moment that our intellectual schema 'differs by definition from that which characterizes the message of the Bible' and that our mental habits have not 'as such the power to bring us to understanding' that message. 'We will keep in mind the qualitative distance subsisting between the thought of the Bible, which always precedes us, and our own thought, determined by some philosophy or other.' Thus our thought will always 'follow in the wake of that of the Bible, not of its own nature, but by virtue of an act of obedience—the act of obedience of the believer who dares to place himself totally in the hands of God's grace'.[2]

Secondly, the methodical and submissive use of the prism will never have, in itself, more than a tentative character. It is for the Word of God to decide what is to become 'of my intellectual categories, in revealing to what extent they will be useful or not to the explanation of Scripture; their usefulness will appear only in the light of the object set before them'. Grace, and grace alone, may properly and freely decide 'which intellectual co-ordinates will prove

[1] *Loc. cit.*
[2] *Loc. cit.*

useful and provide points of reference for the processes of our reflection'. It is the text of the Bible, or, better, the object it reflects, which decides whether our reflection is just or pertinent.

Already we have then, in the foregoing, the implication that one should refrain from setting up any intellectual categories as absolutes; since, as we have seen, our intellectual *schemata* do not possess 'the power of leading us to a comprehension and direct interpretation of the text', it follows that we cannot ascribe to them an *independent* rôle, nor therefore consider ourselves bound to them as much as to Scripture. If we were to do so, the man within us 'stands before the Word of God as a *second* God; he dominates it and disposes of it, thus eliminating the real God. He arrogates the right to discuss the text of Scripture *inter pares.* . . . Any philosophy set up as an absolute can result only in a falsification of Scripture. For the act of setting up as an absolute what is manifestly of human provenance is an act of unbelief, rendering impossible the knowledge proper to faith and excluding in consequence a right explanation of the Scriptures.'[1] Not that it is necessary 'to reduce philosophy to the rank of *ancilla theologiae*' or 'ascribe to theology a power it has not and never will have'. The truth is that both are servants of the same object, the Word of God, which measures and limits them both alike. 'Given that Holy Scripture alone possesses ultimate sovereignty and authority, there can be no "conflict of prestige" between the two disciplines.'[2]

One final rule: we will avoid thinking that any given intellectual *schema* possesses in itself qualities which accord it a preference over any other for the understanding of the Bible: 'It is always in a specific situation that this or that way of thinking may reveal its usefulness for the explanation of Scripture, and if it is to recommend itself at all it will do so at that particular moment.' At the very least we will take care not to elevate 'a purely particular postulate into

[1] *Loc. cit.*
[2] *Loc. cit.*

a universally valid general law', as if one had to interpret the Bible 'from one sole intellectual viewpoint, as if that viewpoint were a norm for all occasions and situations. The Word of God demonstrates its freedom in the fact that it has the constant power of regularly confounding all the norms that one seeks to apply to it, by suddenly acquiring a new and clearer significance—and that within the frame of a philosophy which perhaps will place it at the opposite pole from the one that was going to be made into a general law. No philosophical interpretation of reality could be proposed or dictated to us as constituting the normal form of pre-comprehension of the Word of God'. How indeed 'could one propose a philosophy as being the philosophy *par excellence*, how could one confer on it the character of a general law, without setting it up as an absolute, that is without thereby violating and falsifying the Word of God?' 'There is scarcely any human system which is not *dangerous* for the explanation of Scripture, but at the same time there is scarcely any which God's Word has not the power of using and making fruitful.' That is why 'I will admit that philosophies other than mine may in the event serve as hypotheses worthy of attention, and I will be ready to take into account their contribution to hermeneutics'. That is also why 'we have good reason to take an interest in the history of philosophy. Nevertheless we will not be so simple as to believe that the key to the problem of biblical interpretation is to be found in the frame of that history; we do not expect it to provide us with a hermeneutic method adequate to the Word of God, with a universally valid and necessary system which, because it wields of itself a kind of *potentia oboedientialis*, exempts us from the audacity of obedience. We may expect nothing in that direction from philosophy because, according to the Bible, we have nothing in that direction to expect from man. It is not for man to fix the rules which will permit reflection adequate to the Word of God attested in the text of the Bible.'[1]

In short, the unconditional noetic sovereignty of God's Word

[1] All *op. cit.*, pp. 278-280, ET, pp. 255-257.

in Christ involves two major consequences for our various intellectual *schemata*: on one hand the Word forbids their elevation into absolutes; on the other, that same Word is available to them all upon occasion, and does not allow its content to be imprisoned within the categories of any one among them.

In those pages of the *Dogmatics* where he sets forth his own hermeneutical principles Barth had implicitly rejected in advance the totality of Bultmann's hermeneutics. In *Rudolf Bultmann, Ein Versuch ihn zu verstehen,* where he puts his rejection into explicit terms, he has no need to do more than recall the broad outlines of his *exposé.* Bultmann, it will be remembered, asked if it were possible for us not to impose our *Vorverständnisse* on the New Testament, or to read its text other than in the light of our preconceptions of what is possible and intelligible. In answer to which Barth remarks: of course we all bring to the reading of the Bible a number of rational views to which we are tempted to subject the Word. But this is the temptation to disobey God himself. We have no authority to set against the unfamiliar element of the Word a normative *Vorverständnis,* an absolute 'thus far and no farther'. More particularly, we may not oppose to it a natural anthropology, an image of man and the world, and reduce it to the requirements of that anthropology. We have of course to examine the message for its anthropological content, since it has as its object an event happening between God and man; but we betray it as soon as we relegate to a secondary plane the event of Christ, which in itself is primary and principal, to the advantage of what in itself is no more than secondary: the understanding of man's condition.[1] *A fortiori* we break faith with it when we compare it with the natural conception of man and retain only what corresponds to that. Let us then cease arguing with the Word, on the basis of 'elements of the world' ($\sigma\tau o\iota\chi\epsilon\hat{\iota}\alpha$ $\tau o\hat{\upsilon}$ $\kappa\acute{o}\sigma\mu o\upsilon$, Col. 2.8), about whether and to what extent natural man can or cannot understand the New Testament.[2] Immediately one interposes between

---

[1] *Rudolf Bultmann, Ein Versuch ihn zu verstehen,* p. 40.
[2] *Ibid.,* p. 49.

oneself and the Word a *sine qua non* drawn from human intellectual *schemata*, one deprives oneself of the possibility of understanding it either as testimony or as message. Instead of donning some kind of philosophical armour the reader who believes should ensure that he has the greatest openness and suppleness of mind. Instead of setting up what he considers his 'comprehension-power' (intelligibility defined *a priori*) as a 'catalyst' of the New Testament, he should allow the text of the New Testament to act as the 'catalyst' of his power of comprehension. Let us not forget Luther's warning: '*sacrae literae volunt habere humilem lectorem qui reverenter habet et tremit sermones Dei, (lectorem) qui semper dicit: Doce me! doce me! Superbis resistit spiritus.*' There are two dangers lurking in all interpretation of Scripture: one is to fail completely to understand certain truths (or to express them in existential terms which denature them); the second is to express them truly but to mythologize (in Bultmann's sense). The first is certainly the more to be feared.[1]

All the foregoing amounts to saying that biblical hermeneutics does not simply obey the laws of hermeneutics in general, nor is it merely an application or specific case of the latter. On the contrary it has its own laws, for this reason that God's Word may only be interpreted when it is itself taken as the starting-point. Or if we must establish a relationship between general and biblical hermeneutics, we would rather say that the latter is the model (*Vorbild*) and yardstick of the former. If I wish to understand a text, even merely a profane text, should I not approach it with the greatest openness of mind, in a disposition to receive from it a message for which I might be in no way prepared? At the very least, I cannot impose on it the *a priori* defined limits of my *Vorverständnisse*. Now, such suppleness is not to be taken for granted: the reader must train himself to it. And in that respect, where could he receive better training than in reading the Bible, in which the believer lays himself open to the message of grace, an unhoped-for message which confounds all prior attempts at definition? In truth,

[1] *Ibid.*

Bultmann's doctrine of a *Vorverständnis* conceived as an absolute norm, working simultaneously with the Holy Spirit and subjecting it to its laws, 'is the death of all true and right understanding'.[1]

In conclusion Barth remarks, not without bitterness, that Bultmann's hermeneutics represents a return to Liberalism, to that neo-Protestantism of which Barth himself had hoped finally to cure Christian theology. When, thirty years before, 'he set course for other shores' it was his very purpose to overturn the prevailing concept of 'scriptural comprehension' and 'comprehension in general': it was his wish to found 'human knowledge' in 'man's being-known of God', to free the Word of God from all human subjection, to rescue understanding of the Scriptures from the prison in which philosophy after philosophy had deliberately confined it. In a word, Barth wished to restore to the Christian his sense of the sovereignty of God and to teach him anew that man is not the measure of 'comprehension'. In his hermeneutic principles Bultmann reverts to these former errors. And this is the basic mistake which, much more than his weighty denials of the supernatural or his liquidations of Christian dogma, should draw down our disapproval.[2]

As is evident, the burden of Barth's reproach against Bultmann bears upon the demand for some *Vorverständnis* and more particularly upon the demand for an anthropology of some kind. And of course Barth must be seen as uttering no less specific an accusation when he asks: What would become of the message if one were to believe, with Bultmann, that to understand it one has first to put on 'the armour of Heidegger', if one were willing to retain of it only its conception of man as interpreted by this pre-selected philosophy?[3] Hereby Barth perhaps indicates that he thinks the structures of *Dasein* derived by Bultmann from his existential analysis are inadequate even from the philosopher's point of view. However, Barth certainly does not insist on this

---

[1] *Rudolf Bultmann, Ein Versuch ihn zu verstehen*, p. 51.
[2] *Ibid.*, pp. 52 and 53.   [3] *Ibid.*, pp. 38 and 40.

weakness in Bultmann's theology and does not hold it to
be of prime importance: in his eyes Bultmann's major and
decisive error is to subordinate understanding of the message to a normative philosophy of one kind or another, and
thus to make an attempt against the sovereignty of God.

III

My last remark prepares and even ushers in the verdict
which seems to call for pronouncement in this great debate.
Bultmann appears to be in the right when, differing from
Barth, he expresses the necessity for a certain pre-comprehension of man before one may heed the Word or submit the
Bible to a faithful reading. God's Word in Scripture summons man to pledge loyalty and obey. Now as for the pledge
of loyalty the Word demands faith, which is affirmation;
to believe in the Word is to proclaim that Word authentic
and true; but to proclaim the truth of an object is surely
to recognize that it conforms to the norm of truth immanent
in the human mind, or in other terms that it satisfies a demand—a demand that at the least it shall contain no intrinsic
self-contradiction—which is engraved in the mind and dictated *a priori* by it. As for obedience, the Word imposes itself
with imperative force upon man and demands the response
of faith as a duty, as the fulfilment of an obligation; but can
we recognize the obligatory character of a challenge without in some way grasping its conformity to a norm of goodness, likewise prefigured in our mind?

Indeed, in face of the summoning Word man cannot but
give weight to his mind's constituent requirements. He may
not, to be sure, push his demand too far; he may not require the Word to manifest to him the intrinsic possibility
of its contents. On the contrary, we can know in advance
that the Word, in its transcendence, could not comply with
this particular demand, for in the present order of things
our mind is unable to accede to the very being of God, save
through abstract notions of created realities, notions which
never represent the increate in its proper form. For example,
if revelation informs us of the presence in the divine intellect

of a Word which is the end-term of a generation and thereby
subsists as a Person—a filial person—we are unable to grasp
that intellectual generation save through the analogy of, on
the one hand, our own intellectual *verbum* and, on the other,
our ingrown awareness of ourselves as persons. However,
our intellectual *verbum* does not and cannot subsist as a
Person. It follows that in the way of knowing which is ours
we cannot positively apprehend the intrinsic possibility, the
harmony of those two notes: the divine intellectual generation of a personal life. The perception of this internal harmony is necessarily reserved for the mind which knows the
divine essence *in itself*. We may not therefore legitimately
require the revealing Word of God to *conform to our notions*;
we shall on the contrary understand that it will necessarily
preserve its mystery in relation to essentially defective concepts. Thus to deserve the loyal adherence of our minds the
Word ought not to manifest to us its internal truth; similarly,
to deserve our obedience it ought not to show us in what
way it is good in itself. But when that has been said, there
remains a minimal demand which our mind makes upon
the Word: not to appear evidently contradictory, not to be
composed of elements which the mind would declare to be,
logically, exclusive one of another. Let us put it more generally: if the Word does not consent to having the limits of
our concepts imposed on it, it yet willingly *submits to the form
of our first principles*; and it must conform to that law on
penalty of no longer constituting a possible object of affirmation.

No more is needed to enable us to proceed to a further
statement: the Word does not address us without accepting,
indeed asking, that we should submit and refer it to the
structure of our mind, to the affirmations which the mind
'exercises' constitutionally on Being (and also on itself in
its relation to Being)—without accepting that we should
compare it to what man is and to his mind's imprescriptible
demands. Thus a certain natural light on man, a certain
anthropology, not given by the Word, to which it would
be truer to say that the Word subordinates itself, is the

forerunner and basis of our possibility of obediently hearing the Word or faithfully reading the Scriptures. It is true that in each one of us this anthropology exists at the level not of reflexive but of direct knowledge, or has not, at any rate, been made explicit, and that this condition is quite adequate for a non-scientific reading of the Bible, i.e. a reading which does not seek rigorously to analyse the motives of one's interpretations. But when the reader is transformed into an exegete, he is anxious to make that analysis, and for that reason he should endeavour to transfer his understanding of man from the level of direct apprehension to that of analysis and reflection: in other words he must 'think philosophically'.

We are not of course denying that the Word reinforces our natural light and in particular assists the—philosophical—explication of its content. What illumination has not the mind received from the Christian message, concerning the very notions of truth and imperative goodness! (On this last notion the mind receives particular clarification in the light of the Christian views of God and of our destiny, which is the Kingdom.) And so the Christian philosopher should be incessantly watchful to preserve an attitude wherein he is universally at the disposal of the Word, to follow where it leads, refining under its action and correcting where need be the categories he uses to express on the plane of reflection 'the understanding of existence that comes with the gift of existence' (just as the philosopher —albeit for other reasons and in other ways—refines the concepts of his own philosophy in contact with others, and that without detriment to its firmness and without necessarily falling into eclecticism). But this necessary docility of philosophy before the Word cannot prevent the Word's being constantly referred to the (explicit or implicitly known) natural anthropology. What we have here then is, to sum up, a necessity for reciprocal priority and subordination. Every believer reading the Scriptures, and *a fortiori* every exegete, ought to bear this in mind. If the exegete were to approach God's Word with a philosophy hardened in its

203

concepts and expressions before any true contact with the Word (and it may well be thought that certain theologians are not always sufficiently on their guard against this), there would certainly be no *greater* risk of his betraying the Word than there would be of his missing its sense and intention if he were to open the Bible without a previously awakened interest in the meaning of man's existence; only a person who is already enlightened concerning the problems of man's existence and who uses a man's lights can hope to gauge the full significance of the message—a message which after all is addressed to man. In the absence of some kind of philosophy the reading of the Bible cannot arrive at any more important truth than such as might be afforded by the reading of some historical document relative to an indifferent object. The reproach has sometimes been levelled against certain works of exegesis (otherwise estimable from more than one aspect), that they do not sufficiently bring to light the specifically religious value of Scripture and the meaning intended by the Holy Spirit, and the impression has been given that this insufficiency was being put down to religious deficiency in the authors concerned, to their lack of docility before inspiration and divine illumination. But perhaps one would have done well to indict them too for lack of human disquiet or quite simply of humanity: for want of proper attention to man one may come to fail in comprehension of God's Word.

It remains to be said that in according our mind a sort—a purely relative sort—of priority over the Word we do not in any way seek to undermine the sovereignty of God. In judging all things, including therefore the Word itself, in the light of the first principles of being, truth and goodness (dynamically constituent principles of our mind), it is, at least indirectly, in the light of God himself that we judge. This it is not within the present scope of our inquiry to prove.[1] Let it suffice us to quote St Thomas: '*In luce primae*

---

[1] The proof is outlined in our 'Théologie dialectique, Théologie catholique, Théologie naturelle', in *Recherches de Science religieuse*, Vol. 28, 1938, pp. 540ff.

veritatis omnia intelligimus et iudicamus, in quantum ipsum lumen intellectus nostri, sive naturale, sive gratuitum, nihil aliud est quam quaedam impressio veritatis primae.'[1] Our natural intellect embodies a reflection of divine intellect; it is not an autonomous light-source sending forth its own beams, it exists only by virtue of a constant participation in the divine thought. It follows that when we refer the Christian revelation back to the natural light of our mind we are referring it to absolute truth itself; God himself is, in some way, measuring and judging himself within us.

There is yet more. The natural light of the mind is not so natural that it is not in fact taken up into the Christian supernatural order. If it is true, as Barth himself emphasizes in his Christocentric theology, that the entire universe is related to Christ as to its end (*omnia in ipso constant*: all things consist in him—Col. 1. 17), that applies in the first place to man and intellect: God created man in order to make him his own in Christ: that is in fact the sole ultimate end ordained for our individual and collective history.

From this circumstance certain theologians have thought it possible to infer that the mind of man could not exist save in intrinsic reference to the Kingdom of God. They argue that God's will to adopt us in his Son cannot be conceived as a decree remaining extrinsic to us in all respects; we must have within us a most intimate ordination corresponding to it; we must surely be brought in touch with our end through some attraction, some internal tension, a profound affinity with the Kingdom. This inalienable finalization they rightly call 'the lasting centre of the (supernatural) existential in concrete man'.[2] But if one should feel impelled to dispute this inference one ought however to

---

[1] *S. Th.*, I, q. 88, a. 3, ad 1. Cf. also *ibid.*, q. 79, a. 4, c et ad 1; q. 84, a. 5, c; q. 16, a. 6, ad 1. Cf. *de Verit.*, I, 4, ad 5: *Et quia per eam (veritatem primorum principiorum) iudicare non possumus nisi secundum quod est similitudo primae veritatis, ideo secundum primam veritatem de omnibus dicimur iudicare.* Here *prima veritas* designates what St Thomas calls earlier in the same text *veritas intellectus divini*: we thus judge of all things *secundum veritatem intellectus divini*.

[2] K. Rahner, *Schriften zur Theologie*, Vol. 1, Zürich, 1954, p. 339.

admit, in view of the ordering of all things under Christ, that our mind is related to the Kingdom at least in an extrinsic way or that, as it has been said, our reason is already engaged, externally at least, in the teleology of faith.[1] This, be it noted, is sufficient to produce the following consequence: if, as we have said, when we judge all things and revelation itself in the light of reason it is God indeed judging himself within us, we are now in a position to add that it is not only God the author of nature but God the disposer of the Christian order. Barth has said, 'Revelation is *authority*, that is to say a truth which owes its trueness to no veracity, not even the most profound and truthful; a truth, on the contrary, on which all conceivable veracity depends with ever-renewed dependence; it is then the truth without whose recognition the most profound and truthful veracity can only lie and deceive.'[2] Exactly! Yet if nothing is more exact, just so there is nothing more perfectly compatible with our thesis of the necessary reference of the Word to our reason: when we offer the Christian revelation to our mind that we may judge its truth and goodness, we do not offer it to a thing having existence and magnitude outside it and alien to it. Rather do we judge it by a light which in the final estimate exists only through it and in it, which shines and is manifest only within an order ruled by the divine will to salvation and revelation in Christ. And so for us too the Word remains the sovereign truth, the authority recognizing in the last resort no other outside itself.

In thus taking Bultmann's part against Barth, we do not only accept the psychological sense of his rule of hermeneutics (that to understand the Bible one must bring to bear a certain experiential consciousness of human disquiet, a certain comprehension of man), but, as may easily be seen, we recognize, at least in part, that its critical sense is also well-founded. Still, only in part. For nothing in the foregoing

[1] H. U. von Balthasar, *Karl Barth, Darstellung und Deutung seiner Theologie*, Olten, 1951, p. 294.
[2] Taken from P. Maury's French translation (Éditions 'Je sers', Paris, 1934), *Révélation, Église, Théologie*, p. 16.

vindicates the declaration that the only elements of the message worth retaining are those relative to our understanding of ourselves. Nor have we given support to it in the more restricted sense that among the message's assertions relative to God we should retain only those which shed light for us on God's relations (as judge and liberator) to our existential situation, to the exclusion of any doctrine having God, considered in himself, as object.[1] But in the following limited sense: that the Word should be referred in its totality to the human mind, there to be judged in the light of the mind's immanent principles of being, truth and goodness—a judgment which will decide as to its 'intelligibility' and 'possibility', or at least as to the non-demonstration of its self-contradiction—in that limited sense Bultmann's critical rule is, as we have shown, wholly acceptable; indeed, it is no more than the expression of the necessary first step in the process of our mind's affirmations.

But what kind of creature is this man to whom Bultmann rightly says that Revelation must be related in this way? One may grant that the conception of man, or anthropology, is derived by pure analysis of the understanding of existence exercised within existence, i.e. by existential analytics. But it must be said that error may creep into this reflexive operation. In our opinion that is exactly what happened to Bultmann: the human structures at which his existential analysis arrived are, to put it bluntly, inadequate and even erroneous. There lies the mistake which, far from being secondary as Barth appears to have thought, underlies the aberrations main aberrations of Bultmann's theology.[2]

[1] What judgment may we come to of Bultmann's rule as here understood? Cf. pp. 120-122 and 159, *The Christian Message and Myth*.

[2] Cullman takes Bultmann to task over this error no more than Barth does—in fact, he neglects to mention it. According to Cullman the message of the Bible essentially recounts a history, i.e. an organized sequence of divine events worked out in time and of which Christ is the centre, this centre being connected on the one hand to the divine history of Israel and on the other to the history of the apostles and of the birth of the Church; the whole fulfilling a sole divine economy, a sole divine purpose of election and salvation. In consequence Cullman's

As will be remembered, the dominant feature of Bultmann's anthropology was found to be an emphasis on pure decision, to the exclusion of all substantiality and all existence as a nature; man may verify his authenticity only in a crucial *existentiel* decision which is totally divorced from the world of 'beings'; true human existence, which is free-will and history (*Geschichte*), altogether transcends the plane of nature and phenomena.

The fact is that Bultmann has gravely exaggerated this transcendence. A more prudent existential analytics would have taught him that the structure of the mind to which we refer all our objects of affirmation (and within faith, the Word itself) is not that of an entity wholly removed from the conditions of 'natures' and 'beings': no doubt it is a spiritual reality, but the very form which judgment takes ('this *is*') shows that in its exercise it is united to the world of what is *vorhanden*, to an 'essentialist' reality. It is therefore impossible that, as Bultmann would have it, our authenticity should be realized in a purely ideal decision. No,

chief accusation against Bultmann is of having misunderstood all these features of the message: 'So long as he (Bultmann) fails to see that the New Testament speaks well and truly of a divine *oikonomia*, which concerns a temporal succession of events, we must fear that our discussion will remain absolutely fruitless' (Cullman, 'La nécessité et la fonction de l'exégèse philologique et historique de la Bible', in *Le Problème biblique dans le protestantisme*, by J. Boisset, Maurice Goguel and others; Collection 'Les Problèmes de la pensée chrétienne', No. 7, Paris, 1955, p. 137, n. 4). But there is no doubt that Bultmann would reply that he could see quite well the cardinal outline of the history of salvation as drawn in the New Testament (just as he sees clearly miracle and resurrection, etc.), but (he would add) it is impossible to see in all that the Word of God and to consider this historical frame as essential to the message, in spite of appearances. For according to Bultmann nothing of this has anything to do with the understanding of ourselves before God; none of these elements corresponds with any of the structures elicited through existential analysis and none therefore could determine our adherence to faith; the history of salvation is scarcely more than an external, mythological frame of which the writings of the New Testament ought to be divested. It follows that in any discussion with Bultmann one cannot escape the necessity of discussing his criterion of existential analysis, whether to contest its general legitimacy or, as we are doing, to proclaim the inadequacy of the structures established by his analysis.

rather one should say (as has been written) that our destiny is worked out 'in the course of a succession of real decisions which, without ceasing to represent a creative development of our Self, nevertheless presuppose if not its substantiality, in too static and materialistic a sense, then at least a temporal *continuum*'.[1] This temporal continuum, intrinsic to human *Dasein*, is completely misunderstood in Bultmann's anthropology, where decision takes place in 'the instant', in a constantly renewed present moment and in separation from all antecedent present moments; time ceases to be real time and history is no longer much more than an abstraction: all these deficiencies stem from a faulty analysis of the true characters of our intellectual activities and from an excessive anxiety to distinguish man from Nature, History (*Geschichte*), from objective and phenomenal time.

The first weakness leads to another: just as my history is reduced to 'the historical moments' constituted one by one by my *existentiel* decisions, history as a whole is reduced to my history, at any rate in the sense that Bultmann's anthropology scarcely knows, and can scarcely know, anything beyond the isolated individual. The same excessive transcendentalism which causes him to overlook the temporal continuum of each human *Dasein* prohibits him from properly evaluating the realities of society and tradition, which are thus forbidden to play any part in the realization of our authentic existence. Here, however, Bultmann's negation is not absolute, or rather we must be quite precise as to what society is affected by this negation. We have already heard him telling us that the human being personalizes itself only in intersubjectivity and in responding to the summons of a Thou.[2] He writes further: 'One must not imagine that men are like isolated subjects in a world assimilable to an empty space; nor is it as if one subject looked about him

---

[1] R. Marlé, *op. cit.*, p. 99. Pp. 97-104 of this work ('Remarques et réflexions critiques') are especially penetrating: they will be seen to have largely inspired our final criticism.

[2] Cf. p. 188 above.

to find another, formed relations with him and only there-
after made contact with that other subject. Nor must one
imagine things as if man had first to wonder how he might
approach the other and what he should do with him. My
being is rather from its inception (*von vornherein*) a being
among others; the human being is a being with others
(*Miteinandersein*) and thus a historical (*geschichtlich*) being as
contrasted with the being of Nature.'[1] Thus Bultmann sees
in one's fellow-man and in society the necessary means
whereby the individual existence may realize and conquer
itself. And yet, mark this well, according to Bultmann this
fellow-man comes to us only in the very special mode of
objectivity proper to *existentiel* encounters; or rather, in so
far as he comes to us in the mode of natural objects he does
so without in any way implicating our authenticity or to
any extent affecting its advent. In short, strictly personal
relations are the only ones which hold, and could have held,
Bultmann's interest. Yet these personal relations are sus-
tained by a social reality distinct from them (e.g. tradition),
'which permits them to acquire shape and stature and thus,
as it were, capitalizes whatever they construct or pervert'.
'Quite often they are exercised only within natural relations
(e.g. sexual relations of parentage or union . . .); the link
with "nature" interferes in some (not merely accidental or
occasional) manner with the link between man and man'.[2]
These facts are so many features which Bultmann fails to
appreciate; they are, at all events, aspects of social reality
to which he finds himself unable to allot any rôle in the
realization of our authenticity. His exaggeratedly transcendental conception of *Dasein*, and what one might call his
actionalism, prevent him from owning that they have any
value.

One should now be able to envisage the gravity of the
errors in Bultmann's anthropology. These errors of the philosopher are deeply responsible for those of the exegete. The
transcendence of existence, as Bultmann conceives it,

---

[1] *GV* I, p. 231; also as translated by R. Marlé, *op. cit.*, p. 101.
[2] R. Marlé, *op. cit.*, p. 102.

determines in advance the conditions under which man may meet God in faith. The Word of God summons us for the purpose of ensuring our total authenticity. But precisely because this authenticity cannot be realized save in a pure and ideal decision, in total isolation from the world of 'objects', we may straightway infer that the Word of God will not be able to reach us through the realities of our phenomenal world, through signs or miracles, consecrated realities or efficacious sacraments of grace, nor will it be able to find expression in the forms of our conceptual thought, since these forms are scarcely anything other than generalizations from the objects of experience; the Word can make contact with us only on the very special terrain of *existentiel* objectivity, where alone our authenticity may be located. Thus it is that Bultmann's anthropology, through its emphasis on 'transcendency', has as immediate consequence the demand for 'demythologization' of the Word and more generally all Bultmann's grave mutilations of the message—those mutilations which, as has rightly been said, distort the message to the point of unrecognizability. The conclusion is that the exegete should reject, not the general demand for an antecedent philosophy, but this predetermined anthropology.

NOTE

The reader may be surprised by the line of thought we here attribute to Bultmann. While, earlier in the text (pp. 178ff.), we put words such as these into his mouth: 'Since the Word cannot be either doctrinal or phenomenal it follows that it will be able to reach us only in an *existentiel* encounter,' we appear in concluding to credit him with the inverse argument: 'Since the Word can only come to meet our *existentiel* decision (and that we deduce from its claim to ensure our authenticity), it follows that it will be neither a doctrine nor a myth (an expression of the transcendental in the phenomenal).' Which then is ultimately the author's true thought? The fact is that the two arguments converge, that the first is the more characteristic of the early articles, before Heidegger's influence was felt (in 1927), and that these separate assertions mutually support and reinforce each other.

Historically, this seems to have been the process: at a very early stage there was hostility to a speculative and theoretical conception of the Word, as also a lively repugnance, more ingrown than considered, towards the miraculous and all *manifestation* of the transcendental, i.e. towards a mythologizing form of Christianity. This hostility prepared the way for a theory of the *existentiel* encounter with God and to an entirely actionalist conception of faith: all this was ready-formed before the encounter with Heidegger. (Formed under what influences? It is not impossible that Barth's early theology was in large measure responsible for Bultmann's actionalism, at any rate if that theology was itself decidedly actionalist, as some think. Cf. M. P. van Dijck, *Existentie en Genade; Grondgedachten en samenhangen in de 'Kirchliche Dogmatik' van Karl Barth*, Franeker, T. Wever, 1952; an account of this work appears in the *Nouvelle Revue Théologique*, Vol. 75, 1953, p. 661. On the question whether Bultmann does any more, after all, than simply 'develop' one of the 'potentialities' of Barthian theology, see also R. Marlé, *op. cit.*, p. 16, notes 20 and 21.) Only then did there follow the discovery of Heidegger's anthropology of existence; but thanks to the concepts of 'beings', 'authentic Being', 'two objectivities', 'history' which it supplied, this discovery, however tardy, was nonetheless instrumental in Bultmann's achieving a more elaborate and considered expression of the purely actionalist and demythologized Christianity which he had already accepted. It therefore remains true that Bultmann's anthropology of existence is partially to blame for the aberrations of his theology, since it strengthened them in the mind of the author, providing them with means of expression and even (apparent) justifications which they previously lacked.

INDEX

Adam, 51
Aquinas, St Thomas, 135 n.1, 144, 205 n.1
Augustine, St, 47, 152, 153, 176

Balthasar, H. U. v., 206 n.1
Barth, Karl, 14, 49, 79, 80 n.1 and n.2, 83 and n.3, 86 n.1, 122, 123, 157 n.1, 168, 191-201, 206, 212
Bartsch, H. W., 14
Beth, K., 165 n.3
Blondel, Maurice, 36
Brunner, Emil, 33 n.1, 83 n.4-84, 101 n.1, 122 n.2, 159 n.1
Bultmann, Rudolf
  ambiguity, 67ff., and Biblical Interpretation, 122, 183, 168-212
  demythologizing: argument for, 17-23; objective interpretation of, 71-111; subjective interpretation of, 111-16
  elements in the Christian Message: the Life of Jesus, 71-3; the Cross of Jesus, 73-82; the Resurrection, 82-7; the Gospel Message, 88-92
  existential interpretation of the N.T., 33-43ff., 120ff.
  Heidegger's philosophy and, 29ff., 44, 56ff., 93, 145, 191
  historisch and *geschichtlich*, 73ff., 91, 106, 110, 188 and n.1

and Liberal Christianity, 23ff., 123, 163
and Modern Scientific Thought, 17ff., 125ff., 133-40
myth, conception of, 68ff., 126 n.1; 167
positive elements in Bultmann's thought, 118-23
verdict of author: (i) is a break with the past, 123-4; (ii) based on misconception of relation between Christianity and scientific thought, 125-42; (iii) has not proved that the Christian tradition and philosophy are incompatible, 142-9; (iv) contains a dualistic conception of God and the world, 151-4; (v) impoverishes the Christian Faith, 154-61; (vi) will not stand test of thought, 162-3
Buri, F., 14, 150 and n.1

Caesar, 171
Casalis, G., 15
Celsus, 130
Crespy, G., 132 n.1
Cullmann, O., 116f., 173 n.2, 175 n.1, 207 n.2f.

Descartes, R., 38
De Waelhens, A., 31 n.3, 96 n.1, 187 n.2 and n.3, 189 n.1
Dhanis, E., 133 n.1

213

Eddington, A. S., 139 n.1

Farrer, Austin, 15
Fraine, J. de, 15
Fransen, P., 15
Fries, H., 168 n.2, 179
Fuller, R. H., 14

Gilson, E., 144 n.1
Gogarten, F., 16, 39 n.1, 106-7
n.2, 109 n.1 and n.2, 112 and
n.1
Goldammer, K., 167 n.1
Grandmaison, L. de, 132 n.1,
137 n.1
Gregoire, A. S. J., 134 n.1
Gregory the Great, St, 154 n.1
Guitton, Jean, 140 n.1, 151 n.1

Hamer, Fr J., 15, 112 n.1, 119
n.1, 122 n.1
Harnack, A., 24
Hartlich, C., 14
Heidegger, M., 29ff.; *Dasein*,
29-32, 39, 42ff., 47, 56, 118,
142, 145, 146, 152, 185ff.,
185-6 n.2; Existence, auth-
entic and inauthentic, 44,
50ff., 78; *Geworfensein* 59;
man, 58; *Sein und Zeit*, 37ff.;
Sorge, 31; *Verfallenheit*, 60;
Vorhandensein, 29-32, 47, 56
Heisenberg, W., 133ff.
Henderson, I., 15
Homer, 170

Isaye, G., 134 n.1

Jaspers, K., 14, 25 n.1, 43 and
n.1, 127 and n.1, 129, 149
n.2
John, St, 53, 59, 63, 76, 85, 124,
190

Kamlah, W., 56 n.2
Kaufmann, F., 173 n.1

Kierkegaard, S., 189 n.2
Kinder, E., 112 n.2
Kolping, A., 15
Krappe, A. H., 165 n.2
Kümmel, W. G., 14, 159 n.1
Künneth, W., 112 n.2

Laffoncriere, O., 186
Larock, V., 164 n.1 and n.2,
165 n.1
Lohmeyer, E., 14
Lotz, J. B., 145
Luther, M., 60, 103, 105

Macquarrie, J., 30 n.6
Marlé, R., 15, 154 n.2, 161 n.1
and 3, 168-9 n.4, 179 n.2,
188 n.3; 209 n.1; 210 n.1
and n.2, 212
Maury, P., 206 n.2
Menoud, P. H., 132 n.1
Mouroux, J., 132 n.1
Müller, Max, 29 n.1, 32 n.5,
38 n.3, 118 n.1, 146 n.1, n.2
and n.3

Oepke, A., 133 n.1

Paul, St, 51, 54f., 56, 59, 63,
103, 122, 124, 128, 153, 190
Pfeifer, E., 132 n.1
Plato, 92, 170
Prenter, R., 15, 56, 114, 149
n.1

Rahner, K., 29 n.2, 30 n.2 and
n.5, 32 n.3, 40 n.1, 182, 205
n.2

Sachs, W., 14
Sauter, H., 14
Schleiermacher, F., 22
Schniewind, J., 13, 14, 35 n.1,
105, 106
Schumann, F. K., 48 n.1
Senarclens, J. de, 192 n.1

ABBREVIATIONS

The following abbreviations have been used throughout this book:

B I, B II, B III. The first three volumes of *Kerygma und Mythos*, edited by H. W. Bartsch, Herbert Reich Evangelischer Verlag G.M.B.H., Hamburg-Volksdorf.

KM. *Kerygma and Myth*, SPCK, London. A translation by R. H. Fuller of some of the contributions to *Kerygma und Mythos*.

GV I, *GV* II. The two volumes of *Glauben und Verstehen*, essays by Rudolf Bultmann. JCB Mohr (Paul Siebeck) Tübingen.

ET. English translation.